LUTON AT WA

The story of how the people of Luton wi
war between 1939 and 1945 is largely unknow
who live and work in the town today.

Luton - and its population - have changed so dramatically in the
years since the war that now only a few will recall how the town stood
up to the trauma of those war years.

Because of strict war-time censorship, much of what occurred
during those years was not mentioned in *The Luton News*. Once the
war was over, however, the newspaper staff set about the mammoth
task of presenting a complete and vivid picture of war-time life in Luton.

Luton at War tells of the long anxious nights, the joy and the
sorrow that made even the most terrifying moments bearable thanks
to the tremendous way in which people joined to help each other. And
as well as being a moving personal account, it is also a unique historical
document.

First published 1947 by Home Counties Newspapers Ltd., Luton
Reprinted 1982, 1985 by Bedfordshire County Library

This edition published in larger format
in two volumes by
The Book Castle
12 Church Street
Dunstable
Bedfordshire LU5 4RU

ISBN 1 871199 44 1   vol. 1 October 2000
ISBN 1 871199 49 2   vol. II October 2001

Printed and bound by Interprint Limited, Malta

LUTON AT WAR

VOLUME TWO

Includes an index to both volumes
by James Dyer

Compiled by
The Luton News

Acknowledgments

The publishers wish to acknowledge their indebtedness

To Mr. A. F. Pope, of *The Luton News*, who personally supervised the compilation of this book. His rich store of local knowledge, gained through close personal contact over many years with all phases of Luton life, has been invaluable.

To Alderman John Burgoyne, O.B.E., (Mayor of Luton through the greater part of the war), to officers of the Corporation of Luton, local officials of Government departments, ministers of religion, educationists, industrialists, traders, social workers, and all others who, as leaders of some branch of the local war effort, have willingly given valuable help in the provision and checking of information.

To those members of the Editorial staff of *The Luton News* who undertook the responsibility of writing articles, and were thereby involved in much painstaking research among records, published and unpublished, during the last eight years.

To their colleagues of the Photographic staff, whose daily work throughout the war provided some thousands of pictures of all aspects of Luton's war-time life, from which most of the illustrations reproduced here have been selected.

To the Photo-Engraving staff of Home Counties Newspapers, Ltd., and the staff of Gibbs, Bamforth & Co. (Luton), Ltd., whose craftsmanship contributed to the technical production of the book.

1947

Contents

To the People of Luton, who showed, not only that they could "take it", but that they could hit back...hard.

Introduction

The war effort of the people of Luton is, to some extent, recorded in the files of the Luton newspapers between 1938 and 1946. Yet anyone who would seek the background to those years in the history of this thriving industrial town, who wished to measure its determination to play a full part in the onward struggle to final victory, could search those voluminous files in vain. Newspapers normally chronicle events as they pass. They could not, in 1940, speak of the grim events of that year from the viewpoint of 1946. They could not, in fact, record many events as they happened, because of a stringent war-time censorship, and much information had perforce to be filed away against the time when it could take its place in the broad canvas of an historical record.

The story of Luton at war, therefore, had to be written. It had to present the vivid picture of local war-time life in all completeness. More than 100,000 residents of Luton make up its community life, and those who in future years study the history of that community life must not find that a gap exists with little or no record of the effect of a great world upheaval on local life and habits.

It is appropriate, too, that wherever and in what form may be enshrined the Roll of Honour of Luton in this second World War, the names of those who gave their lives, whether in the Services or as civilians (for total war comes right into the homes of the people) should be attached to the story of their times.

The roll has been compiled from particulars sent to the publishers, from inquiries made, and from records kept by *The Luton News* throughout the War. It is as complete as it has been possible to make it, but some who died may not have been recorded here. That does not diminish the honour they share with the host of the Fallen.

They paid the price - theirs is the Glory.

1947

Fifteen Million Pounds

WHEN "Thanksgiving Week" ended in November, 1945, War savings in Luton since January, 1940, had reached the total of £15,255,321.

A very nice nest-egg, you may say, but it isn't quite as big as it sounds. The reason? In every special "Week" there were big investments by the banks, insurance companies, etc., and although they do business in the town, their investments cannot be regarded as the money of the "ordinary people."

All the same, "ordinary people" had a big finger in the Fifteen Million Pie for, with the exception of that "Thanksgiving Week," about half the total in each special "Week" came from traders and small savers.

When to that is added the thousands put into war savings every week by small savers, and for the collection of which group secretaries were so largely responsible, the "ordinary people's" share of the nest-egg must be pretty good.

Added to this is the deferred value of those "tax credits," which, we are told, will not be realisable until all the shops again have all the goods we want, so that money represented by these credits can be spent without forcing up prices still more. Then it may even be a useful stimulus to industry.

The big stepping stones towards the fifteen millions were :—

1941—War Weapons Week (jointly with Luton Rural District and Dunstable). Target, £1,000,000. Result, £1,420,423.

1942—Warship Week. Target, £1,000,000. Result, £1,421,714.

1943—Wings for Victory Week. Target, £1,425,000. Result, £1,442,299.

1944—Salute the Soldier Week. Target, £1,500,000. Result, £1,522,635.

1945 — Thanksgiving Week. Target, £1,000,000. Result, £1,084,757.

* * * *

The money didn't just fall into the bag. It took a lot of campaigning, the introduction of the competitive spirit at home, and the stimulus of challenges thrown out to, or accepted from other towns. At times there had to be even an approach to the spectacular.

Luton had had a Savings Committee since 1917, and even in the year preceding the start of World War II there was quite a number of Savings Associations, whose members were putting away something like £150,000 a year. The new war was not many days old before the Savings Committee was enlarged into a Savings Council, and made as representative as possible of every phase of life and industry in the town.

The days of austerity were, at that time, still a long way ahead. All spending was not suspect. In fact, Alderman John Burgoyne told the inaugural meeting of the Savings Council—" Saving can be just as big an evil as spending if pushed to foolish extremes. How to strike the balance between wise spending and wise saving is what we have to determine and try to get across to the people."

Plans for a National Savings Week early in 1940 were soon maturing, with the establishment of 200 savings groups a practicable aim. The theme for the first special " week " was—" Only a few can do a lot, but most of us can do something." The aim was to encourage the many who could " do something " to do something a little better.

National Savings Week actually produced £25,058, which was above expectations. Only once before had £20,000 been exceeded in a single week, and that was in the previous March. No doubt employees of Vauxhall Motors, Ltd., could easily give the reason for a record week that March. The £25,058, however, was only a preliminary canter. The time was to come when Luton could be regarded as falling from grace if normal weekly savings fell to anywhere near £25,000.

By July, 1940, savings groups numbered nearly 250, and the schools were doing particularly well. Street groups had still to come into existence, but a move to establish them had been initiated. Luton had already reached second place in the Eastern Region and before long it was possible to report 410 savings groups, putting Luton over 100 ahead of any other town. Of 250 street groups aimed at, 134 were formed in four weeks. Immediately the aim became 500 groups By the time the war was a year old there were 510. Then it was asked, Why not 500 street groups, alone ?

Luton was then averaging £100,000 a month in current savings, and was far ahead of any other town in the Region. Before the end of October that year it was possible to say that Luton had saved a million since January 1st. We were not far into 1941 before the cry was " Why not 1,000 groups ? "

*   *   *   *

Then came the first of the really big ventures—" War Weapons " Week. Luton, Dunstable, and Luton Rural District banded together in a first effort to raise a million in a week. It was regarded as a tremendous effort even in combination. Sir Nevile Henderson, British Ambassador in Berlin until the war began, came to Luton to inaugurate the effort. He said—" National savings mean the saving of the nation. Better to pour your money out like water if it is going to save one drop of English blood."

That Sunday saw the first of those big parades which were thereafter to be a feature of all the special wartime weeks. The total rose and rose. The result showed that for the combined districts it was not really such a bold objective after all. People did not merely put up the million—they added nearly another half million to be on the safe side. They set a standard for the future. The total was more than enough for two large destroyers. It covered a third but smaller one. There were high hopes that they would bear names of local significance. The Lords of the Admiralty eventually decreed otherwise. Then one local speaker went so far as to suggest that the money had been obtained under false pretences. Be that as it may, the Royal Navy never included H.M.S. Luton, H.M.S. Dunstable or H.M.S. Whipsnade.

*   *   *   *

After this, " Million " weeks became an annual feature of the savings campaign, but they were only the highlights of the years. The real saving was done week by week. The Savings Council were always alert to ideas for maintaining enthusiasm between the " Million " week of one year and that of the next, and the suggestion of a Town League eventually developed into an Industrial League, to give wider scope to the inter-departmental competitions already running in some of the larger works, and to bring others into the fold.

*   *   *   *

A knight, attended by a herald and page, created a stir in 1942 by riding into Luton on his trusty steed and throwing down the gauntlet at the foot of the Mayor. He introduced a new note into the savings campaign. He brought a bold challenge that Watford would beat Luton in " Warship Week." For Watford it was claimed that there was no audacity in the challenge ; that it was merely perspicacity, and that the men and women of Watford would dig deep into their pockets and bring out a weight of metal that would crush Luton.

" Luton braggarts," said the challengers, " need not think we shall fight with kid gauntlets. We shall not spare them from receiving the full weight of our mailed fists. If they think to overcome us with knavish tricks we are equal to them. We, too, realise that all is fair in love and Warship Week."

The gauntlet was hung from the Town Hall balcony, and the knight was told to return to Watford and there proclaim that there would be only one winner, and that not Watford.

Some time later bold pirates, complete with skull and crossbones nailed to the mast, set sail from Luton by lorry for Watford, to give the challengers opportunity to withdraw. It was rumoured that they also aimed at capturing " Miss Watford "—maybe this was one of the knavish tricks expected of Luton—but from coyness or wisdom the lady evaded this honour.

Perky messages passed between the two towns on the opening day. Luton, with a target of £1,000,000, got off with a flying start. The young King Peter of Yugoslavia was the centre of tremendous interest when he came on the Sunday and took the salute at a great parade which for the first time in Luton included representative of the Allied Nations. The Americans had yet to arrive, but there were Czechs, Poles, Yugoslavs, Norwegians, Dutch, Free French and

ABOVE: *Sir Nevile Henderson, pre-war British Ambassador in Berlin, and Mr. Maurice Healy, K.C., visited Luton to inaugurate Luton, Dunstable and district War Weapons Week in March, 1941.*

BELOW: *A section of the large crowd in George Street who heard the Mayor, Councillor John Burgoyne, announce that 1941 War Weapons Week had raised £1,385,000.*

Clad in a suit of mail, a "Knight" rode over from Watford, to issue a challenge to Luton for Warship Week in 1942. Here, the gauntlet, thrown down by the Watfordians, is hoisted in front of the Luton Town Hall, for all to see.

LEFT: *King Peter of Yugo-slavia outside Luton Town Hall, at the Warship Week parade march past in March, 1942.*

BELOW: *Admiral Sir Lionel Halsey inspecting Sea Cadets on Wardown Sports Ground.*

LEFT: *One of Luton's own "Battle of Britain" heroes, Wing Commander Christopher Currant, D.S.O., D.F.C., opened the town's "Wings for Victory" week in May, 1943. He is seen with Alderman John Burgoyne, then Mayor, and the Wings Week "Queen," Dilys Evans.*

ABOVE: *Straw boaters for victory. The fact that the late Dr. Leslie Burgin, then Member for Luton, and Ald. John Burgoyne were wearing boaters when they came out to make the final announcement showed that Luton had achieved its "Wings" target*

RIGHT: *The salute at the Sunday parade in "Wings" week was taken by Colonel Milton Turner, United States Acting Air Attache in London, representing Mr. John Winant, the American Ambassador. He is seen speaking after the parade.*

Belgians in the parade. It also included women munition workers in the distinctive overalls of their particular factories, to indicate the part they were playing in the productive capacity of the nation.

As the week progressed there were dark rumours that Watford was really after two millions, but at the end of the week Watford was well and truly beaten. The figures were :—Luton, £1,421,724. Watford, £1,203,040. Watford was generous with congratulations. Luton replied that the challenge had been a wonderful spur.

As a sequel to the " Week," Luton " adopted " H.M.S. Ceres, for which H.M.S. Diadem was later substituted. A considerable time elapsed, however, before this substitution could be announced. No mention could be made of the fact that Ceres, a veteran of the 1914-18 war, had been retired. The enemy had to be allowed to assume that the gallant old lady was still a useful unit of the British Fleet. Another long period elapsed before a small party from Diadem could visit Luton to present a plaque, and even that involved silence, so that the enemy should not be told that temporarily Diadem was not at sea. It was not until December, 1945, that the Captain could bring a large party to sample the hospitality of Luton, to say " Thank you " for £250 which had been sent for the benefit of the ship's complement, and to tell something of Diadem's part in the war at sea. Later still, a small official party from Luton paid a visit to Diadem.

*   *   *   *

After " Warship Week " the savings campaign pursued its steady, normal course until the time came for another Million Week. Then Luton savings became a matter of Transatlantic importance, and a straw boater attained a new significance.

" Wings for Victory " Week could not be made the subject of a challenge to the Luton on the other side of the Atlantic, so the English Luton challenged New Bedford, Massachusetts, to a savings battle, and set its own target at £1,425,000, or £15 per head of the total population. New Bedford accepted the challenge. So much interest was aroused that the Ministry of Information and the American Embassy arranged for daily totals to be exchanged. They were displayed side by side at the Luton indicator, and did much to stimulate interest, particularly in the early days, when Luton led. Another new departure was the selection of a " Wings " Queen.

There was no need to look outside for an opener for Wings Week. There was an obvious No. 1 choice in Wing-Commander Christopher Currant, D.S.O., D.F.C. and Bar, one of those who in the Battle of Britain inspired Mr. Winston Churchill to make his historic pronouncement—" Never in the field of human conflict has so much been owed by so many to so few."

Wing-Commander Currant told a vast crowd at the opening ceremony that they had the chance of a lifetime to do a bit to help crush the foulest tyranny that ever befel the world. It had been his honour to live and fight with comrades who had gladly made the

Great Sacrifice with gallant courage and selflessness. All wanted victory and freedom; but, as " The Few " had fought, so all in their own way would have to fight, by being ready to sacrifice their most treasured possessions, luxuries, comforts, above all even lives. There were now, he said, hundreds and thousands of lads who had done, were doing, and would do when opportunity offered, bigger and better things than he had been lucky enough to do. " Let us be worthy of them, and worthy of victory."

Before and after his speech three planes gave a wonderful flying display over the town, coming down almost to the roof tops of George Street and the Town Hall, where the British and American flags were flying.

On the Sunday there was another great parade, in which the Air Services were naturally given pride of place. It included, for the first time, a contingent from the American Army Air Force, of which subsequently we were to see so much, in and over Luton. Fortresses flew over Luton during the parade, and the salute was taken by Col. Milton Turner, an Air Attache from the American Embassy.

During the week Lord Halifax sent a very encouraging message from America. Mr. Henry Morgenthau, junr., Secretary of the U.S. Treasury, cabled from Washington congratulating Luton on originating such a friendly competition with New Bedford.

For a few days Luton kept ahead of New Bedford. It had to acknowledge defeat in the end, but it had again beaten its own target and that was what primarily mattered. This is where a straw boater took on a new significance. When Alderman Burgoyne came out of the Town Hall to announce the figure as far as it was known on the Saturday night, he did not need to tell the crowd the target had been passed. He wore a straw hat, as did other members of his party. The crowd cheered him on sight. Had he been wearing a black hat, they would have known that he was mourning a Luton which, for the first time, had let him down.

The final figure was £1,442,299. New Bedford put up £1,833,829. There £569,218 had been added on the last day, and that saved the Stars and Stripes. They would still have been beaten had the terms of the challenge not been modified in the closing stages. There was at the time no bond issue in which the big firms and industrial undertakings of New Bedford could invest. Therefore it was agreed that it should be an " all in " contest, and whereas the whole of the Luton total was made up of " money on the drum," New Bedford was allowed to include promises of big investments to be made when there was a suitable issue.

How much the small savers through the groups helped towards beating the target can be gathered from the fact that their own target was £38,000; their result, £110,341 5s. 3d.

Papers received here during and after the campaign showed that if nothing else had come out of the challenge, Luton secured tre-

LEFT: "Miss Luton of 1943"—Miss Dilys Evans—sticks a savings stamp on one of three bomb cases which were on exhibition in the town during "Wings for Victory" Week in May, 1943. The bombs were later filled and dropped on Germany.

BELOW: Making a tour of Luton works, "Miss Luton" stops to chat to the finalists of the Beauty contest at the Davis.

LEFT: *One of the many bright ideas of the Publicity Committee of Luton's "Salute the Soldier" week in 1944 was this poster at the top of the Town Hall tower . . . standing cut against the drab camouflage background.*

RIGHT: *A "Naval man" takes a peep through the sight of an Army gun at an exhibition of weapons during Luton's "Salute the Soldier" week.*

BELOW: *Baseball was an unusual game to see on Luton Town Football Ground in the "Salute the Soldier" week. There was a good crowd to watch the Brooklyn Dodgers and the St. Louis Cardinals in their "battle."*

ABOVE: *"Miss Luton of 1944"—Mrs. Nellie Robinson battled with a giant straw hat measuring seven feet across, when the Mayor, Councillor J. Burgoyne, announced that Luton had smashed its "Salute the Soldier" target of £1,500,000.*

LEFT: *The indicator at the Town Hall showed how Luton had beaten both the target and the figure for the Savings Week of 1943.*

BELOW: *Part of the large crowd which formed a solid mass in front of the indicator to hear the speeches after the "Salute the Soldier" procession.*

RIGHT: *A view of one of the aisles at the Luton Industries Exhibition, at the Winter Assembly Hall, held in connection with Luton's Thanksgiving Week in November, 1945.*

BELOW: *The Rt. Hon. Arthur Greenwood (nearest camera), Lord Privy Seal, inaugurated Luton's Thanksgiving Week in November 1945, appealing for £1,000,000 in savings. At the microphone is the Mayor of Luton, Councillor W. G. Roberts, with the Town Clerk, Mr. W. H. Robinson, and the Deputy Mayor, Councillor H. C. Lawrence.*

mendous publicity in news, pictures and even cartoons on the other side of the Atlantic, and many friendly messages were exchanged between people who otherwise would have had no point of contact.

*   *   *   *

The Navy and the Air Force having had their Weeks, it was the turn of the Army in 1944. Plans for " Salute the Soldier " Week were actually being made when plans for the Army's greatest adventure—the landing in Normandy—were being completed. It was therefore fitting that the target should be higher than anything so far achieved. It was fixed at a £1,500,000. Again, and despite the first effects of P.A.Y.E., Luton did it, and again added a few thousands for luck. This was just a month before D-Day.

The opener was General Sir Kenneth Anderson, who had led the First Army in the Tunisian Campaign, and had returned and temporarily resumed his former appointment as G.O.C.-in-C., Eastern Command. He cheered a big crowd by telling them that unlike four years earlier, when it was hard to see what the end of the war was going to be, complete victory could now be seen as the only possible end. He was wisely cautious, however, when he said the Germans knew they had earned all that was coming to them, so would not readily give in, and people must not be disappointed if the end of the war did not come by the end of the year.

Instead of a " Queen," there was a " Miss Luton," the young wife of a prisoner in Germany. Again the Sunday was made the occasion of a grand parade, and first place was given to over 300 veterans from overseas. It was Luton's first opportunity to welcome home some of the men who had helped to clear the enemy out of North Africa, made possible the landings in Sicily and Italy, and opened the Mediterranean again to our ships. All along the route these veterans were loudly cheered. One great contrast in this procession is worth recalling. There were Churchill tanks. There were also G.S. waggons that might well have seen service in 1914-18, drawn by smartly-groomed horses—they were a reminder that even in this mechanised age the Army has not entirely deserted the horse for horse-power.

Field Marshal Sir Cyril Deverell, who took the salute, was in prophetic mood. He recalled the grim and difficult times of Dunkirk, Greece, Libya, Hong Kong, Crete, and other setbacks. Now, he said, we were all set to stage a great come-back. The Army would receive tremendous support from the Navy and R.A.F. ; but it was the Army which would go in and deliver the knock-out, and soldiers away fighting had the right to expect the utmost backing from those who had not been called up.

Later it was said that Luton had never been known to set its heart on anything and fall short. The result of the Week was £1,522,733. Again it was an occasion for straw hats. They were worn easily by the men, but " Miss Luton " was nearly lost under a 7 ft. straw hat

P

made some years earlier for exhibition purposes. She made a gallant struggle to wear it. Then, decorated with the black and amber of the County Regiment, it was hoisted on to the indicator, before which there were two symbolic figures—one of a soldier in the full dress of the original 16th Foot, the other a typical infantryman in battle dress.

* * * *

In " Salute the Soldier " Week the street groups did it again. Asked for £150,000, they produced £217,282. And people still kept on saving afterwards, without any special stimulus. There came a time early in 1945 when their normal weekly savings reached £50,450.

* * * *

The last great effort was " Thanksgiving Week." The war in Europe had ended, Japan had given in. All sorts of celebrations had been held. There came the inevitable reaction.

For various reasons " Thanksgiving Week " was deferred until late in the year. It was not a good time. Bad weather and dark nights told against the work of the street group collectors. The wage-earning peak had passed. Big investors were not so promising. There was a feeling that Saving for Reconstruction had not the appeal of earlier causes. For the first time a target was fixed which did not equal the result of the previous effort. It was reduced to the round million. There was no " Queen " no " Miss Luton." There was no big Sunday parade—the substitute was a not very well attended Thanksgiving Service at the Indicator. The one outstanding visitor was the Lord Privy Seal, Mr. Arthur Greenwood, who came as opener.

Otherwise the week proceeded as usual and, as usual, Luton did what it set out to do ; but it took a big effort on the last day to make the total £1,080,757, and so take Luton's War Savings past the Fifteen Millions mark.

* * * *

Of the many who contributed to this total achievement, but one received official recognition. Mr. W. A. F. Hearne, honorary secretary of Luton Savings Council from July, 1940, until business took him away to Northampton towards the end of 1944, received the M.B.E. in the 1942 Birthday Honours.

* * * *

No review of the war savings effort in Luton would be complete without reference to what the schools did. In the early war years school groups were the chief savings groups. There were groups with membership figures of 1,099 ; 691 ; 618 and 542. It was obvious that they were handling more than the children's own money. Peak membership in any one half-year was 11,746. It naturally decreased as street and works groups sprang up.

Schoolchildren, however, saved in other ways than through their school groups. A check-up throughout the schools, and covering those of every category, showed that through these groups, the Post

Office, the Trustee Savings Bank, or the Co-operative Society, 95 per cent. of the children were saving through one channel or another. Some schools reported 100 per cent. savers.

In the big weeks they were very active, and returns made public showed that some schools, as distinct from groups, had totals of over £3,000, £2,000 and £1,000. The £500 total for a school was fairly common, and the achievements of some infants' schools in passing the £500 mark was particularly praiseworthy. Best effort of any school in one half year was £4,339.

Up to September, 1945, £214,537 had gone into National Savings through the schools. In " Thanksgiving Week " they added another £10,000, and they still go on saving.

The Christian Spirit

IN the years before the war, a frequent topic of discussion in public and private was the influence of the churches on the problems of everyday life. Much was written and said on the subject. It was pointed out that congregations at Sunday services were diminishing, or at best it was becoming increasingly difficult to maintain them, and that there were few young people coming in to church life to interest themselves in the work.

To the superficial observer all was not well with the churches. Were they facing up to the responsibility of the age ? If, as it appeared, they were unable to hold their own in the face of the other interests that jostled for a place in family and social life, what would the future hold for them ?

The prospect was disturbing. Thirty, forty years ago the church or the chapel was the centre of social life. It spread its wings over the family, and indeed the community, but, by the fourth decade of the twentieth century, the development of entertainment as an industry in its broadest sense had widened social life and provided an easy temporary escape from the problems and anxieties that crowded thicker and faster on the human race. The tempo was fast. There was little time for reflective thought, and, too often, the instinctive call of conscience had sunk to a mere whisper.

The war brought to the churches supreme difficulties but also a supreme opportunity. The difficulties were material only. The churches' worst enemy was the black-out. Church-going, it cannot be gainsaid, was more popular with the middle-aged and the old than with the young, and the older folk, or the great majority of them, did not care to venture out after dark unless it was absolutely necessary.

Then there was the difficulty, the impossibility in some cases, of completely blacking out places of worship. Afternoon services had to be substituted for evening services. Change is not always welcome or convenient, and church attendances suffered. The withdrawal of Sunday morning transport was also a particular handicap in Luton, where so many of the churches, sited in what were once populous districts, but now almost entirely given over to business, draw their still faithful congregations from areas at a distance.

Many churches lost valuable officers and members through the call of the Services—although Luton did not suffer so much in this way as some places. The town's many war industries, Home Guard, Civil Defence and Firewatch duties, not forgetting the many who had to carry on with their war work on Sundays, interfered greatly with attendances, though the influx of evacuees and some war workers offset this to a certain extent.

A great blow to some of the churches was the loss of their premises by military requisitioning. This caused curtailment of many activities, the suspension of others, and they were unable to put into operation projects that would have had a social value or could have helped the many Service personnel who at various times were stationed in the town or made a habit of visiting it. In almost every case halls were requisitioned, and churches possessed of basements had them taken over for A.R.P. shelters or first-aid posts.

But it is not the object of this record to enlarge upon the difficulties that beset the churches during these six years. Rather should stress be laid on the magnificent way in which they rose to their great opportunity.

The outbreak of war had a sobering effect on the nation. The churches sensed the road they must travel. They saw that the fundamental principles of the Christian life, and the freedom of the spirit of man were the heart and roots of the impending struggle. They saw, dimly stirring in the souls of their people, the deep ingrained philosophy that they had always felt they could not have taught for two thousand years in vain.

Then in the thunder of the German advance, in the holocaust of Dunkirk, in the blood and toil and tears and sweat of 1940, they saw the vision of their great purpose. Their pathway lay through the hearts of men, to steel them against fear and adversity, to sharpen the sword of their courage, and to clothe them in the full armour of God.

*   *   *   *

To some extent, perhaps, the difficulties of the churches were a blessing in disguise. They spurred those who remained to greater efforts to keep things going. At any rate, sceptics who might have thought that a second big war in twenty-one years was going to mean the end of something they had declared for years to be dead or dying were confounded. The churches of Luton carried on, maybe with lesser activities in some directions, but still with vitality enough to launch out into new avenues.

Foremost in everyone's thoughts was, naturally, the idea of helping those who had gone to serve their country in uniform, and many ways presented themselves. They were remembered in the services, they were written to, and parcels and other gifts were sent to them. Thousands of messages must have passed to and fro, and expressions of gratitude came from far and wide.

There was also a keen desire to meet the social and recreational needs of the men and women stationed here. One of the leading ventures was the provision, by the clergy and members of Luton Parish Church, of a rest house and social centre, at a roomy old house in Church Street.

The idea originated with the Rev. G. B. Gerrish, then a curate at the Parish Church and afterwards a Chaplain to the Forces. With the ready consent and backing of the Vicar, he formed a small committee consisting of himself, Mr. Cyril Hyder, Mr. A. C. Fellingham, and Mr. Jim Wing, and they got the necessary workers together and carried on. At first Mr. Gerrish acted as Warden, assisted by the Rev. R. K. Miller, and later he was succeeded by Mr. Hyder.

St. Mary's House, as it was known, came into being in January, 1940, when it was declared open by Miss Elsie Green and dedicated by the Vicar, who acted as its President, and its good work was carried on until after the end of the war with Germany. It was the first canteen for the Forces to be opened in Luton, and thousands of men and women found pleasure in its welcoming atmosphere. They particularly appreciated the lounge, with its brightly glowing fire on cold days, and the " quiet room," where they could gain some of the peace not always to be found where Service people foregather.

Another centre for quietness and reflection was the little chapel tucked away at the top of the building. Evening prayers were always said there, and there were services, too, the most notable being held at the Christmas when Mr. Gerrish was on leave. Then the place was full.

On the whole, though, the workers at St. Mary's House found that the call upon them was mainly for material things. Games, reading and writing facilities and refreshments entered into the scheme of things. Christmas was naturally marked in a special way. Both on Christmas Day and Boxing Day tea was free for all, and annually an order was placed for a thousand mince pies.

One difficulty a good many Service men experienced while stationed in Luton was in finding accommodation for the wife or " best girl " whenever she wanted to pay a visit. This led to the establishment of a room at St. Mary's House which became known as " the creche." Wives, families and sweethearts could be taken there, instead of walking about the streets. This, and all the other activities at St.

Mary's House, were thoroughly appreciated by the Service men. Their thanks were expressed personally to the workers, and in letters which came after they had left Luton.

The Free Churches, gravely handicapped by the requisitioning of premises, were not behindhand in their desire to do something for serving folk, but it was only those in the central part of the town that could really be looked to for action, because it was there the uniformed visitors were mostly to be found.

Chapel Street Methodist Church, not having the use of its school buildings, extended a special invitation to troops to attend concerts given after the Sunday evening services, but the response was so small that the concerts were discontinued after one season.

Beech Hill Methodist Church started a club, but it was only sparsely patronised, probably owing to the fact that it was not centrally situated.

The Salvation Army adapted the old Bridge Inn in Bute Street into a Red Shield Club for troops. Being opposite one of the largest buildings in the town in military occupation, it was most conveniently situated.

Union Church was in a more fortunate position than some. It did manage to retain its Lecture Hall, and carried on a regular Sunday evening social for the Forces, with musicians from the district offering entertainment and the ladies of the church providing refreshments. Usually the minister, the Rev. E. B. Keeble, conducted a short epilogue, and this and the friendliness shown were so highly appreciated that letters of gratitude were received from soldiers who had moved to all parts of the world. This good work was carried on for five winters, and it was only when the need was obviously diminishing that it was discontinued.

Union Church, incidentally, had very good basement facilities for shelter, and these were much sought after by people in the neighbourhood at the height of the enemy attacks. When less attention was concentrated on Luton, and it was thought that the bombers were only passing over to a more distant target, the desire to seek shelter out of the home became less.

While catering for the safety of the shelterers, the church also had some thought for the comfort of the families—from grannies to little children—temporarily in their care. The shelterers themselves subscribed the cost of heating, the church held services for them, and members of the choir went down to sing to them.

*   *   *   *

While many of the churches could do nothing on their own premises, their members were not idle. The town's voluntary canteens were very largely supported by workers from the churches. The latter also provided helpers for all kinds of flag days and house-to-house collections which had their origin in some war emergency.

During the blitz times, when evacuation was at its height, the

RIGHT: *There was free tea for the troops who attended the opening ceremony of the Red Shield Club in Bute Street, Luton, in February, 1940. This was one of the many Salvation Army Welfare centres which sprang up all over the country.*

BELOW: *A typical evening scene in the lounge of St. Mary's House, Church Street, which was run as a canteen and rest house for the Services. On the right is the Rev. G. B. Gerrish.*

ABOVE: *Led by the Vicar of Luton, Canon W. Davison, a procession of clergy and ministers of all denominations paraded with sandwich boards during Luton's Religion and Life Week, in June, 1942.*

BELOW: *10,000 spectators packed Luton Town Football Ground, together with 3,000 people who had marched through the town in procession for a United Nations Day Service on 14th June, 1942.*

LEFT: *Canon W. Davison, Vicar of Luton, with the Rev. W. H. Sansom, of King Street Congregational Church conducting an open air service on Wardown Sports Ground, on June 13th, 1943.*

BELOW: *"This magnificent crowd—one of the finest I have seen here yet in my seven years in Luton," said Mr. Sansom, to which the Vicar rejoined, "John Wesley would have rejoiced could he have seen this crowd to-night." 3,000 Lutonians from many churches in the town attended this service.*

churches were again able to render valuable aid. People arriving hungry, tired and dispirited were catered for in the matter of temporary accommodation, and found fresh friendships in the life of the churches. Quite a number of church members also did a wonderful job of work in helping to clothe and house evacuees and, in a number of instances, in showing them a different standard of life from what they had known before.

The Baptist churches coped with a big influx of evacuees received voluntarily through the West Ham Central Mission. Baptist homes were circularised and asked for volunteers, so that when the visitors arrived it was already known exactly who would receive who.

All the Sunday Schools were considerably increased for a time by evacuees, and even now there is contact with some of the children who grew up in the homes of Luton people and joined various youth organisations. This was only a temporary growth, however, for Sunday School work was badly affected by the war. The tendency for children not to go increased, beginning with the daylight sirens, which naturally led to parents wishing to keep their little ones under their own roof. On the other hand, some of the older-established youth organisations showed definite growth. The Boys' Brigade offered a notable example. The Battalion more than doubled its membership, and the few remaining officers did a noble job in holding these young people during such difficult days.

Financially it may be said the churches of Luton did not suffer because of the war. Wages were high, and people were wonderfully generous. Christ Church was able to invest £252 of church funds in support of Warship Week in 1942, and earlier in the war had installed a new organ, although, as the Rev. G. B. Carlisle, who was then Vicar of the parish, said at the annual parochial church meeting in 1941, some might think this was tempting fortune !

*　　*　　*　　*

One of the greatest signs of vitality shown by the churches during the war years was the emergence of the Religion and Life Movement, in which an unprecedented measure of unity was achieved. Its activities were held up for a time by war conditions, but on June 14th, 1942, Luton saw the opening of the Religion and Life week, marked by scenes of wonderful enthusiasm and the visits of many notable people. It was a week during which, to use the words of the Vicar, Luton people had an opportunity of knowing all that was meant by the impact of the Christian religion upon the social, educational, civic and industrial life of the community.

Virtually every section of industry, every form of social welfare, and every phase of religion was enlisted to ensure success. This success was abundant and religion in Luton was proved to be neither dead nor moribund. Over 5,000 people attended the inaugural service on the Town Football Ground on the Sunday evening, and on week-

235

The scene inside Luton Parish Church on Sunday, September 3rd, 1944 . . . the National Day of Prayer . . . when the Archbishop of Canterbury, the late Dr. William Temple was preaching. The service, which included singing by Luton Choral Society and the B.B.C. Singers, was broadcast on the National programme.

nights, crowds ranging from 1,500 to 2,000 were attracted to the meetings at Chapel Street Methodist Church.

Highwater mark was reached when the Bishop of Lichfield and the Rev. Donald Soper spoke on " The World of Nations." A quarter of an hour before the meeting began the Chapel Street church was filled with 2,000 people, and an overflow meeting at King Street Congregational Church for another 600 had to be improvised.

As was said at the time, the Week was only a beginning. Commissions dealing with the home and social work, industry, education, and evangelism were set up, and the Crescent Club, which has done and is doing such good work for girls, was the direct child of the Home Commission. The Rev. H. E. Frankham, then on the staff of the Parish Church, was the first secretary of the Club, which was established in a large house in Crescent Road formerly run as a private hotel.

Thousands of pounds were raised to secure the premises and to get the Club in running order, and it was typical of the spirit of co-operation which prevailed between ourselves and the U.S.A. at the time that a notable contribution came from friends on the other side of the Atlantic. The Ministry of Labour and the big works also proved most helpful, and hundreds of girls who came into Luton during the war years to help the industrial effort had very good reason to be thankful for the social and recreational facilities of the Club, and for the friendships it enabled them to form.

An advisory bureau on marriage difficulties was another outcome of the work that followed the Week, and in wartime, with its hasty marriages, its separations and infidelity, the bureau had many knotty problems to tackle.

Out of the Industrial Commission, following long conferences at the Skefko Works with leaders of industry, came works chaplains, whose work has been spoken of as highly encouraging.

The Educational Commission provided courses in religious training for both day school and Sunday School teachers, and the Evangelistic Commission did a good deal of work in the way of open air services at Wardown and also in arranging brains trusts and conferences.

Handsome tribute was paid by the B.B.C. to the vigour of the Religion and Life Movement in Luton when it asked the Council of the movement to inaugurate a series of inter-denominational services to be broadcast in the General Forces programme, other services of a similar character following from Leicester, Bristol, Leeds and other centres. The broadcast took place on the morning of Sunday, April 16th, 1944, and all denominations were represented at the service. The King Street minister, the Rev. W. H. Sansom, read the Lesson, and the address was given by the Rev. Wilfred Wade, of Beech Hill Methodist Church.

Services at the Parish Church are always marked by a dignity and an excellence in music and singing that cannot fail to be noted by the visitor, and the world in general had opportunity of taking in this point on more than one occasion, for this was not the first time the Parish Church had been " on the air." It was estimated that more than six million people participated in a service broadcast in the Home Service in July, 1944. The congregation included a large number of Service men and women, and the Vicar officiated and preached.

Most notable of all broadcasts from St. Mary's, however, was that on the first Sunday in September, 1944, when Dr. William Temple, revered Archbishop of Canterbury, led the nation in its Day of Prayer. It was possible by that time for the church's fine peal of bells to be heard heralding the service, and the service gained additional distinction by the fact that the singing was led by the church choir, Luton Choral Society, and the B.B.C. Singers, under the conductorship of Mr. Leslie Woodgate, with Dr. Thalben-Ball at the organ.

*　　　*　　　*　　　*

Firewatching may have been one reason for people being absent from church or from their duties in connection with churches, but firewatching also took people to church. The Parish Church, with its rich historical associations, its many interesting architectural features, one of the few buildings, indeed, to which the Lutonian can point with any sense of pride, naturally loomed large in protective measures taken to guard against damage, either from high explosive bombs or incendiaries. From 1941 to 1944 the church was never left and it was a tribute to the affection in which the old building was held that all the many people who watched over its safety in those fateful years were volunteers. The clergy, in the midst of their many other duties, were ready to play their part. As early as 1937 they had been trained as Wardens, etc., and in 1938 they underwent a refresher course. They also helped in the distribution of gas masks.

Fortunately there was never any great call on their services although the Parish Church did not escape scathless, and many others had windows and roofs damaged. Park Town Methodist Church was the most seriously affected, and had to be closed for some time, while the Methodist Central Hall, after a daylight bomb which fell in Midland Road, had to be re-roofed. Considerable damage was also caused by an oil bomb which penetrated the roof of the Bury Park Congregational Memorial Hall in September, 1940, causing a fire inside the building. North Street Methodist Church suffered when another daylight raider destroyed factories in Old Bedford Road. Oak Road and Bailey Hill Methodist Churches also had their quota of damage, and the Rev. H. Goldstone Edwards, of St. Margaret's, lost his home when a rocket fell in Biscot Road in November, 1944.

*　　　*　　　*　　　*

The Rev. G. B. Gerrish has been mentioned as becoming a Chaplain to the Forces. Another to go was the Rev. N. Goodwin Burndred, who had charge of the Methodist Churches at Church Street, Round Green, and Stopsley. He went to France in January, 1940, and, attached to a Clearing Station, experienced " Dante's Inferno "—his description of Dunkirk. The Casualty Clearing Station with which he was working was the last to leave Dunkirk, and he had many narrow escapes, coming safely through between 70 and 80 raids.

Of the clergy and ministers who remained here, several undertook chaplaincy work. During the war years Canon Davison was, and still is, chaplain to the Church of England troops in Luton. He was also chaplain for about two years to the R.A.F. at the airport, and acted in a similar capacity to the Home Guard until the Stand Down. Further, he was, in conjunction with the Rev. E. Allan Roberts, chaplain to the A.T.C. all through the war, and for five of the war years was chairman of the Luton and Dunstable Hospital, work which he took up definitely as war work.

Regularly there were parades of uniformed men to the churches and chapels ; the A.T.C. attended in force one church a month, and the Home Guard on frequent occasions. Members of the Forces were also regularly to be found at services they were not called to attend, and it was not unusual to see a Salvation Army band parading through the streets with a man in khaki, navy blue or Air Force blue taking part as an instrumentalist. There were also parades to churches other than St. Mary's for members of the Forces, and Luton clergy and ministers took part in services at Luton Hoo, both when it was a hospital for officers and after it became Eastern Command Headquarters.

Contact was maintained with the military to obtain lists of men who might be visited, and there were also " Padre's Hours," at which the men could shoot questions at whoever was conducting the proceedings, an opportunity of which they freely availed themselves.

In an educational series put on by the Army Welfare Department music courses were included, and at least one Luton church organist took part, giving piano evenings, with duets and talks.

The presence of Service people in the district led to one innovation. For the first time in the history of the Parish Church a midnight Communion Service was held on Christmas Eve, 1944. It was specially arranged at the request of Service members, and the congregation included a goodly number of them, and also a number of Americans. The experiment was repeated in 1945, but time alone will show whether it is to become a permanent feature of the Christmas Services.

*   *   *   *

These are the known facts of the churches' contribution to the war effort in Luton, but the thoughtful will read much between the lines.

Unobtrusively, and often at the expense of physical well-being, the clergy and ministers of the town, supported by countless men and women of high Christian principle, devoted themselves through six years of war to work for others that will never be recorded except in the Great Book.

Scarcely a home in Luton during those years but was visited at some time by sorrow, anxiety and distress of a personal and intimate kind. In the dark hours of the black-out, when spirits were at their lowest ebb, friends came and brought comfort and solace to stricken homes, loneliness was dispelled, and courage re-born. This was a service performed not as a duty, but because of an instinctive consideration for others. It was a great work, a necessary work. The war could not have been won had not the high ideals and spiritual well-being of our people here, as throughout the nation at large, been so consistently maintained.

6,000 Women

WHILE the Services and the war factories made big calls on thousands of Luton women, there were many other war responsibilities which women were best fitted to shoulder, and which they carried well in a voluntary capacity.

By far the largest group was the Luton W.V.S. The Women's Voluntary Services came into being primarily to provide a second line of Civil Defence as and when regular Civil Defence was depleted by other war demands. While waiting the call to serve in this capacity they managed to do a thousand and one other jobs nobody else found time to do. Working in close collaboration with the local authorities, they saw to such things as the provision of comforts for the troops and shelter for the homeless. They assisted with evacuation, clothing and welfare schemes, transport and clerical work, salvage and savings collections. In doing these things they displayed a team spirit with which women had not before been credited.

The Luton Centre came into being early in 1940, following a meeting addressed by Lady Reading, chairman of the national organisation. Lady Keens was appointed Centre Organiser, and did valuable preliminary work with Mrs. P. Stanbridge, who later became Joint Centre Organiser. Membership grew rapidly, and within a few months 3,000 Luton women had enrolled. In February, 1942, Mrs. R. O. Andrews, who had been head of the Leagrave and Limbury branch, became Centre Organiser, and continued in this capacity to the end of the war. From 1943, Mrs. Bart Milner acted as Deputy Centre Organiser.

In this period membership reached a peak of 6,319. Of these, 400 were Rest Centre personnel, 4,000 belonged to the Housewives' Service, and the rest were canteen workers, knitters, work party members, or carried out the many other duties allotted to them. Central offices were in Gordon Street, and parallel activities were carried on at two sub-branches. These were Leagrave and Limbury, under Mrs. Turner and Mrs. Hyde, and Dunstable Road West, under Mrs. Clews and Mrs. Coombs.

*   *   *   *

Surveying W.V.S. activities in connection with A.R.P. during the war years, one has to bear in mind Luton's comparative luck in the matter of air raids. Although after a few bad months Luton had considerable immunity, the emergency organisation for the feeding, clothing, and general welfare of bombed-out people was always " on its toes," and on occasions which put it to the test it worked smoothly and well.

Continuous practice at the twelve first-line Rest Centres made members familiar with the geography of these places under black-out conditions, and steps were taken to ensure that all stores, covering feeding, heating and sleeping equipment, were available at a moment's notice. Mrs. J. C. Venniker was in charge of all Rest Centres.

One factor which was of immense value in equipping members to face emergency was a scheme which provided basic training in cookery, home nursing and first aid, with qualifying tests for every intending wearer of the W.V.S. badge.

The Housewives' Service, which covered every street in Luton, gave opportunity to lend a helping hand to the busy housewife who was tied to her home by family responsibilities, but the most important work was done by mobile teams ; these rendered invaluable assistance after raid incidents. They visited bomb-damaged houses, gave a hand in getting things cleared up and the home life started again, and sometimes did all the clearing up for the woman of the house. They assisted those rendered homeless, and in many ways gave that human touch of sympathy so essential in circumstances of tragedy and distress. The provision of clothing for bombed-out people, who often lost everything except what they were wearing, was in charge of Mrs. Bart Milner.

The W.V.S. Clothing Exchange was another valuable activity. Started early in 1941, when the clothing shortage was beginning to make itself felt, it proved a godsend to mothers of growing children. The depot in Melson Street was organised by Mrs. R. Hickman, who had the help of a staff of eight. It opened two afternoons a week, it helped not only Luton people but many from surrounding districts, and by the end of 1945 the depot had an index of well over 1,000 people to whom it had proved of great benefit.

*   *   *   *

Figures from the books of the W.V.S. Wool Depot are proof of the great contribution this department made to the war effort. From May, 1941, to December, 1945, 32,391 garments were knitted for the Navy Army, and R.A.F. personnel, 1,282 for the Red Cross and 1,450 for

240

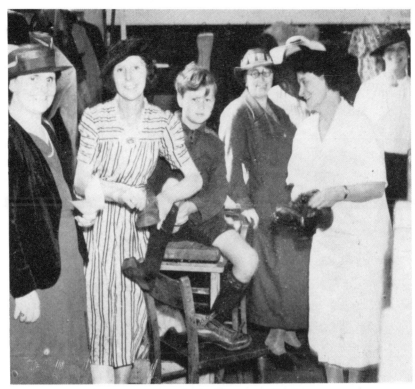

ABOVE: *A young evacuee is fitted with a new pair of shoes at the Waller Street centre.*

BELOW: *Luton women interested in a demonstration of emergency feeding, held in Wardown Park, in June, 1941. Steam for heating was supplied from a traction engine.*

A member of the A.F.S. receives a hot meal from a woman helper at the Waller Street canteen, which catered for the town's A.R.P. services.

Lady Keens serves a cup of tea to Mr. Northam L. Griggs, special representative of the American Red Cross, from the Luton W.V.S. mobile canteen.

ABOVE: *The Luton W.V.S. wool depot, where workers issued wool to knitters, and received and packed garments made for members of the Services. At the telephone is Miss Cumberland, who was in charge.*

BELOW: *Nimble fingers make do and mend at the W.V.S. workroom at Waller Street Methodist Church.*

The Dowager Marchioness of Reading (also inset), National Chairman of the W.V.S., addressing Luton W.V.S. workers at the Central Mission in February, 1942.

Christmas cheer for the kiddies at a Luton W.V.S. party.

overseas relief of children, a total of 35,123 garments in all. Over 10,000 lbs. of wool were issued to knitters, and to these figures must be added a further 4,000 garments knitted by work parties at Gordon Street and the sub-branches.

Local war canteens owed their efficiency in great part to W.V.S. workers. The Civil Defence canteen in Waller Street, run so successfully and for so long by Lady Keens, was staffed by voluntary helpers, while the W.V.S. also supplied staff for the British Restaurant in New Town Street, and provided a rota of 80 helpers for the American Red Cross Club in George Street.

The Food Emergency Van Service was also operated by the W.V.S. Hot meals prepared at the British Restaurant were taken out daily to men working on isolated constructional jobs, and to other workers without canteen facilities.

Another transport job was efficiently done by the Voluntary Car Service Pool, of which Miss Read was in charge. There were 30 members, and this Service proved its worth after air incidents in moving homeless people and their belongings, and in answering constant calls from local hospitals.

Another task undertaken by the W.V.S. was keeping an " accommodation register " to facilitate the billeting of Service personnel sent here for special purposes, and also for factory workers and evacuees. Credit for its smooth working is due to Mrs. Thripp and Mrs. Eaton.

No account of W.V.S. activity would be complete, however, without reference to the part they played in recruiting for the Women's Land Army, the visits they paid to old age pensioners, the bandage work they carried out in our hospitals, and the help given to the Blood Transfusion Scheme in looking up lapsed donors. In addition, the W.V.S. Savings Group handled over £25,000 during the war years, and by various efforts raised the whole of the Campaign Funds—a total of more than £5,000—for Luton's Savings Weeks.

Health Services

ONE September morning in 1939 Luton's Medical Officer of Health, Dr. Fred Grundy, seated in his office in the Town Hall, placed a file in his out-basket and started to make notes.

It was the end of one era and the beginning of another.

The story in the file was of the general progress that had been made in Luton's health services; there were the blue-prints, if such an unmedical term can be pardoned, of future plans. The fact that the file was in the out-basket indicated that these plans were to undergo a radical change.

So Dr. Grundy made his notes. First things were about to come first.

About the same time, at his office in the Luton and Dunstable Hospital, secretary R. E. Lingard was holding a serious conference with the Matron, Miss Redman.

There was still the smell of new paint about this modern streamlined hospital, with the sunny outlook and green approaches, and it had been open for only six months. Now there were new responsibilities to be added to its teething troubles.

Both Borough Council and voluntary organisations had a share in a significant task—ensuring the health of a community during a war of unknown length, against a threat of unknown dimensions, in conditions calculated to undermine the resistance of the population to disease, while dealing with a substantial quota of service and civilian casualties. They had to accept as a *fait accompli* a population swollen by evacuation and the influx of industrial employees.

It was true that all departments of public life had added responsibilities in war. But the successful functioning of industry, supply and communication pre-supposes an efficient medical service ; it is a factor which is common to the planning of each. Just as a military commander assumes a proper medical arrangement in his operational planning, so all the facets of civil defence take for granted that the health organisation is 100 per cent efficient.

And in the wards, not only at Luton's premier hospital, but in the smaller institutions, they made ready . . . just in case. Dr. Grundy called his conferences . . . and made his notes. He made so many, and led his department at the Town Hall into such a state of organisation that for five days he remained shut in his office, perfecting the technique of Luton's health defensive.

One difficulty was that of co-ordination, and we shall appreciate it better if we examine the " set-up."

*　　　*　　　*　　　*

Certain medical services in Luton were the responsibility of the Bedfordshire County Council—they included public assistance and tuberculosis arrangements—but the greater part of the health provision devolved on the Town Council, who took under its wing extensive maternity and child welfare schemes, nurseries and laboratory facilities. In addition to the Luton and Dunstable Hospital, there was a Children's Hospital run on similar voluntary lines.

We have said this was the end of an era in health development. In fact, when Luton switched from peace to war, the plans which were left on the stocks were part of an enlightened growth and advancement which had been proceeding since the middle thirties.

The town's arrangements were on the crest of a wave when war broke out, and were well fitted to take the transition in their stride. A policy of zealous application to necessity had given Luton a health service comparable with the best in the country.

The end of an era ? Yes, but if plans had to be shelved, progress was made in other directions. The graph maintained the upward curve, and we propose to show not only how, but why.

*   *   *   *

For the first three years of war, Luton Corporation's Public Health Department deliberately concentrated on maintaining services, and adopted a policy of consolidation, while placing priority on civil defence. Only after that period did the department begin seriously to plan for the future.

The file which we left in Dr. Grundy's out-basket had the outline of a new health centre, a larger maternity centre, and better hospital facilities. The energies which would have been expended on these things had to be directed to other channels.

As the Public Health Department was not able to build, it concentrated during the last two years of the war, when defence matters no longer required 100 per cent. attention, on laying down the basis of a future policy by developing health education both for children and adults. The resultant scheme was something considerably in advance of anything else in the country.

The important thing was that the Department recognised that this was not a time in which advances could be made requiring bricks and mortar.

What could be done was to develop those services not dependent upon building, and to put the Department in the most advantageous position, by the collection of facts, to build on the best plan as soon as it was possible to do so.

Further, war propaganda made the public receptive to new ideas. The Department seized the opportunity created by the readiness of the man in the street to co-operate, to push quietly ahead with a number of campaigns and at the same time to watch current tendencies for evidence of an increase in the incidence of diseases.

Laboratory arrangements were steadily improved, there was a successful crusade in the cause of immunisation, a Health Education Week offered new opportunities for capturing the imagination of the public, and youth in particular ; nurseries were built, health centres expanded, and the evacuees from London and the East and South coasts were invited to share the benefits enjoyed by their new neighbours.

*   *   *   *

One of the first to be open to Luton's new population was the Department's maternity scheme, which had been improved consistently since 1936.

The Maternity Hospital was an up-to-date building dating from the start of Luton's medical renaissance—it had been opened in 1936—

but with the evacuee public and a Luton growing from natural causes, it was hardly expansive enough to cope with the first war-time winter. In 1940, the Grove Road extension of the county-controlled St. Mary's Hospital was opened, and the Borough Council succeeded in negotiating its use as an Emergency Maternity Unit.

In the dying days of the war a further extension was added at Chaul End, in a building originally intended as a war-time nursery.

Institutional confinement had become much more accepted in Luton immediately prior to the war. In 1936 only one birth in 10 took place outside the home, and municipal midwifery was non-existent; in 1940 half the births were institutional, while no birth was notified by a private midwife. There was a similar trend throughout the country as a whole, but it was more marked in Luton because the Corporation had anticipated it by providing the facilities.

The Department's scheme for training midwives went on throughout the war.

The second wave of evacuees in 1940 again set the experts thinking. The Luftwaffe brought fresh terror to the East End in mass raids, and low-flying enemy aircraft bombed and machine-gunned the coastal belt daily. The expectant mother, rushed from these surroundings to safety, needed sympathetic treatment and understanding. Routine billeting was no answer for a woman whose admission to the maternity wards was probable within a short time of her arrival, and on November 19th, 1940, a hostel for evacuees who were expectant mothers was opened at 48, Napier Road.

Ten women were received there each week. They arrived by coach, and the scheme worked happily from its inception.

Progressing hand in hand with the maternity services had been the Health Centre scheme. Two of these centres were in operation throughout the war. One, at Dallow Road, was used principally as a clinic in co-operation with the schools, with some maternity and child welfare work thrown in as a secondary issue. At Beechwood Road the reverse was the order of things. They were well-appointed buildings, and represented the start from which war-time progress was made.

Premises were hurriedly requisitioned in widely separated districts for use as temporary infant welfare centres as the work increased, and at the same time, came the demand for children's nurseries.

*   *   *   *

The real story of the nurseries is that they were not an unmixed blessing. To begin with, they were essentially a war development in which the Department had little experience. But they were a national departure, and Luton toed the line. The town's contribution to the war effort did involve a high percentage of female labour, and on the face of it, day nurseries were a definite requirement.

So six of them were built on sites which were widely distributed.

Four were brick structures, modern in design, and two were "pre-fabs."

Although considerable pressure was brought to bear by the Ministry of Health, Luton successfully resisted the attempt to provide temporary and pre-fabricated nurseries in many other parts of the town. With the exception of the first two in London Road and Manor Road, where the urgency of the situation demanded something temporary, the Council, with an eye on the post-war possibilities, provided structures of a permanent character. Labour was at a premium; it could not be wasted.

In siting, the Nurseries were placed with an eye to possible future Health Centres and Clinic needs, and the existence of these four ready-made buildings may mean that certain clinical requirements of Luton's post-war policy will be completed five years earlier than would have been the case.

Were the war-time nurseries a success? In their limited sphere, they achieved what they set out to do, but it is doubtful whether they justified the outlay. They were, as has been said, essentially a war-time feature, and the Health authorities were not anxious to encourage their retention. They were costly—£3,000 apiece was the charge for their erection—and it cost £150 a year to maintain each child at a nursery.

Considering the cost, staff, amount of labour which had to be diverted to build them, the number of children which they received, and the relatively small number of women they released for war work, it is doubtful whether they were in themselves a material contribution to the war effort. But they did provide the Corporation with some excellent sites for future Health development.

*   *   *   *

In the meantime, what was happening to the birth rate in this town which made such elaborate arrangements for babies arriving?

It did some remarkable things, and finally earned Luton the title of a boom town for babies!

It sank to 13.83 in 1941, the lowest figure since 1933, but thereafter climbed steadily until in 1944 the birth-rate was 22.7, the highest since 1920.

Why did this happen? The story behind statistics is often simple, and in this case, the rise in the birth rate was due probably to the spate of early marriages which the town experienced during the war. These reached their peak in 1941-42, and the babies from these marriages began to arrive in 1944. Answer, then, is that there was not so much an increase in the size of families but rather an increase in the marriage rate; he who searched for bachelors in Luton in 1943 searched hard.

We have said that the Department campaigned. Generally it campaigned for prevention rather than cure, and this was true particularly of the Health Education Week which was organised in 1943. The main aim was to support the Government's anti-V.D. campaign, and in conjunction with the County Council, public meetings, film shows, lectures, exhibitions and conferences were held.

Most productive of results was a conference to which teachers were invited. The outcome was a plan for a system of long-term health teaching in the schools on human biology and sex education. An agreed policy was formulated and a year later, in September, 1944, a whole-time biologist was attached to the Health Department, to complete arrangements for biology teaching in the schools. A health education theatre was opened in Napier Road, and a system of adult education worked out.

*   *   *   *

Luton led the field again in the drive against diphtheria, for efforts to popularise immunisation had been made long before the Ministry of Health policy was formulated. Results had not been startling; even in 1939 only 112 children of indeterminate ages were immunised, and in 1940 the number was only 204.

Prevention rather than cure . . . the war years laid children open to more treacherous conditions, and 1941 became the anti-diphtheria year. In those 12 months, 7,838 children were immunised.

The first indication that the drive had paid a dividend was in 1942, when Dr. Grundy was able to tell the Corporation that diphtheria had reached a new low level, with only one fatality in the borough—a child who had not been immunised. A diagnosis had been established in 18 cases, but only one had been in a person immunised. During the year, 2,874 more children were immunised.

The diphtheria incidence was even lower in 1943; 16 civilian cases were notified, and there was only one civilian death—a person not immunised.

And in 1944 there was not a single death in Luton due to diphtheria. The only two reported cases recovered. That was Luton's war-time diphtheria story.

*   *   *   *

Still, the watchers kept watch, for diphtheria was not the only complaint to be feared in war. If mothers and teachers watched in the homes and schools, the wardens of health were out at night just as much as the wardens of the air raid precautions.

Frankly, the Department was worried. It is, for a conscientious department, a disturbing thing to have to accept a breeding ground for disease as an integral part of your defence scheme. The source of the worry was—the tunnel shelters.

The story goes back to 1940. The sirens wailed nightly and London burned in the south, the red of her wounds reflected in the night sky. The angry glow on the horizon was a testament to her suffering. Hitler had promised blitzkreig, and this was it.

Underneath Luton four tunnel shelters had been built, and as the blitz intensified, these were used as dormitories.

The health of Luton's shelter population was a constant source of

RIGHT: *Dr. J. W. Bone, president of the Luton and Dunstable Hospital showing the Mayor of Luton, Councillor John Burgoyne, part of the new laboratory opened at the Hospital in January, 1942.*

BELOW: *Some of the seventy-five children evacuated with the Alexandra Orthopaedic Hospital to Stockwood, Luton, bask in the sun on the lawn in front of the house.*

ABOVE: *A bombed-out Luton family, whose home was left roofless and uninhabitable by a raider, slept at nights in one of Luton's public shelters.*

LEFT: *Luton's tunnel shelter folk, had their Christmas brightened by the Salvation Army, who provided decorations and held a party for the children.*

To enable Luton mothers of young children to carry out war work, day nurseries were opened in various parts of the town.

LEFT: *Children looking at picture books at the Linden Road Day Nursery.*

BELOW: *Toddlers play in the sand while their nurses look on.*

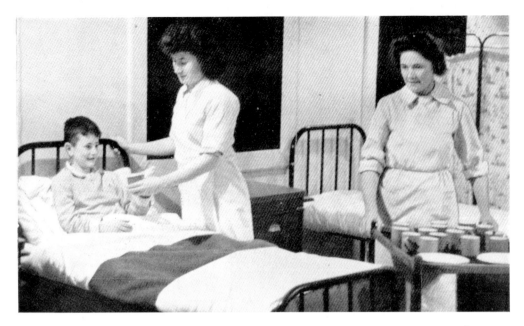

When half the Luton Children's Hospital had to be closed in February 1944 owing to an acute shortage of domestic and nursing staff, a number of Luton war workers, of whom these ladies are two, volunteered and carried out domestic duties there in their spare time.

H.R.H. The Duchess of Kent chats with Sister M. M. Hopkins, Assistant Matron of Luton and Dunstable Hospital, when she inspected members of the hospital's nursing staff, who with other units of the women's services, formed a guard of honour, during the Duchess's visit in April 1943.

concern, and at the same time provided one of the freaks of the war.

Tackling the job from a factual angle, the Department computed that there were 1,277 people sleeping in the tunnel shelters on October 2nd, 1940, and that 404 were under school age. Most of the children came from poorer class homes, and there was no immediate evidence that they were suffering. However, a panel kept watch, and in January, 1941, a survey of the child population was conducted.

Anxiety was relieved when this revealed little to indicate ill-effects, and the story remained unaltered until the end of " shelter-sleeping." The degree to which infectious disease could be attributed to contact in the shelters remained negligible.

Indeed, infectious disease in Luton never reached the heights expected. Vigilance did not relax, and an Emergency Committee remained in office to keep an eye on unusual tendencies, but war ailments and war diseases left Luton alone.

In common with the rest of the country, Luton experienced an increase in tuberculosis during the early years of the war. A similar experience had occurred in 1914-1918, but this time the peak was not accentuated to the same extent, due probably to a wiser nutrition policy on the part of the Government.

Luton did not suffer severely from the increased incidence of scabies which occasioned alarm in some parts of the country, but the Department opened a cleansing station at Bury Park Memorial Hall, at which some cases were treated, and through which whole communities passed when it was considered that there was a risk of infection.

*   *   *   *

Why was it that Luton escaped war infections ? First, it must be remembered that Luton shared this comparative immunity with the nation as a whole. It is largely a matter of conjecture, but the more ordered habits of the people probably had something to do with it. Whatever other effects the black-out had on our lives, at least it was one of the primary causes of getting people to bed early. It kept children at home and advanced their bed-time to an hour which would be considered unusual in days of improved transport and street lighting. During the war many people were schooled into the frame of mind which accepted 9.30 p.m. as a late hour to be out.

People tended to move about less, herded together less in public places, and diminished the risk of contagion. There is evidence, too, that the Government's nutrition policy increased resistance to infectious disease.

During the last two years of the war, however, there was a general medical impression in Luton that the vitality of the adult population was falling off. It was difficult to place a finger on the cause, but the impression was that the ordinary cold, for example, seemed to take longer to shake off, and to hold the victim in its grip for an indeterminate number of days.

It is not beyond the scope of this review to discuss to what extent

Governmental policy in the calling up of men and women affected the vitality and resistance of those left behind.

Local medical opinion, taking Luton as a typical industrial section, questioned whether mobilisation and the call-up had not gone too far. It had placed an immense strain on civilian social services, and especially medical services, and had reduced the capacity of the ordinary family to withstand crises that would have been unimportant in peace time.

The amount of time lost by women workers on health grounds, by male workers to look after sick wives, and by both to take care of children was an example. There were two instances of the strain in local organisation.

Anticipating that the demand for home help in cases of sickness and confinement would exceed the supply, the Council prepared an excellent scheme on paper. But home helps were not forthcoming. The St. John Ambulance Brigade, the W.V.S. and V.A.D. were among those answering the Mayor's request for an emergency force in case an epidemic broke out. But they had to tell the Council that they hardly knew how to meet their own commitments.

The fact, brutally and frankly, is that had there been a serious epidemic of influenza during the last two winters of the war, it is difficult to see how the authorities would have coped with it. It is a fact to be faced, and one which few people realised at the time.

Another example of the shortage was at the Maternity Hospital, where accommodation, too, was restricted. In the last two winters of the war, premature births presented a dilemma. Mothers could not be retained because of the limited number of beds and the shortage of staff, and on the other hand they could not be sent home to what nurses knew would be inadequate heating and unsuitable domestic conditions.

But providence was on the side of the people, and whatever retrograde tendencies may have been evident to the medical mind in the later stages, the town came through largely unscathed and the Health Department never had to face the expected crisis.

*　　*　　*　　*

If the air-raids threw a heavy responsibility on the municipal health services, what effect had they on the Hospitals ?

So far we have taken no account of the part played within the framework of the health organisation by the voluntary institutions, whose sisters and nurses were on call night and day to deal with the casualties whenever the enemy struck.

It was a difficult time for Luton and Dunstable Hospital. In February, 1939, Queen Mary had opened this fine modern building on the Dunstable Road. It was a tribute in bricks and mortar to the progress which the voluntary hospitals had made since 1872, when Luton's first cottage hospital opened with three beds !

The new hospital had 170 beds, and a further 44 were provided under a government scheme.

The hospital's war-time record is an impressive one ; not only was it called on to deal with local patients ; it was a valuable auxiliary as well for London, from where casualties were evacuated. From Luton's raids, 271 casualties were admitted, many of them severely injured.

Many people walking in Luton to-day owe their lives to the skill of the staff of Luton's hospital, and to brilliant surgery often performed under arduous conditions. The staff was under a constant strain, and shortage of nurses was aggravated by the fact that the hospital was serving a growing area.

During the war, between 70 and 90 beds were reserved for service and civilian casualties under the Emergency Medical Service scheme. The fact that they were not always utilised does not mean that the pressure was appreciably less ; the planning to meet the contingency had to be there.

The hospital attended to 4,530 service patients, and these figures pale into insignificance beside the civilian returns. The number of in-patients treated was nearly 23,000, while over 127,000 out-patients came on to the Hospital's books during the same period. The total out-patient attendances were 332,134 and the in-patients and out-patients served under the Emergency Medical Service Scheme amounted to 6,393 and 10,413 respectively.

It was an inspiring performance. But figures and charts do not tell the story of heart-aches and battles for life that were the routine of the war-time hospital ; they do not tell of the exhaustion and mental fatigue suffered by a nursing and medical staff taxed to its limit.

*　　　*　　　*　　　*

The Hospital's biggest success of the war was the production of penicillin in workable quantities.

This episode came at the end of the war-time story, in the spring of 1944, but it is worth telling at this stage, for it put the Hospital on the national map. Once again Luton was first in the field.

It was the first time in the history of voluntary hospitals in Britain that penicillin had been produced for civilian patients. The drug had been very much in the news, but so far its use for civilian purposes had been restricted.

March, 1944, was the month in which it was produced for the first time in Luton, and since then thousands of civilians have benefited from the Hospital's enterprise.

In early 1943 the Hospital was handicapped by the scarcity of penicillin, and it was decided to try to produce it locally. Months of research produced no result. There were searches for mouldy green cheeses, among other things, to see if the mould could be found, but the results were always nil.

Not disheartened, the Hospital persevered. Then, in March, 1944,

Mr. H. Alison Blundell, a member of the Board, succeeded in obtaining a small culture of the mould. This was merely the start of the work.

Night after night Mr. Blundell and Dr. Seiler, the hospital's pathologist, worked in the pathological laboratories. It was an anxious time, and there were many disappointments. But at last success was announced.

The staff of the Hospital will remember the first occasion on which their penicillin was used. A patient was suffering from a disease of the hand which had resisted all known treatment and which was, to all intents and purposes, incurable.

In April penicillin treatment was started, and the patient responded; at the end of a week's treatment the infection was gone. This was the first of a long chain of successful applications of penicillin made within the walls of the Hospital itself. The equipment to produce it was elaborate and the technique complicated. Yet soon after its initial production, enough was being manufactured for 25 local treatments a day.

*   *   *   *

This is near the end of the story. For the rest it is not all the romance of laboratory research, but the story of realities, which at the time were grim enough.

Turn back the clock to 1939. The work of the hospital had already increased by 72 per cent., and people were saying " The Hospital is too small."

In 1940, casualties started to insinuate themselves into the routine cases in the wards; the hospital was administering to the needs of a six-figure population. It was a time for action.

In the winter of 1941, when nurses worked with the distant thunder of the London barrage in their ears, the first plans were formulated for an extension to the Hospital. At this time as many as 94 beds were vacant, under the control of the Ministry of Health. It was a relief when the extension was opened in October the same year.

To take some of the pressure, the Hospital called on auxiliary accommodation, and Emergency Medical Service patients were directed to Ashridge, Arlesey, Friern Barnet and Hill End.

Reserve base was Luton Grammar School. In 1941 a scheme was announced for it to be converted into a reserve hospital in the event of Luton and Dunstable Hospital being damaged, but fortunately, the necessity for this scheme to be put into operation never arose.

A further extension, this time to the casualty department, was opened in 1943 at a cost of £800, and in April of the same year, the Hospital was visited by the Duchess of Kent.

Staff difficulties became more and more acute in the later years of the war, and assumed serious proportions in 1944.

When, in the summer of that year, the first Allied forces were storming Normandy's beaches, and the toll of the V-bombs mounted on the home front, there were signs that the staff shortage might make it

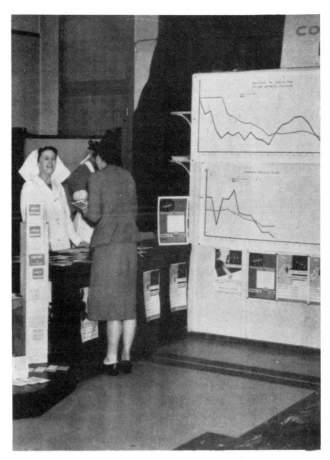

RIGHT: *A nurse answers questions at an exhibition at the Electricity Showrooms during Luton's Health Education Week in September, 1943.*

BELOW: *Luton's Medical Officer of Health, Dr. Fred Grundy, (right) taking part in a recorded discussion on the town's health services for a broadcast in the B.B.C.'s European Service in March, 1945. He is standing in front of a graph illustrating Luton's increased birthrate . . . the rising line can be seen above his companion's left shoulder.*

difficult to meet a major crisis. In the following spring, when the Canadians and the British were going down through the Reichswald, the Hospital was coping with even more patients than before. When Montgomery was carrying the battle across the Rhine a few weeks after, the nursing position was being described as " acute."

Not until June, 1945, was a staff improvement reported, and by that time other Hospital news took priority. There were rumours of a changed constitution, of a merger with the Children's Hospital, of a doubled capacity when building was possible again.

*   *   *   *

That was no part of the war story ; the Hospital had done its job, and written some notable additions to the history of voluntary medicine. Big things had been done, but to conclude this miniature hospital saga, here are two of the smaller stories . . . two of the human pictures which illustrate the inner greatness of a country at war.

In September, 1941, an effort was being made to raise £1,000. One day in that month, three small children, rather shy, but determined, were ushered into the Secretary's office.

They waited, and then the eldest stepped forward. His little hand clutched an envelope, which he thrust towards Mr. Lingard.

The secretary opened it, and inside was a note :—

> " Please accept this small effort. We have had a little concert and collected from a few friends. Enclosed 5s. K. Churcher, V. Churcher, A. Pearson."

The three children had given a concert in their front room to an admiring audience of relatives and friends. And the complete proceeds of this command performance had been given to the Hospital—and the sum, was in fact, the first amount to be credited to the new fund.

The second of the stories concerns the staff itself. In the rush and pressure that was war-time hospital work, the nurses could still spare time to think of the welfare of those who were in uniform and facing terrible dangers on active service. It is a story not without its tragedy, and not without its happy ending.

In 1940, the nurses decided to " adopt " the submarine *Undaunted*. Adopting it meant sending, originally, the gift of a few books. These the nurses obtained by saving amongst themselves. Gradually the gifts grew—it was no longer only books, but harmonicas and gramophone records. They sent their cigarettes, and they sent Christmas presents.

They formed pen friendships with the men of the *Undaunted*, and many were the letters exchanged between the crew and the nurses of the Luton and Dunstable Hospital.

Then, quite suddenly, in 1941, the correspondence stopped The *Undaunted* was missing. The nurses never saw their friends of the submarine . . .

They decided to try again. This time they adopted one of the sister submarines—the *Unbending*. Again they sent gifts of books, and again they collected, through their social club, to send Christmas boxes. And more pen friendships were formed.

In July, 1945, seven members of the crew spent a 48 hours leave at the Hospital as guests of the staff, and were given a royal time. They were welcomed by the Mayor, Alderman Lady Keens, and highlight of the visit was a dance held in their honour. They presented the matron, sisters and nurses with a silver fruit basket, and a replica of the submarine's " Jolly Roger " flown from the periscope whenever it entered harbour after making a " kill."

In the nurses' home, there is a replica of the submarine's crest.

Perhaps some of the crew of the *Unbending* will see this. If they do, this incident is recalled in the hope that it will provoke reminiscences of a happy association, and for seven of their members at least, memories of a leave spent at Luton, with their friends the nurses at the Hospital.

*   *   *   *

At Luton Children's Hospital, the first rush of evacuation was felt at a time when the staff was busy converting one of the wards into a first aid post, in preparation for the possibility of heavy casualties.

In 1940 an influx of bombed-out children caused a problem. At the same time, Luton had its own taste of air-raids, and the Hospital suffered some structural damage. However, it carried on, and when the real crisis came in 1944, it was not from the air.

In common with other institutions it was feeling a staff shortage. The handicap became so serious that eventually the position was reached where nurses were doing domestic work. The position worsened and one ward containing 26 of the 56 beds had to be closed.

Then there came a demonstration of the spirit of mutual help which was so often manifest during the war. Workers, their energies taxed by a heavy day at the factory, might justly have claimed that they were already making their best possible gift to the war effort, but they volunteered to work for the children during their off duty.

Rangers and guides came forward, and the principal industrial concerns of the district provided teams of helpers. Twenty employees from Electrolux were early volunteers, and Vauxhall Motors started an organisation to promote regular help. Soon the ranks of applicants to help had swollen to such an extent that a meeting had to be arranged at the Town Hall to fix a rota !

St. Mary's Hospital, under the aegis of the County Council, was another institution which suffered both from shortage of staff and accommodation. Luton Area Guardians Committee was responsible for the direct administration of both the institution and the hospital, in Dunstable Road. The days of the institution pictured in the crusades of Dickens had gone, but the new Master, Mr. J. A. Green, came in 1941 to find a legacy of accommodation rendered inadequate by war demands.

In 1940 Hitler's planes started their machine-gunning and mining attacks on the East Coast . . . the low-lying Essex beaches facing the North Sea, were no longer a playground for the young. Crippled children of Clacton were evacuated to St. Mary's.

The story of St. Mary's is briefly one of more patients than beds, and appeals for more nurses. In 1943, for example, there was reached a situation where six nurses were attending to 123 cases. The accommodation situation was eased when in December, 1944, a wing of the old Bute Hospital was taken over.

Not all the Hospitals in Luton during the war were local organisations. To St. Margaret's, formerly the New Bedford Road Casual Wards, came the Home and Hospital for Jewish Incurables.

The inmates of the home had been refugees since the first air-raid sirens. They evacuated from Tottenham to Essex in the early days—providentially, for their home was badly damaged by bombs. Then, their new home in Essex was damaged by an explosion.

They arrived in St. Margaret's, bringing about 60 patients, and later a further 40 were accommodated at the request of the Middlesex County Council.

Another refugee hospital was the Queen Alexandra Orthopaedic, from Swanley, Kent, which evacuated to Stockwood. Swanley was a railway junction, destined to see most of the Battle of Britain. Moreover the tentacles of greater London spread towards it and close by the chimneys of industrial Kent belched their smoke into the Thames skies. It was a legitimate target, and on the road to even better targets. It was also no place for a Children's Hospital.

To Stockwood, home of the Crawleys for 500 years, came the children of the Alexandra Hospital. They played on the smooth, green lawns, and the house echoed to their laughter. Few of them will forget their first Christmas at Luton . . .

*   *   *   *

A far cry, perhaps, from Luton's planned health campaign, from a record of municipal achievement to a little child playing in the summer sun on Stockwood's lawns . . . a far cry, perhaps, from a chemist working hard into the night to produce life-saving penicillin, to three little children shyly handing 5s. to the hospital secretary.

But it is not, perhaps, an inappropriate note on which to end Luton's war-time health story, for the children of those days will be citizens of the town which will see the Public Health Department's plans brought to fruition, and the vision of a bigger Hospital realised.

For the Hospital which made the penicillin found that it progressed not in spite of, but because of, the war.

And in the Town Hall, a file has come back into Dr. Grundy's in-basket.

The Stream of Life

THE transfusion of blood to fortify the vitality of the human body is a comparatively modern development of surgery.

In the public mind it is still believed widely, but quite erroneously, to be a " last resort " to which recourse is taken when a patient is *in extremis*. That is not so now. It is a valuable aid to surgical science and its use is so widespread that it has become a commonplace treatment in all cases where the natural resistance of the human constitution can be—not necessarily must be—strengthened.

By experience, too, it has been found that the donation of a pint of blood by a normal healthy human being leaves no ill effects; so responsive is the natural function that the deficit soon disappears.

The Red Cross started their Blood Transfusion Service as early as 1921, but the imminence of war in 1938 and early 1939 demanded a lightning expansion of the facilities.

The fruits of this have been the saving of countless lives. Men, women and children, hundreds, nay, thousands of them, are alive to-day only because this great national service was at hand when it was needed.

The Emergency Blood Transfusion Service began to operate in Luton early in 1939, when preliminary tests were made of volunteers. When war started Luton became one of twelve centres where a depot was established, and one of four intended to serve London and the Home Counties in a national emergency.

The emergency came, and blood given by Luton people helped to save the lives of hundreds injured in air raids. It had been collected at regular intervals from the numerous donors and stored in special cooling chambers at St. Mary's Hospital. This was Luton's Blood Bank.

During the war the Luton depot, of which Dr. J. Shone was director, collected over 170,000 bottles of blood from volunteers in this area, and all demands for civilian air raid casualties in London and the Home Counties, and for the vast needs of the Navy, Army and R.A.F. in all theatres of war, were met. Blood was also provided for the Merchant Navy, U.S. Forces, for Malta, and for the Chinese, Belgian and Dutch Red Cross Organisations.

Local donors came from all walks of life. They were mainly factory workers. Nearly every Luton factory had its own panel, and periodically had " blood drives " for new donors. Quite a number of the donors were housewives.

The week before D-day saw the peak in the number of donors offering their blood. Good attendances were maintained throughout the early months of the invasion, so inspiring were the events of the time.

RIGHT: *A section of the blood bank at the old Luton Bute Hospital, later known as St. Mary's Hospital, where blood was preserved in specially built cooling chambers, ready to be sent out at a moment's notice.*

BELOW: *The way it was done. The donor's arm is bound up and from a punctured vein, blood is withdrawn into a specially sealed bottle.*

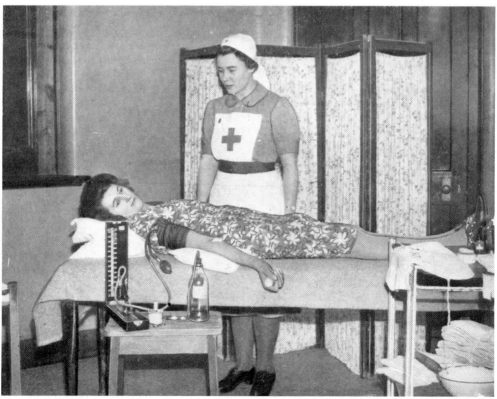

Some interesting figures of the work of the Depot during that period can be given. In May, 1944, 2,485 new donors were enrolled, 5,002 were called upon, and 4,859 responded. In June another 2,005 donors were enrolled, 8,007 were called upon, and 6,741 responded. In July, although new donors had increased, the need proved to be not so great for the Normandy casualties were far fewer than had been anticipated. New donors totalled 2,937, 7,821 were called upon, and 6,392 responded.

In the three months of June, July and August, 1944, 1,700, 1,800, and 1,600 bottles of whole blood (liquid blood) were sent from the Luton depot to meet war needs.

There was much enthusiasm among donors in the Luton area. Many a person was seen proudly exhibiting the small blue and gold card recording the dates on which blood had been given. For every ten occasions the donor received a special certificate, and although no person could give more often than once in three months, a sort of competition developed among many as to who could put up a record.

Blood transfusion has long since proved its worth. Although for the last seven years it has been essentially a wartime service, the need for its continuance exists in peace as in war.

The donors of 1939-1946, unlike members of other war organisations are not standing down. They are still at hand and the stream of life is in their keeping.

War Against Waste

OLD iron caused more bad tempers in Luton than anything else concerned with the salvage campaign.

It was not the old iron for which the itinerant collector formerly shouted, when he also wanted rags, bones, and bottles. It was the iron garden fences and the front garden gates from thousands of Luton homes. People were not asked whether they would like to surrender them. It was announced that they would be taken, unless they had definite artistic or historical value, which would have to be substantiated, and that a very modest value would be allowed,—if the owners claimed it. Whether claimed or not, it was nothing like the probable cost of reinstatement.

The average Luton fences and gates had no claim to art or history. They disappeared. The immediate result was to give a pretty forlorn appearance to many a hitherto neat frontage. The householder's willingness to stand the loss might have been greater but for a considerable doubt as to whether the sacrifice was really necessary. He heard of dumps of this old iron accumulating for months, for no apparent use or reason. He heard that after the metal had been collected it proved unsuitable. No wonder he asked whether his fences and gates were a real contribution to the war effort.

He was told that the old iron in the dumps was not the same old iron all the time—that it was going to the foundries as well as coming to the dumps. He still doubted the truth of this, and looking at neighbours' fences and gates which remained because they were wooden, had a feeling that he had been hardly used.

Where people could afford it, and could get it done, there was considerable activity in getting brick walls and wooden gates erected, so what was gained in one material was lost in others. For the majority, however, this kind of replacement was impracticable.

In Luton, there are two main objections to the open garden. One is that people in general are rather conservative. Their gardens always have been enclosed and they always must be enclosed, otherwise, they feel, they are robbed of their privacy. The other reason, a much more cogent one, is that a few people are no respecters of unprotected gardens. What happened was a peculiar form of vandalism. Not only were flower beds trampled down, but shrubs were stolen or torn to pieces, and saplings were broken and irretrievably damaged. There was no rhyme or reason for it.

But it was not only the individual householder who suffered at the hands of hooligans after the fences and gates went. Immediately it ceased to be possible to close the parks and recreation grounds at dusk a wave of wanton destruction began. Further reference is made to this elsewhere, but it will cost the ratepayers as a whole thousands of pounds if these pleasure grounds and open spaces are ever to recover their pre-war beauty.

Those are some of the things about the salvage campaign which have left unpleasant memories. It is an ironical comment that some old iron abandoned in Pope's Meadow by the Army even before the fence-grabbing started remained there for years, although for a long time Luton was the headquarters of the Army Salvage Training School. That old iron remained until it ceased to be worth salvaging. It may still be there.

*　　　*　　　*　　　*

Happily other aspects of the salvage campaign were free from any such repercussions. They can be regarded as an asset to the war effort, with no debit.

The Luton News was the first in the town to organise a waste paper collection scheme. The first entry in the books was three-halfpence paid for a small parcel on October 5th, 1939, The following day, 10d. was paid for waste paper, and thereafter the scheme grew like a snowball. By May, 1940, *The Luton News* scheme had been adopted

ABOVE: *Any old iron? Luton children enter into the spirit of Luton's Salvage Week in 1941.*

LEFT: *Part of a week's accumulation of waste paper at Luton Corporation Depot.*

BELOW: *Mrs. Day, of Kennington Road, receives yet another saucepan to add to the pile of aluminium in her front garden.*

LEFT: Food waste collected from bins in the streets of the town, being fed into the boiler at Luton Corporation depot.

BELOW : The finished "meal" . . . fit for a pig.

by practically every provincial newspaper in the country, and thousands of tons from newspaper offices alone were finding their way back to the mills.

One of the features of *The Luton News* scheme was a weekly collection from the schools. A van went round, the bundles brought to the school by the children were weighed, cash was paid on the spot, and the money went to some special school fund. A league table was published, and the enthusiasm of the children was tremendous. The record of collection goes to Maidenhall Junior Boys' School, who collected over 23 tons while the league was in operation. The league aggregate from the schools of Luton was over 114 tons, and this takes no account of the quantity afterwards collected by the schools and handled by the Cleansing Department's Salvage Collection Scheme.

The most comprehensive contribution in Luton to the general salvage campaign was made through the Public Cleansing Department. When the Government launched the salvage campaign in November, 1939, the Town Council acted at once. Facilities for collection and disposal were provided at the Cleansing Depot in Windmill Road, an advertising campaign was started, and early in 1940 a leaflet was distributed to every house urging people to prepare a weekly parcel for the dustman. They were asked to save every scrap of waste paper, and also rags, bones, bottles, jars, and anything in the way of of scrap metal.

By the time a Defence Regulation made it obligatory on local authorities to salvage waste paper, Luton's voluntary scheme was well under way, and in the three months to June, 1940, salvage collected totalled 280 tons, worth £1,122. It was a good beginning, but nothing to what was to follow.

To increase recovery of waste, the Town Council varied a long-standing policy to enable certain classes of waste to be collected from trade premises without charge.

At the meeting where this decision was made, the Director of Cleansing, Mr. John Stephen, reported that he had initiated another move, destined to put Luton right into the forefront as a pioneer salvage authority. This was the special collection of kitchen waste which could be prepared for feeding pigs and poultry, and so supplement or take the place of imported feeding stuffs. To begin with, collection was only possible in certain parts of the town. In these areas each house received a card to hang in the kitchen, as a reminder of the need to save the food waste, and as a guide to what was useful and what was not. If, as town dwellers, they were not certain, they learned from the card that pigs and poultry did not appreciate rhubarb leaves, tea leaves, coffee grounds, or orange peel, but that there were a lot of kitchen odds and ends they would like. Collection was combined with the usual collection of house refuse.

Happenings of 1940 and 1941 made it difficult to extend the salvage effort. Manpower was short; transport was short. Many of the employees were key A.R.P. personnel, and had a lot extra to do when there was bombing. A mortuary for civilian dead had to be established and maintained. It had a heavy duty in the first big raid of August 30th, 1940 The department was responsible for a lot of other jobs in connection with Civil Defence. The winter brought a heavy snowfall.

It became clear that the regular collection of food waste would become increasingly difficult, and to obviate people having to keep it for unduly long periods in their homes, the communal bin system was adopted. Then the whole town was covered ; 1,000 bins were provided.

Out of this expansion came the installation of a concentrator plant, to process the waste and provide a ready-cooked food for pigs and poultry. The livestock liked it, and it found a ready market, so much so that Luton began to import the raw waste. In addition to the direct collection of a small amount from the villages, food waste was received from the local authorities of Dunstable, Leighton Buzzard, Harpenden, St. Albans and Welwyn Garden City, and from the Service and prisoners-of-war camps in Bedfordshire and Hertfordshire. At the end of the war 250 tons a month were being collected in the town, and 140 tons received from these outside sources. By evaporation about a third of the weight was lost in the concentrator plant, but there remained about 260 tons a month for sale to farmers and poultry keepers.

Some other figures are enlightening. During the period of the war the Cleansing Department collected and returned to industry 17,199 tons of essential raw materials, of the value of £76,011. Food waste totalled 10,522 tons, value £41,248. Waste paper took second place with 4,793 tons, £27,025. Scrap metals were third, 1,240 tons, £2,092. The scrap metals must not be associated with those fences and gates, with the removal of which the Cleansing Department had no concern.

The total weight was roughly equivalent to a whole year's collection of household and trade refuse. The value was equivalent to £12,880 a year, or a 4d. rate. At £76,000 the total was only about £8,000 less than the net cost of running the Public Cleansing Department for the last three years of the war.

As a sideline, help was given with the occasional book drives, which had a threefold object—to get books for the Services, for blitzed libraries, and for salvage. These campaigns brought from the shelves books which had probably never been read for decades, and just over 360,000 were of no better value than to go for salvage ; but 2,605 were picked out for blitzed libraries, and 26,661 were of a type it was felt the Services would appreciate.

The Army Salvage Training School, during its three years at Luton, made good use of the Windmill Road depot as a practical instructional centre. Mr. Stephen lectured to officers and men on municipal

ABOVE: *Sign of the times . . . 1. Luton Parish Church was denuded of its iron railing when the call for scrap iron was made . . . but somehow the gateway was left behind.*

BELOW: *Sign of the times . . . 2. The war years increased hooliganism in Luton's public parks. Taken in Kingsway Recreation Ground this picture of a shelter shows broken windows, woodwork ripped away, and tiles smashed on the roof.*

salvage, and from time to time there were distinguished visitors to inspect the methods of handling, sorting and grading salvage. They included Field-Marshal Lord Milne, General Sir Walter Venning, Quartermaster-General; Major-General Buckley, Director of Economy, War Office; and Brig.-General Badcock, Director of Salvage, War Office.

From 1942, at the request of the Ministry of Supply, and having got the Luton Salvage Campaign well established, Mr. Stephen was lent to the Ministry's Salvage Department, and was Deputy Assistant Director of Salvage and Recovery until recalled in April, 1945. He still acts for the Ministry as honorary district salvage adviser for Bedfordshire and Hertfordshire.

*　　*　　*　　*

It has been noted that it was around the collection of waste paper that the salvage campaign originated. The war created new uses for paper and cardboard. Many sources of raw materials for the paper industry were cut off. Dutch board went off the market until early 1946. Waste had to be utilised. Old newspapers largely went back to newsprint mills, although only a limited proportion could be incorporated with new material. Rough waste was just as important. Sent back to the mills, it emerged again in quick time in new forms. As board, it largely superseded metal when made into containers for the transit of certain types of munitions. As coarse paper, it had many war uses.

It was easy to collect in the early stages. When newspapers were reduced in size and restricted in numbers, when many magazines came down to diminutive size or disappeared altogether, when papers magazines, and books, once read, were sent to menfolk overseas, when traders were no longer permitted to wrap their goods, quantity collection of waste became far less easy.

Most of the waste paper passed through the hands of Messrs. Mitchell and Outen for transfer to the mills, and they handled 10,290 tons. It is clear that this salvage activity saved a considerable amount of shipping—and dollars. But even that figure was not the complete total. A considerable quantity of used newsprint went by rail direct to the mills, and there were consignments of printed waste so secret that lorries came from the mills to fetch it, and a special escort had to accompany the waste to the mills to ensure that no bundle was opened on the journey.

*　　*　　*　　*

Supplementing the salvage campaign Luton was covered by the Container Recovery Service, a co-operative effort by manufacturers to collect from retailers cartons, tins, wooden boxes, drums, sacks, and any packing material good for further service. Luton made its fair contribution to the six years' total of two hundred millions for the whole country.

The Fruits of the Earth

IN 1940 and early 1941 the food situation in Britain began to look rather grim, and the Englishman was faced not only with the necessity of tightening his belt, but with the prospect of pulling it in even further in the future.

There were no early potatoes coming from the Channel Islands or sources farther away. Tomatoes did not come from warmer climes. Spanish and Egyptian onions were off the market. Cauliflowers could not be brought from the Continent. We had no bananas, and for these there was no home-produced substitute. Other things for the table were cut off, for ships were going down at the rate of one a day, and those that stayed afloat had more vital cargoes to carry. So, lest we should go shorter than need be, people had to set to and dig.

Some of the diggers, of course, were old hands, cultivators of long-established allotment fields. But they were few, whereas wartime diggers became legion. At the peak period they were estimated to number 5,000.

They dug, and did other related work, in about 60 allotment areas often in the most unlikely quarters. They dug up corner sites which had not been built upon. They dug up patches of ground so cluttered with rubbish that it seemed almost hopeless to try and bring it back into cultivation. Old bedsteads, bicycle remnants, rusty parts of antiquated prams, and so on, came up with the forks. Never was there such a clearance.

It was recognised that the nearer a plot was to a man's home the more attention it would receive, as the minimum of time would be wasted in getting to it, and there was scarcely a part of the town which did not have some plots handy.

Individual plots were often larger than the recommended ten poles, so that part could be devoted to vegetables suitable for winter storage. A cup materialised to stimulate interest in winter greens particularly, as these were of special value at a time when so little else could be got from the ground.

Many plotholders were more enthusiastic than expert, but as the plots were in groups there was usually somebody handy who had the knowledge and, what was more important, was willing to share it.

Lectures, films, brains trusts also helped, and as time went on even those who had been novices could exhibit their produce at the shows held annually, with more than reasonable hope of winning awards.

And those shows ! Well, village folk know what their annual show meant in the years when they were at the height of their popularity. The allotment holders' shows eventually bid fair to rival the glory of those old village shows.

Allotment associations increased to seven, and were linked in a

S

ABOVE: *Week-end volunteers putting sheaves into stooks on one of Luton Corporation's farms.*

LEFT: *Cabbages among the flowers, in Luton Parish Churchyard.*

BELOW: *Four air raid wardens were the founders of the first Luton pig club, and are seen admiring their proteges in the piggery near Wardown Crescent.*

RIGHT: *Girls of Surrey Street School, Luton, hoeing and watering the crops on the allotment, which was their contribution to "Digging for Victory."*

BELOW: *The result of their efforts. The produce on view at the Harvest Festival, in the school.*

ABOVE: *Mr. C. H. Middleton, the famous broadcaster, congratulated the people of Luton on their great efforts when he opened the Ministry of Agriculture's exhibition at Wardown in August, 1945.*

LEFT: *Exhibits at a produce show arranged by the Dallow Road and district allotment holders.*

BELOW: *A smart detachment of Land Girls parade round the arena at Wardown Sports Ground on Farm Sunday in June, 1943.*

Federation. The various Association shows not only stimulated the production of good quality vegetables, which was their primary aim, but also raised considerable sums of money for the Red Cross Agriculture Fund and for local charitable causes.

They were generous people, those plotholders. They put the pick of their plots into the shows. They generally ended with all the exhibits being sold for charity, and more than one prize-winner bought another man's non-prizewinning exhibits—all could not be winners—for the good of the cause.

Meanwhile home gardens were not neglected. There were fewer flowers and more vegetables. The latter sometimes monopolised even front gardens ; but this does not mean that a few flowers in the corner were frowned upon.

Did not the late and great Mr. C. H. Middleton, who more than once visited Luton in connection with " Dig for Victory " weeks, always advise that in seeking the useful one should not wholly ignore that which was beautiful, and that even to grow more vegetables one should not uproot all the roses ?

*　　*　　*　　*

While allotment holders were busy on their plots, and home gardeners on their patches, some of the larger factories started allotment fields for their employees. Thirty schools had allotments or large gardens, and the Parks Committee practised what they preached by doing similar things, but on a larger scale.

On 30 sites they cultivated about 500 acres which had not been producing food crops. There was a large area at the Airport, and another at the Chalton site for the new Electricity Works.

Smaller areas were scattered about the town. All were open and there was no provision for storing the necessary machinery, which had to be driven miles to and fro. Skilled agricultural labour was practically unobtainable, and crops produced probably cost far more than they would have done under other conditions. Nevertheless they were grown without loss to the town.

Off this land came wheat enough for about 1,400,000 loaves of bread. 12,860 cwts. of additional vegetables, and considerable quantities of barley, rye, oats, and cattle food.

At the same time, through getting the allotment holders organised, the Committee was able to arrange for the distribution of fertilisers and seed at specially favourable prices, and, from Wardown, etc., to supply a lot of hardened-off young stuff ready for planting on the allotments.

*　　*　　*　　*

Extra food production was helped in the town in other ways. They had nothing to do with digging, but they justify mention here. Pig clubs were started, and although they did not become very numerous, those who had a stake in one found themselves well provided when in due time a pig went to a bacon factory. The factory kept part and returned part for clubbers to share.

277

But, if pigs did not become numerous, back-garden poultry did. Many people who found it difficult, and sometimes impossible to get eggs through normal channels, decided to become poultry keepers. Neighbours often benefited by registering for eggs with the amateur poultry keeper. They passed over their food scraps, and got a more regular egg supply than they would have done through the shops. It all helped the food supply.

*   *   *   *

While all these efforts at increased production were going on in the town, the countryside was not ignored. People were encouraged to go to farm camps and lend the farmers a hand in harvest or other busy seasons ; some went to help lift the potato crop ; some even know now what it means to help lift sugar beet.

" Dig for Victory " was the slogan of the times. The result through six years of war was staggering. The allotments alone in Luton, provided vegetables for sixteen million meals, according to the statistics and report prepared by Mr. R. J. English, Luton's Director of Parks.

" Dig for Victory " in Luton was much stimulated by Mr. English's help. It was intended as a personal encouragement to the individual to fend for himself and grow, as far as possible, his own needs. In fact it became synonymous with every aspect of food production, and nothing was of more value in offsetting war shortages and keeping the kitchen well supplied.

Whatever the monetary value of these homegrown vegetables, they had a far greater indirect value. They maintained the vigorous health of the individual not only by their own nutritive properties but by the benefit they brought through exercise and an open air occupation to many a stale or jaded worker. They were in a large measure the regenerating agent for industry.

Rationing and Prices

THE story of rationing is the story of the retailer, and the story of the consumer. We can leave out of it for the moment the unapproachable and often unpredictable Government departments responsible. The retailer was their instrument, and he got the kicks from the consumer. Both were harassed in mind and exhausted in body. The retailer tried to cope with crowds of disappointed shoppers, hopeful shoppers, bullying shoppers, wheedling shoppers, legally-minded shoppers, sinister shoppers, what-have-you-under-the-counter shoppers, and those wolves in sheeps' clothing, Government inspectors disguised as shoppers.

He tried all the time to keep tabs on the latest rationing regulations, and writhed as " registrations " and " directions " abstracted from his employment, one by one, his well-trained, experienced, and always helpful assistants whose successors, more often than not, were inefficient and sometimes irresponsible. Some seemed only too regrettably unaware that however long the war might last, courtesy and helpfulness need never be included among the things " in short supply."

The consumer, the housewife charged with feeding the family and clothing the children, found her responsibilities and difficulties growing steadily as the years of war went by. Here is the view of one of them who, in addition to bringing up some small children, also went out to work :

The war, she maintains, could never have been won without the scheming and planning of the British housewife to get the best possible value out of the rations. Yet the housewife was probably the only " war worker " who had no official recognition of her services, which, at times, taxed her patience and ingenuity almost to the breaking point. Apart from the problems which faced her within the home, there were the added troubles of shopping under great difficulties. When queueing was at its worst, and because the things which were wanted were at their scarcest, it was a heartbreaking and tiring task . . . one which took three or four times as long as before the war. This, plus doing war work to make good the absence of a man in the Forces, usually meant early to rise and late to bed, with the home tasks squeezed in between work and shopping.

And to this particular housewife, as probably to many others, it came as a shock to find that the worst period of rationing seemed to be when one really expected things to become a bit better, the world war having ended. Meals, if adequate, had been no more. Their sufficiency for young and growing people, she had always thought was open to question, and their value was not increased by their monotony. Having learned kitchen economy in the hard school of experience, however, and having hoped for some easing of her burdens, the housewife saw this hope fade, and submitted to the imposition of more cuts, and talk of still more, because after the liberation of Europe all the food that could be spared was not enough to feed Europe's hungry mouths.

*   *   *   *

Rationing had no prophet to honour ; few people had any concrete idea of what it would be like after the first three years. It has not gone without its historians, and they have not been tardy in pointing out errors in the system.

Nobody will pretend that everything attempted by authority was a complete success. The lessons were too often learned at the expense of the consumer and the man behind the counter.

Rationing was a necessary evil. Any cross-section of life in Luton would show that it succeeded largely because there was, from the first day of the war, an acceptance of the fact that this was 1917 again ; there was another war afoot in which a priority target for the enemy would be the larder of the ordinary housewife. But there was this fundamental exception—this time we knew more, and rationing started almost with the first sirens of 1939. As a result, there was no outstanding shortage of food in Luton.

Some commodities were occasionally difficult to secure. Transport difficulties started a small bread scare in January, 1940, and many bakers still remember the sudden outbreak of panic buying which took place, as the impression gained credence that there was a serious shortage. For once many Luton shoppers were fooled by rumour.

Policy in higher quarters was not free from blame for the periodic difficulties which arose in the supply of unrationed foodstuffs to Luton. At no time did it seem that the problem of ensuring a fair supply of these foods had been solved to satisfaction. Account did not appear to have been taken of Luton's inflated population. Luton retailers will tell you that supplies of unrationed foods never followed the people that moved into the town to an adequate degree. As a result proper allocations could not be made. Shopkeepers were supplied in many cases on a datum basis, that is, according to quantities bought in 1939, which meant that subsequent movements of the population were not considered.

*   *   *   *

Generally, Luton's position as regards rationed commodities compared favourably with other districts. The prompt introduction of food control in 1939 was on the whole welcomed by the retailer. Control meant legislation, it meant restrictions, it meant officialdom. It meant many unpleasant things, all of which spelled headache for the man serving you in the little shop on the corner.

But it also meant something else. It meant that his supplies of rationed commodities to meet his registered customers' allowances became the responsibility of the Ministry of Food, and for that he was thankful. The little man was freed from the task of searching any-where and everywhere for someone who could and would supply ; it limited the purchases of those with more time on their hands and more money in their pockets than others less fortunately placed. So far as rationed goods were concerned, it stopped shop-crawling and unequal distribution.

*   *   *   *

The retailer may have grumbled about rationing, but that was not his biggest headache. That came from the spasmodic and uncertain appearance on his shelves of the unrationed goods. It is when one draws a comparison between the easy way in which rationed items were obtained from the shops, and the muddle which frequently attended other commodities, that the value and success of rationing became clear. Often the problem of obtaining equitable distribution of other foodstuffs to complete the family shopping list assumed nightmarish proportions.

Action was inevitable, and a nation-wide demand for the Ministry of Food to regulate the provision of non-rationed goods in short supply resulted in the introduction of the points rationing scheme. This was delayed until November 17th, 1941, and by that time most of the larger establishments in Luton had instituted schemes of their own to ensure a fair share-out.

After retailer and consumer had mastered the routine of points rationing, the benefits of the scheme were evident. But this did not end the retailers' troubles. Certain branded foods such as canned salmon and canned meats, were very popular, and to secure these goods on points customers started to go from shop to shop. The problem of the retailer was this. If he sold these goods to all and sundry, his registered customers stood a poor chance. If he reserved goods for them, it was against the expressed desire of the Ministry of Food that the public should get points food anywhere. Eventually, the Minister ruled that it was in order for retailers to reserve goods on points for registered customers.

With the points rationing system came the points banking system. Under this scheme the retailer's bank opened for him a points account, which he worked in all respects as if it were a current account in pounds shillings and pence.

*   *   *   *

One of the earliest phenomena of control was the institution of meat distribution centres.

The scheme was introduced in November, 1939, and was put into operation for the first time during the second week of January, 1940, when all private slaughtering ceased.

From that date, livestock were taken over by the Ministry of Food through collecting centres. The wholesalers were permitted to form a body called the W.M.S.A. (Wholesale Meat Supply Association), and this distributed the meat on behalf of the Ministry.

Luton was one of the local centres selected for the grading of cattle ; from the slaughter-houses the meat went to the distribution centre in Crescent Road, from where the butchers were provided with their requirements.

The ration to the public varied from time to time but even during the worst shortage the butcher was able to provide his customer with a bigger ration than at the time of the gravest shortage in the previous war, when prices were higher.

*   *   *   *

The unrationed wares of the fishmonger were more than ever in demand in Luton to eke out the ration, and a system operated to ensure that inland towns received their fair share of the catch. As a result of a zoning scheme, Luton's fish generally came from Fleetwood, although a few retailers received fish from Grimsby, through an inland wholesaler at Hitchin.

The zoning system, however, had one great drawback, a drawback which accentuated queueing. In pre-war times Luton's fish arrived early in the morning, and was on sale from the time shoppers began to get about. Under the zoning delivery it often did not arrive until mid-day. Shops did not open until they had the fish, and then the pavements were already being blocked by queues. And the kinds of fish! Many a housewife has banned for ever from her household menus the name of salted cod. For this inoffensive fish familiarity bred the utmost distaste. At one period also catfish had risen so much in the social scale that it lay unashamedly on the fishmonger's slab.

*   *   *   *

The arrangements made for meat rationing, points, and canned foods, however, were simple compared with the problems which arose when milk rationing was introduced in October, 1941.

A complicated business from the start, it involved a complete record of the constitution of every family, as the quantity of milk was regulated according to the number of children, adolescents, and adults in each home. Then the price was dependant on the economic conditions of the home. Free milk was provided where the financial position was acute, cheap milk was supplied for children under five, while full price was charged for the remainder.

Special allowances were allocated for medical cases and some classes of workers were also regarded as priority consumers.

The remainder of the milk went to non-priority customers—that is people not in the special classes already enumerated, and as the amount to be supplied to priority classes varied considerably at differing periods, it followed that non-priority consumers found their allocation fluctuating frequently.

A number of farmers were allotted to each dairyman, and where the supply allocated was insufficient to meet demands, as in the case of the larger distributors, the deficit was made up from big creameries at a great distance, and transported by road and rail, with price margins severely controlled.

Not only did the authorised allocation vary, the yield from the farms varied with the seasons, and this meant an occasional surplus after the dairyman had effected normal delivery. The retailer could never regard the position as reliable and the system, necessary though it was, involved an elaborate recording system, throwing considerable strain on milk producers.

Later, in order to economise in labour, petrol, tyres and vehicles, a scheme of block distribution was introduced, and with the exception of the Co-operative Society the customers of all the Luton dairymen were placed in a common pool. They were then re-allocated to each dairyman within a limited compass, so that instead of travelling all over the town to deliver to his clients, the dairyman was given the same number of customers within the radius of a few streets. Registrations were frozen, and only in exceptional circumstances were customers allowed to re-register.

When the block distribution system worked hand in hand with the rationing system proper, a tremendous amount of labour was involved, and in the transitional stages there was some confusion. Rationalisation of delivery started early in 1943, and for a few days some householders found they had insufficient milk, or even none. Others found they had too much.

Ultimately the scheme settled down to organised working, and although it was never perfect owing to the high level of administration required, it was a step towards economy, and contributed to the sharing of the milk resources on an equitable basis.

*   *   *   *

Bread was unrationed until 1946, but Luton bakers were confronted with a peculiar situation almost immediately on the outbreak of war. The first influx of evacuees created a demand which it was impossible to meet with immediate labour and materials. There was, of course, no transfer of these from the home area. It meant, too, long hours for the master and the operatives.

Local bakers found the call-up of the men for the services affected delivery rather than production, and getting the bread to the customer was the chief worry. Three-day delivery, though it brought a saving in rubber and petrol, was not the complete answer.

Bread became darker as the war went on. It was found necessary to increase the extraction milled from the wheats, which, to the man in the street, simply meant that darker coloured flour was used. With less choice of wheats, the flour varied considerably, and the baker had continually to alter his process to produce a satisfactory loaf.

Luton bakers were well prepared against the emergency which would have arisen had the yeast supply failed. They were generally instructed in the use of barms, and arrangements were made to store considerable quantities of yeast with the local brewers. Facilities would have been available to manufacture a considerable quantity at the breweries had the need arisen ; the arrangements included the installation of special water tanks.

A mutual aid scheme was devised by the bakers, and an outline issued to all concerned, but happily it was never found necessary to bring this plan into effect. The scheme was co-ordinated with other areas in Eastern Region.

While Luton bakers had their difficulties, they were all surmountable, but there remained the human element with which to contend. The manufacture of bread was one thing which could not be postponed from day to day ; it had to be continuous despite staff shortage.

283

Yet the bread supply never failed. The bakers could echo the sentiment of a London theatre and claim that they never closed. Production rose, and in most cases output was doubled compared with pre-war figures. It was almost impossible to assess public demand, whether upwards or downwards—but the bread supply never failed.

*　　*　　*　　*

Luton had certain advantages when it came to the supply of fruit and vegetables. Situate in an agricultural surround, it was favoured to an extent which was never true of the larger industrial towns of the North and Midlands, and when items were scarce, it was generally attributable to climatic conditions. Of course, there were the inevitable disappearances—oranges, lemons, grape-fruit, bananas, etc. ; but the district was usually fortunate in the supply of the home-grown article.

Rationing of foodstuffs brought with it barter on a small scale, and the inevitable black market. The country districts were a favourite prey for the mobile black marketeer ; rural food inspectors could not check up on every pound of grain threshed, or every egg laid.

During the Christmas period, chickens which could be bought at 7s. 6d. before the war were fetching 35s. ; a goose might easily cost £3. It was said that one could go to certain farms in some areas and buy all the milk, butter, and eggs one required . . . at a price. But there was little evidence of organised black marketing, except in poultry-stealing, which was worked on planned lines.

*　　*　　*　　*

Rationing has so far been reviewed in relation to necessities. There were, however, other retailers, whose goods, if not claiming the same priority as food, were in demand by an extremely high percentage of the population.

Behind his counter, the Luton tobacconist soon found that his stock of cigarettes was not going to meet the call. The first real signs of a shortage occurred in December, 1940, but it would be more accurate to say that what actually occurred was a big increase in consumption. This increase, which started in September that year, was consequent upon the great expansion of night-work and the nervous tension of air-raid vigils, and was one of the first signs of war strain.

Subsidiary causes of the shortage were the reduction of bonded stocks, and the dislocation or diversion of distribution through bombing and moving populations. Another was labour reduction.

When the air-raids slackened in 1941, this first deficiency ceased, and there were no real difficulties in Luton shops until June, 1944. In that month, at the time of the Normandy invasion and the onset of V-warfare, tobacconists found that cuts had to be made in the civilian supply owing to labour difficulties, and absence of materials. A further cut was made in September, 1944, and the result was a heavy and false demand.

The curtailing in 1945, of " duty-free " cigarettes for troops abroad

ABOVE : *Food rationing . . . the housewife's headache! This picture of a week's ration for one person at the end of the War speaks for itself.*

RIGHT: *No this . . . and no that. How often this was seen on the doors of Luton's shops, during the War and after.*

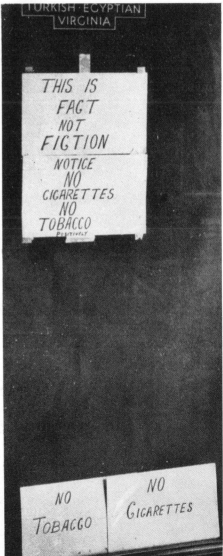

BELOW: *The worst has happened!*

ABOVE: *The food storage depot between Luton and Dunstable, where reserve stocks for the area were held.*

RIGHT: *"Almost as good as mother's" .. some youngsters tuck in to a square meal at Luton's British Restaurant, in New Town Street.*

BELOW: *Drawing contentedly through their straws, these Luton schoolchildren drink their daily one-third of a pint of milk.*

Qu·ues, queues, queues . . . Luton housewives, in common with those all over the country, became queue conscious during the shortages brought about by the war. Here cakes were the attraction.

Ration books became a housewives' headache . . . the first pains came with the queue to obtain them.

Victory is ours: it is March, 1946, and there is peace on earth if not plenty. Bananas make a welcome re-appearance after an absence of six years . . . but only for the 18's and under, and then there were the queues, queues, queues.

caused a slight improvement, but this was soon nullified through the requirements of returned demobilised men and women.

Tobacco manufacturers have been, and still are, selling more goods than ever before in the history of tobacco, but have yet fully to meet the greatly increased demand, and this with prices higher than ever before.

*　　*　　*　　*

Luton's licensed houses never experienced the acute beer shortage of the war of 1914-1918, and there was generally enough beer to satisfy customers. Here again a favourable comparison with other towns of similar size can be made ; the opinion of many connected with the trade was that Luton, where houses rarely had to close because they were sold out, was one of the most favoured towns in the kingdom from the point of view of beer supplies.

The war years saw Luton provided with an output which exceeded by hundreds of thousands of barrels the pre-war figure.

To achieve this, the sale of heavier gravity beers was discontinued, and J. W. Green, Ltd., the local brewers, concentrated on two beers representing a penny increase on what was previously the cheapest gravity beer. This meant that materials formerly used for brewing the heavier gravity beers were available for increasing the output of the new beers, which were a light bitter and a mild at the same price. The Brewery plant was therefore kept at maximum output, which would have been impossible with a more varied range. An extension to the brewery made just prior to the outbreak of hostilities was capable of adding 1,000 extra barrels a week to production.

The result was that although retailers on isolated occasions had to admit an inability to cope with demand, there was nothing like the all-round deficiency existing in the bars of other districts.

Luton-brewed beers were very popular with the Americans, who came from all parts to obtain supplies. Characteristic ruses adopted to persuade the company to increase individual quotas included the story that a certain unit, having brought down a large number of enemy planes, qualified for extra supplies !

When the Battle of the Atlantic was at its height, beer was considered so important to the Americans that supplies of their native malt and hops were shipped to England for delivery to Luton, so that the quota for their forces could be maintained without interfering with the materials allocated for the production of Luton's own beer.

*　　*　　*　　*

Other items, considered to be luxuries, became subject to an entirely new impost in the form of a Purchase Tax. It was intended to be not only a revenue-producing tax, but a deterrent to spending on non-essentials and an encouragement to saving. Goods were graded for this tax according to their degree of necessity. Some commodities carried no tax at all. Others, such as jewellery, furs, and cosmetics, were subject to as much as 100 per cent. tax. As a deterrent to spending, however, the tax was to some extent ineffective. So much money was in circulation that on the sales of many classes of goods appealing particularly to the less thrifty it had no limiting effect. Footwear was a case in point. Cosmetics, too, kept up their sales, even though the prices rocketed, even though the goods were sometimes of unknown origin and doubtful quality. Even the 100 per cent. tax could not persuade girls educated to lipsticks to forego these adornments.

Regularly the price tabs of cigarette cases, pipes, and leather goods, were altered ; regularly the retailer watched the reluctant figure rise higher, but he never saw the demand decrease. Ornaments and handbags were constantly required ; coupons were not needed for their sale, and they made good presents at a time when coupons made gifts difficult to choose. All types of gramophone records, heavily taxed, had an eager public. The spending power of the purchaser seemed competent to cope, according to his or her particular weakness, with the rise in prices in these markets. An effect particularly notice-able was the tremendous boost given to the secondhand market. Many owners cashed in nicely on things which in pre-war days they had regarded as practically unwanted junk.

*   *   *   *

Legislation confronting the retailer of clothes was hardly less impressive than that affecting the grocer, the butcher, and the milkman. Clothes rationing was the Government's present to the nation at Whitsun, 1941.

The austerity restrictions imposed on suits and shirts probably accounted for the lack of popularity of men's utility clothing. For example, the single-breasted style became universal ; there were only eight pockets for the whole three-piece suit, and even the number of buttons came within a prescribed margin. Trousers were shorn of turn-ups although, singularly enough, they were still permitted on ladies' slacks. Tunic shirts had to be single cuff only, and regulation lengths were imposed with geometric precision. Socks dwindled in length. These rules came into force almost immediately, and were baffling to the retailer who had not previously regarded his merchan-dise as such an elaborate and complicated piece of machinery. And everything, except hats, was on coupons.

When restrictions were removed, the quality became quite good, but towards the end of the war, a government claim of over 80 per cent. of cloth and garments led to a temporary shortage. The basic reason for this latest development was the demand for suits for ex-servicemen.

The retailer of footwear found that utility shoes for men, were popular to an extent never reached by those for women. The reason is not hard to seek ; they were of an austerity pattern, and female technique is to regard the shoe as something more than a machine for walking. A wedge heel, for example, is held to double the attraction. Such artistic adventures in footwear have more often than not been

289

T

out of stock, since they are not manufactured under utility grades, and this, logically or otherwise, added to their value in the assessment of Luton ladies.

When it came to clothing, the ladies were more tolerant. After the first sighs had been offered up, they accepted the situation very well. Fashion quite failed to thwart feminine intuition where a bargain was concerned, and it was necessary always to remember that the non-utility product was subject to heavy purchase tax, although frequently equalled by the utility product.

When this word utility first reached a new public, women's and children's outer garments were unattractive, and often poor both in quality and style, but they improved considerably as time went on.

Popular wartime lines were ladies' and children's gloves and hose. Most glove lines were well made and were at a reasonable figure, compared with non-utility articles bearing $33\frac{1}{3}$ per cent. purchase tax or, if trimmed with fur, 100 per cent. tax. The hose were good value for the price, but of course, the range of colours was not so all-embracing as in the halcyon days when shopping was really shopping. But the public was practical about it, and utility hose never remained on the counter very long—or under it either, for that matter. Re-tailers found growing difficulty in meeting the heavy demand for fully fashioned hose.

Corsets became a subject to be discussed with due solemnity in the House, and the technical complaint was expressed that there was a lack of support in articles which had to be made without steel. And so the Board of Trade deliberated, and manufacturers in due course became acquainted with an order to prepare better and stronger corsets, especially for larger figures.

The clothing coupon system had many peculiarities and some anomalies. It also had a curious flexibility. Any one could buy anything, provided the appropriate number of coupons were surren-dered. There was no question as to whether or not one already had a sufficiency of what it was proposed to buy. The coupons were pri-marily for the use of the individual, but in the family they could be pooled. They could not be offered loose over the counter, but could be cut out and sent loose through the post on a mail order. Women who didn't mind what they spent on clothes found that there were ways and means of disposing of part-worn clothes in a manner that helped them to get something new. Where the law stepped in, however, was where new goods were sold without the surrender of coupons, and where the coupons were bought and sold. In proved cases heavy fines and penalties were imposed; nevertheless the racket continued. There were stories of deals in coupons at prices which varied with the district. Other things supposed to be done in the black market were to sell lengths of material at double price and no coupons, or for double coupons and no money. But it was always a risky deal.

The problem of children's clothing became acute almost immediately coupons became necessary. After a time an extra allotment of 20 was given for children who had reached a certain age or stage of growth, but even these were quite insufficient when children were growing visibly. The extra eased the situation, but there still had to be handing down within families, each child being merely the temporary lessee of clothes which another had outgrown. Where children, on admission to a new type of school, required a special outfit, somebody else had to go short of coupons : many a young man who carefully stored away his civilian clothes when he went into the Services found when he returned after a period of years that a younger brother had " inherited " them.

Another very sore point with the housewife was that although household furnishings, linen, towelling, etc., were all on coupons, there were no special coupons for these things. Where the inevitable wear and tear of the war years necessitated renewals, somebody in the family had to go short of clothing coupons, or there could be no new towels, bed-linen, or whatever might be needed.

*   *   *   *

Setting up home was a serious business in war-time. Luton had about 1,200 empty houses in 1939, but it was not long before accommodation was at a premium, and later, renting a house became practically impossible. Property prices soared. By 1945, a pre-war £600 house would fetch £1,000, if offered with the magic words, " Vacant Possession," while in a better residential district a house for which £1,000 would have been taken in earlier times would fetch over £2,000. In a number of cases better class houses costing £1,600 or so pre-war fetched nearer £4,000 at auction.

As far as furniture was concerned, the man in the shop, doing his best to help, was only too painfully conscious of the fact that he could not do very much. Furniture was obviously going to be one of the biggest sufferers in a world where raw materials were at a premium and the war effort claimed labour and stocks.

In 1943, in order to make the best possible use of timber available, and to ensure a reasonable price, utility furniture came on to the market Generally, an official permit was necessary to buy it.

It was sold against units, and those eligible for these units were bombed-out people and newly-married couples. The quality on the whole was good, the retailer did not hesitate to advise his customers, and usually he could recommend it. Sixty units were the stipulated supply, but only 30 were valid at a time because of the long waiting list which every retailer had for furniture. And yet, as the man in the shop knew, as he showed you what he had for sale, those 30 units just furnished one room. And the remaining 30 could not be used until a further six months had elapsed.

Second-hand and antique furniture prices shot up into the clouds. As far as the former was concerned a control order fixed maximum prices for types of furniture, and these governed the shops and the auction marts, but bargains between private buyers and sellers remained uncontrolled. In the result a second-hand three-piece Chesterfield suite worth pre-war about £20, might easily fetch £70 or £80. Carpets, part worn, of a new pre-war price of £10 to £15, commanded £60 to £70 and many other items of furniture were quite unobtainable.

But if you had been lucky enough to buy some furniture, your next problem was to get it home. The family who furnished one or two rooms—it is too much to say they furnished a house—had their furniture delivered to the door on the pool scheme.

This idea of pooled delivery was not confined to furniture dealers. The objective saving in labour and transport and such vital materials as petrol and rubber was achieved through the co-operation of all the firms taking part, and the first scheme in March, 1942, covered 36 different businesses supplying furniture, drapery, musical instruments and hardware.

When the scheme was extended to include butchers, retail delivery within the borough by motor vehicles ceased. Five vehicles were available to deliver outside Luton once a week, and deliveries inside the borough by cycle and hand were made on the basis of once per house per week.

The pooled delivery scheme was symbolic of the whole of the attitude of Luton retailers towards the war. True, there were grumbles, and often they were justified; true, there were mistakes made—how many of the customers would have been foolproof in similar circumstances? Many of the mistakes were the result of the system, in any case.

But generally, the retailer accepted an organisation of rationing which he knew aimed at ultimate fairness and a solution of the distribution of available resources. Because he accepted it, and because he knew his own responsibility, whether he was a manager in a big store, or the man in the shop on the corner, the rationing system worked in Luton, and worked as well as it did anywhere.

*   *   *   *

There are two other aspects of rationing which ought to go on the record, one general, one affecting Luton in particular.

That which affected Luton was not perhaps so much the rationing itself as getting the rations. So many women were at work in the big factories, and the shops closed so much earlier, that an agitation arose about the impossibility of their doing their necessary shopping and also going to work, and it was urged that this was having a prejudicial effect on output, and causing absenteeism. The matter was taken up officially, a special committee appointed to investigate the need for some special arrangements, and in due course the traders arranged to co-operate by keeping open late one night a week particularly for factory women. This scheme was in fact put into operation in the very early days of 1942. It was not a success. The shops were open for the service only of women factory workers. The extent to which this facility was utilised did not justify the shop assistants' time, the lighting involved, or anything else. After a trial it was abandoned. The women had been given their chance. The agitation was never renewed. There were not even any protests that the experiment was not continued.

The other aspect of rationing was one that affected Luton only as it affected every other place. Those who had the time, and the money, could economise on their rations by going out to meals, which, unlike what happened in the latter part of the 1914-18 war, did not involve the surrender of coupons. Sometimes, when wives had insisted on their menfolk getting meals out, the men got their own back by describing the wonderful meals they got in their particular canteen, for perhaps 1s. or 1s. 2d. Perhaps the stories had some sub-stratum of truth in the early days of the war; but, like Army cooks, there are canteen cooks and canteen cooks, and of some canteen meals towards the end of the war the teller of tales had to be able to tell a convincing fairy story if he hoped to be believed. But where canteen meals were really, or only reasonably, good, and where more than one member of a family could utilise such a canteen, then the family had an undoubted advantage over another which had to make the week's rations last the week.

Wastage of food was quite properly made a criminal offence, but proceedings in court were rare compared with those which arose out of selling articles of clothing without coupons.

*   *   *   *

So that some future generation which may be exempt from rationing may know with what we had to be content, not only during the six years' war but also afterwards, here are some things to enlighten them. Meat ration, 1s. 2d. a week (some canned, if necessary); butter minimum, 2 oz. a week; cheese, 2 oz.; bacon, 2 oz.; cooking fats, 1 oz.; jam or other preserves, 1 lb. a month; tea, $\frac{1}{2}$ lb. a month.

Things like canned fish, fruit, peas and beans, dried peas and beans, rice (when obtainable), dried fruits, and biscuits were on " points," and any marked run on a particular article was usually countered by an increase in " points " value, to divert demand to something which was less attractive but temporarily more plentiful. Sweets were rationed by a " personal points " scheme, after some retailers had adopted their own rationing system.

Coal, coke, gas and electricity were never actually rationed, but if a 1943 appeal for a voluntary cut in consumption had not been heeded some drastic action would have followed. There was an immediate drop in consumption and the situation was tided over . . . temporarily. In the following years, however, the mining situation became so critical that coal, coke, and patent fuel were put on an allocation basis, which meant " if available." The maximum allowance for a household was 34 cwts. a year. There was no guarantee that even that quantity would be available.

If an old proverb is to be believed, the war did not encourage an approach to godliness, for soap was a commodity that was rationed. Shaving soap was exempt, so some women bought that.

Eggs were an " allocation," on the basis of one a month. There were months when not even the one egg made an appearance. In consequence, many housewives became poultry keepers. Lack of experience did not seem to affect their success.

To supplement the official rations there were some unrationed foodstuffs. Where they went puzzled many people, for they were rarely to be had in the shops. Even fresh fish was sometimes practically unobtainable, except for privileged back-door customers, and the humble bloater and kipper became almost forgotten.

Children grew up without knowledge of a banana, and when they did reappear in March, 1946, for children only, some children needed much persuasion to try this novelty. Oranges became an allocation, tomatoes became an allocation. There were times when there wasn't an onion for the kitchen, times when in regard to many things we just had to " do without."

Clothes rationing was so severe that two major articles for the wardrobe could not be bought in a year. A man's suit needed 26 coupons, which were more than were available in the first rationing, and more than half the year's issue. Other coupon values were :—Overcoat, 18 ; raincoat, 16 or 18 ; shoes, 9 ; pyjamas, 8 ; shirt and two collars, 7. Underclothing, socks, pullovers, gloves, ties, handkerchiefs, all called for coupons ; everything wearable, in fact, except hats.

It was much the same with ladies ; Costumes and coats took 18, raincoats 15, and slacks 8. If they were extravagant with stockings, as many were until they joined the bare-legged brigade, they had to go without other things. Household linen, referred to earlier, was all on coupons, it suffered considerable wear and tear in the course of the six years, and there were no separate coupons for its replacement.

The slogan of the times was " make do and mend." Where people had " made do " with the minimum before clothes rationing came in, as they were officially urged to do, they had to do the maximum of mending afterwards. The wearer of new clothes became conspicuous and to an extent embarrassed. To go shabby became a virtue.

The Red Cross and St. John

THE war efforts of the Luton detachments of the British Red Cross Society and of the Luton Corps of the St. John Ambulance Brigade ran on parallel lines in many respects, while in others they became a joint effort. To many the Red Cross may suggest merely a women's nursing organisation and the St. John Ambulance Brigade a band of men volunteers who, in emergency, are always at hand to help the physically distressed. Yet the intensity of their joint work under war conditions and its far wider ramifications made up a contribution of the highest value to the nation.

*   *   *   *

Members of the men's Red Cross detachment in Luton put in many thousands of hours on voluntary duties during the war. They made it their particular duty to relieve the porters at Luton and Dunstable Hospital during the weekends. Every Saturday night two members reported to the Hospital for this purpose, and from 1939 onwards they put in a total of 8,000 hours. Members also reported to the Hospital when there were raid incidents, day or night, and, following the rocket incident in Biscot Road, they were on duty at the Hospital from the time the casualties arrived until the following morning, assisting in the operating theatre. Four men were also on duty every night for stretcher-bearing and fire-watch in emergency.

Between 1939 and 1945 members put in over 35,000 hours on fire-watch duty, and over 17,000 hours' duty at public events. In addition they did 3,000 hours of A.R.P. duty, plus an average of 2,300 hours a year at the Red Cross surgery.

Cadet duties in 1944 and 1945 alone totalled 13,730 hours.

The war effort of the Women's detachment of the British Red Cross Society really began in 1938, when members helped to fit gas masks during the November crisis. Lectures in anti-gas measures had started early that year, and of the 250 women who attended, 35 became new members of the Red Cross, while others went on to the A.R.P. reserve.

Numbers so increased that the original detachment, becoming unworkable, was divided into three, each with an average of 40 members. They trained for the Civil Nursing Reserve, working 50 hours in Luton and Dunstable Hospital. Some worked in First Aid Posts, on Mobile and Light Mobile units, at the Blood Transfusion Depot, at the Ray Therapy Institute, and in industrial nursing.

In the 1939 'flu epidemic members helped to nurse sick Service personnel in halls and at a sick bay in Brantwood Road. The latter proved too small, so " Uplands," London Road, was taken, and for sixteen months Red Cross officers and members worked there, only giving up when R.A.M.C. personnel took over.

In conjunction with the magnificent work done jointly by the Red Cross and St. John for prisoners of war, a Next-of-Kin Bureau was opened in October, 1942, when so many Luton homes had menfolk in the hands of the Japanese, and news of them was so hard to obtain. Located at the St. John Ambulance headquarters in Barbers Lane, it was open weekly for relatives of prisoners to meet there for information and advice, and it served a very valuable purpose. Its activities did not end until early 1946, when practically all the prisoners who had been freed in the Far-East had come home.

Those from the Continent who were home much earlier had found it a place where they could get some much-needed things at less than the customary price, although they still had to surrender coupons. This form of service was even more valuable for the later arrivals from the Far East, as they had particular need of extra supplies of warm underclothing, etc.

Two parties were also arranged for homecoming war prisoners.

Joint efforts by the Red Cross and the St. John Ambulance Brigade for the Prisoners of War Fund produced about £6,000 from street collections, while collections at local cinemas added another £2,406.

*　　*　　*　　*

The earliest war activities of Luton members of the St. John Ambulance Brigade were of an anticipatory character. As early as 1937, officers from Luton were specially trained at the London head-quarters to become instructors in air raid and anti-gas precautions. This was followed by two years of intensive training of large numbers of A.R.P. volunteers and of the general public, both in the town and in the large works, in first-aid and anti-gas treatment.

Brigade members were appointed official instructors in all branches of the Casualty and Ambulance services, and assisted in training air wardens, the police, and the Home Guard. When the Luton A.R.P. Service was formed, all members of the Brigade immediately volunteered for service in one form or another, and from the start of the war the first-aid posts and stations were largely manned by them.

In the first-aid parties the men rendered valuable service during the bombing of Luton in 1940 and 1941. Later these parties were combined with the Rescue Service, and Brigade members continued regular stand-by duties throughout the war, attending all incidents. Certificates of merit were presented to two members in recognition of specially meritorious service at the last incident of all, when a rocket did such damage in Biscot Road. About 130 members were attached to the rescue parties in 1943-44, several holding principal executive positions.

Stretcher-bearer parties provided for Luton and Dunstable Hospital not only served during bombing incidents, but also carried out a regular rota of orderly duties.

In spite of the large amount of time taken up by their Civil Defence duties, normal duties were not neglected. Members continued their

ABOVE: *Dame Beryl Oliver, D.B.E., R.R.C., who was in charge of Red Cross personnel, inspecting local V.A.D.'s during her visit to Luton on January 10th, 1943.*

BELOW: *Lady Louis Mountbatten, Lady Superintendent in charge of the Nursing Divisions of the St. John Ambulance Brigade, inspecting members of a Luton unit during the same month.*

Early in 1940 a stretcher bearer corps was formed. This picture was taken at a practice, but they were later called upon to carry out the real thing when bombs began to fall on the town.

attendance at cinemas—a particularly important service during the raid periods—at football matches, sports meetings, and the Open Air Pool. They were always on duty where there was any big public assembly, and the Holidays-at-Home seasons created extra duties. All this was carried on despite the fact that mobilisation in September, 1939, had taken away those members who were in the Military Hospital Reserve or the Royal Naval Sick Berth Reserve.

Figures of the wartime growth of the Brigade are illuminating. In 1939 there were four ambulance (men's) divisions in Luton. These were combined in 1941, together with one nursing division and two cadet divisions, to form the Luton Corps. Since then, and in spite of the call-up of men for the Services, the Corps has continued to grow. Now there are eight ambulance divisions, four nursing divisions, and six cadet divisions—plus an independent Corps at Vauxhall Motors, Ltd.

All the activities connected with Civil Defence were continued until the Stand Down, and the services of the Brigade in that connection were so well appreciated that two trophies originally presented for competition among A.R.P. personnel have been passed on to the Brigade for their peacetime competitions. The Burgoyne Trophy will in future be a stimulus for the ambulance divisions, and the Pakes Cup for the nursing divisions.

*   *   *   *

The nursing personnel also found the war years a period of great activity, which was reflected in membership. At the beginning of 1939 there was one division with 44 members. At the end of the war there were four divisions with a total strength of 108, peak membership having been 140 in 1944.

Many women in local factories were trained in first-aid, and some increased their knowledge by attending lectures on home nursing and A.R.P. Certificates awarded to women candidates included 505 Senior First Aid, 262 Senior Home Nursing, and 66 A.R.P. St. John instructors gave 110 lectures on first-aid to W.V.S. members alone, and as a result of the interest aroused several members of the W.V.S. joined the Brigade.

During 1939 and 1940 many members trained at Luton and Dunstable Hospital for the expected emergency. This enabled a rota to be on call for bomb incidents, day and night, so that in their special capacity they could render service as valuable as the men's section were trained to render. Later a similar rota was formed for St. Mary's Hospital, and members continue to supplement the nursing service at both hospitals in the evenings and on Sundays.

Women members of St. John were attached to all first-aid posts during the whole of the war, some on full-time work, but the majority as part-time volunteers. In many cases they also staffed factory first-aid posts. Like the men, they also still carried on their peacetime activities, attending cinemas on busy evenings, doing duty at the

Swimming Pool in the season, establishing first-aid posts for all big public events and during the Holidays-at-Home seasons, while during the VE and VJ-Day celebrations, posts were maintained at the Electricity Showrooms and at Wardown Park throughout each day and night.

*　　*　　*　　*

Although, in view of the operations of the Luton Nursing Association, and the fact that in an industrial town few members are available until the evening, it is not possible to establish in Luton the Nursing Aid Scheme which is found of much value in some places, the voluntary worker of the St. John Ambulance Brigade still goes on. The Medical Comforts Depot in Barbers Lane is still open three times a week to issue comforts in case of illness, the articles there made available having been in great demand during the period when there was such an evacuation from London to Luton. Training classes for recruits are another continuing activity.

*　　*　　*　　*

In addition to the good war work done by Luton members of the Red Cross and of the St. John Ambulance Brigade, as separate organisations and jointly, Luton people can also feel justifiably proud of what they themselves did for the Duke of Gloucester's Red Cross and St. John Appeal.

Principally through what was known as the Penny-a-Week Fund although few gave the minimum and many willingly doubled their regular contributions when D-Day made even greater liabilities probable, an original collection of £28 in the first month was developed until by the end of 1944 it was over £1,000 a month.

In January, 1945, the £50,000 mark having been passed, there was a special celebration. To this came Lord Iliffe, chairman of the Appeal. He considered it " a wonderful success," and probably a record for the country on a population basis, as it represented over a penny a week from everybody, including infants.

It was emphasised by Lady Keens, the then Mayor, that the £50,000 had been raised without deduction of a penny for expenses, and acknowledgment was made of the great help received from the schools, and particularly the elementary schools.

That celebration was not to be the end of things, but a spur to further effort. In fact, £70,000 by the end of the year was regarded as practicable, the £3,000 of the first year having been quadrupled in 1944. However, the sudden ending of the world war resulted in the appeal being closed in August, 1945, and the Luton effort ended with its pennies having totalled £65,000.

They Went to War

IT is officially estimated that by the time the war ended 12,000 Luton men and women had joined the Services. There would have been 12,001, but one man who received his calling-up papers for September 22nd, 1939, and duly reported to Kempston Barracks as directed, was sent home again. The military authorities did not regard him as likely to make a useful soldier . . . he was 86.

From the days when the British Expeditionary Force went to France until the end of the war with the Japanese, Luton men were fighting on and under the sea, in the air, and on every land front. For an inland town Luton seemed to have an extraordinary number of young men with a preference for the sea. They chose it even before the R.A.F., numerous as were the volunteers for the latter.

The war was an epic of desperate adventure. Convoys to Russia battled their way through the bitter gloom of the Arctic night. Tankers and food ships ran the gauntlet of U-boats in tropic waters. Ceaseless patrols kept watch and ward over the drear Antarctic wastes. With them all were Luton men.

Hitler's Fortress of Europe stood menacing behind seeming impregnable ramparts while patient fearless men were probing, ever probing for the weaknesses they knew were there. Snakes stirred in the hot foetid slime of the insect ridden Burmese jungle. The merciless sun beat down in brassy waves of heat on the long road from Alamein to Tunisia. Luton men were there.

High in the black night air, penetrating deeper and ever deeper into the Third Reich were the bomber aircrews of the R.A.F. Luton men were with them too.

These men, trained in a new technique of war, proved themselves possessed of all the skill and resource needed to combat the obstacles they had to overcome. Some who were away in lonely outposts like Iceland, the Faroes, and the Azores, even if their contribution was less spectacular, were nevertheless playing an essential role in the master strategy which led surely, if more slowly than could have been desired, to the ultimate goal.

Losses from a smaller Luton, in the four-and-a-half-years of the 1914-18 war, are commemorated by 1,285 names on the Memorial which stands in front of the Town Hall. The total for the six years of the Second World War was much smaller, and, on the whole, Luton men and women came through those six years with extreme good fortune.

*   *   *   *

Two months before war broke out a new militia was brought into being. It was really the beginning of general conscription, but it did not start as such. It was to be a preparatory step in the training of young men, and it began with the compulsory registration, under the Military Training Act, of the 20-year-olds. The date fixed for the first registration was Saturday, June 3rd, 1939, and it was announced that after June 2nd no one in that category could join the Territorials.

This did more to stimulate local recruiting for the Territorials than all the propaganda of the between-war years. Many young men made certain of getting into the Territorial unit of their choice while they could, rather than chance where they would be sent after registration. The first batch of those who did register was called up for training on July 15th, 1939, and Luton men were among the first to report at the depot of the County Regiment at Kempston.

Whether men had enrolled in the Territorials, or were compulsorily registered for the new militia, in fact made very little difference two months later. Before the second batch was due to register for the Militia in the October, the Territorials were on a war footing . . . active participants in a struggle which was to prove for this country the longest within living memory.

In due course the Military Training Act was succeeded by National Service Acts. Men of more and more mature years were brought in as also were the youngsters as they reached Service age. Eventually, also, they conscripted women.

*   *   *   *

After the first batch of Militia had reported for training, the reservists were the next to be on their way. They were recalled from their peacetime occupations when war, though not declared, was considered inevitable. The Territorials were mobilised, although this did not necessarily mean that they all went off immediately.

The Territorials of 1939 were somewhat different from those who left Luton in August, 1914. Then they were the 5th Bedfords, a company of Royal Engineers, and the Eastern Mounted Brigade Field Ambulance, R.A.M.C. They all took part in the Gallipoli adventure, and afterwards in the successful Palestine campaign.

When, after that war, the Territorial Force was re-established as the Territorial Army, Luton was again a base for the 5th Bedfords and an R.E. Company, but the R.A.M.C. unit ceased to exist. Instead, there was a battery of Field Artillery. Yeomanry, as a cavalry force, were deemed to have had their day, the Bedfordshire Yeomanry were transformed into the 105th (Beds. Yeo.) Brigade, R.F.A., and Luton, which in earlier years had provided only a few men for the Dunstable Troop of the Yeomanry, produced the 420th Battery. Other changes followed when, in a complete re-organisation, the Royal Horse Artillery, Royal Field Artillery, and Royal Garrison Artillery, had to abandon their separate identities and become just Royal Artillery. A somewhat anomalous result was the creation of Artillery Regiments within the Regiment. To this end batteries were combined, and, when the Luton battery went off to war it went, not as a battery, but, in conjunction with the Dunstable battery, as a Field Regiment of Artillery.

This, however, was not the only respect in which the 1939 Territorials differed from those of 1914. Under Mr. Hore-Belisha's scheme for the expansion of the Territorial Army, the 5th Bedfords had expanded into the 5th and 6th, the 5th being allotted the northern half of the county, and the 6th the south. Similarly, the 249th Field Coy. R.E., had the 289th Field Park Coy. as offshoot. There was also an R.A.S.C. Coy., only a few months old when the war started. There was a not-much-older company of W.A.T.S., later to become just A.T.S. It was one of the first companies of women Territorials in the country.

All these were units, but they were not all. There was also a preliminary training centre for the R.A.F.V.R., whence Luton men, with some training as pilots, air gunners, observers, and navigators were gradually absorbed into squadrons, and only as individuals could afterwards be traced. Many of them became very successful members of aircrews, and as such collected a substantial number of decorations. They became scattered all over the world. Of some, alas, their story ended when an " aircraft did not return."

*   *   *   *

The war history of the units which went away as units varied very considerably. They did not even remain in the same higher formation. For instance, the Artillery went to Singapore. Other Luton units did not, but the 5th Bedfords, who had the sticky job at Gallipoli in the previous war, also landed into the Singapore fiasco. If the fortunes of the Artillery and the 5th Bedfords, whose subsequent experiences were so terrible, are therefore reviewed as one, the general story may also be told of many other Luton men who, having originally joined the Bedfords, found themselves transferred to other infantry battalions brigaded with the Bedfords—the Royal Norfolks, Suffolks, and Cambridgeshires. They all went through the same preliminary of ranging up and down the country, combining defence with further training. When they embarked for the Far East, they all went in convoy, by a route which took them right across the Atlantic on the way to the Cape, they had a brief break in India, then on to Singapore where they all landed when matters had become hopeless.

Orders to go abroad as part of the 18th Division were received on September 24th, 1941, and they sailed from Liverpool on October 29th. First port of call was Halifax, Nova Scotia, the next Port of Spain, Trinidad ; then on to the Cape, for a three-days' shore break and a taste of South Africa's boundless hospitality. It was believed, and apparently correctly at the time, that they were bound for the Middle East, but plans must have undergone a sudden change, for the next stop was Bombay. Then Singapore, too late for other than a brief part in a battle which was already lost, too late for everything except years of terrible experience and endurance as prisoners of the Japanese.

The 5th Bedfords were the first to land. They reached Singapore on January 29th, 1942, and when the order to cease fire was given on

February 15th, many in the battalion had not even seen a Japanese soldier. This was because the battalion was split up after arrival, to meet the urgencies of various local situations. It was understood that they would reassemble later and go into action as a battalion, but that time never arrived. There were only two brigades of fresh troops. These two brigades, with units split up, and further handicapped by always meeting tired troops who were being driven back and back by an enemy who knew everything about jungle warfare and camouflage, could do very little. The only consolation was that in the fighting in which some were permitted to engage the casualties were very few. The major casualties were to come in those grim years while they were prisoners.

The Artillery fared no better. Major C. H. B. Grotrian, who commanded the Luton Battery until he left for other duty, was subsequently killed in action in Burma. Major W. H. Merry, who commanded at Dunstable, was killed in the fighting at Singapore while endeavouring to reorganise some other troops who were in a bad way. The maps available for the Gunners were very unreliable. The Gunners did their best—that was all they could do—before they, like the 5th Bedfords, were driven off into the years of captivity.

*　　*　　*　　*

After Singapore was all over, and formal official notification had been received by relatives that their men were " missing," months passed without news. Then came brief official notification that men were prisoners. It was April, 1943, when this news began to filter through and much later before the men themselves were allowed to send printed cards. These cards contained very cheering messages, the general tenour being that everything was as it should be, that they were working for pay, and that there was no cause for any anxiety. Relatives, however, were advised not to put too much faith in these statements. Evidently there was reason for the authorities to believe that conditions in the prison camps were anything but what they should be, and although there was an apparent official desire not to cause despondency, there was still the suggestion that any cheerful messages from prison camps, and particularly those in Malaya and Siam, should be taken with reserve.

Later revelations proved only too fully how bad things really were. The conditions under which prisoners had to live and work in the jungle caused far more casualties than were sustained in the fighting, and the men who managed to survive had some grisly stories to tell. The real fate of some could only be ascertained, or assumed, when there had been searching investigations after the war with Japan had ended. The lot of the prisoners was made still worse by the prolonged refusal of the Japanese to let Red Cross relief workers have access to the camps, either to provide comforts or investigate conditions, and the prisoners, in addition to having to wait an almost unbearable time for their first mail from home, were also denied those things which helped to make life bearable in the prison camps of Germany. Their ultimate release, too, was longer deferred.

Of what they suffered in the meantime there are innumerable stories. It will be sufficient to give one or two as typical. Here is what a young officer of the 5th Bedfords said when he came home :—

"There were bad periods—as bad as they could be—especially when the big push to build the Siam-Burma railway was nearing the climax. The Japanese policy was summed up in a remark I heard from one Japanese area commandant to whom protests had been made. He said, 'If prisoners working on this railway die, it does not matter. There are still thousands more to take their place.'

"Prisoners at that time were pushed beyond the limit of endurance, and no humanitarian considerations were allowed to interfere with the progress of the railway. Sick prisoners were evacuated to camps where conditions and food were a bit better, and under the care of Allied doctors who were among the prisoners, and who did magnificent work under terrible conditions, many of the sick men recovered their health, only to lose it again when sent back for a further period of forced labour."

A Luton Gunner sergeant was able to keep a copy of an order issued at another camp by a new commandant, one of those later charged with atrocities. It was a camp of ill-fame, and the effect of the order was that prisoners only continued to live at the goodwill of their captors, that ill-health was really their own fault, and therefore no excuse for not doing enough work. The day after this order was issued 14 men died from malnutrition. That day's diet consisted of half-a-pint of "rice pap", half-a-pint of rice with a bit of dried fish, and another half-a-pint of rice with pumpkin water. On this diet men had to work from 6 a.m. till 4 a.m. next day. At another camp where this sergeant spent some time there was a list of things for which prisoners could be shot. No. 1 on the list was "Man who pretends to be sick and does not work." Many were sick unto death. There was no need to shoot them. In fact, of about 650 gunners of this Regiment alone taken prisoner, 251 died in captivity.

These were the experiences not alone of men in the two units specifically mentioned, but shared commonly by men of all arms whose fate it was to be prisoners of the Japanese, and while those who had to work on the construction of the "Death Railway" fared worst of all, there were none who escaped grievous treatment. Many who lived to be released were in such pitiable plight that they could only be brought home by easy stages, and then had to go into hospital. Even those who were in better shape had to be safeguarded against themselves on the homeward journey, lest the ample food should do them harm. There were few who had not lost many stones in weight. A strange yellowness of countenance had not disappeared on the journey. Only too often men gave the impression that they were still in fear and afraid to express their thoughts. Pausing in the middle of something they were saying, they would lose the thread entirely, and be unable to continue.

The authorities recognised that these men had suffered even more than those who had been prisoners in Europe, and merited special consideration. Because of this, when their home-coming leave had expired they were all automatically demobilised, whereas prisoners from Europe who had returned earlier had to rejoin their units until their due demobilisation date, even though their active service was over. There were some who after return to this country died in hospital from the effects of their treatment in their jungle prisons. Some were a long time in recovering their health sufficiently to be able to resume their normal occupations. It is good to be able to say that there were some who appeared to make a quick recovery, but time alone will show to what extent they have been prematurely aged by their three-and-a-half-years in the hands of the Japanese.

Tribute to the 5th Bedfords who had returned was paid at a county gathering at Bedford on December 16th, 1945. The survivors paraded under their commanding officer, Lieut.-Col. D. R. Thomas, O.B.E., M.C., and marched through crowded streets to St. Paul's Church, opposite the Town Hall, for a memorial and thanksgiving service. The church was packed, and the service was relayed to a crowd outside. The service was followed by a march past, the Lord Lieutenant, Lt.-Col. D. C. Part, O.B.E., taking the salute. With him were the Mayors of all three boroughs in the county, Bedford, Luton and Dunstable, General Sir Henry Jackson, Colonel of the Regiment, and many high military officers. Two returned prisoners who had each lost a leg were provided with special seats on the dais.

For the Artillery a similar service was held at Dunstable Priory Church on Saturday, January 12th, 1946. The men paraded under their Commanding Officer, Col. S. C. Harris, and marched to church from Grove House Gardens through flag decorated streets. They came principally from Luton, Dunstable and Leighton Buzzard, and all the local authorities in the area were well represented in the congregation. In the subsequent march past the salute was taken by Major-General C. W. Norman, C.B.E., Commanding the East Central District, who, with the civic heads of Luton, Dunstable and Leighton Buzzard, was among the principal guests at a reunion dinner in the evening.

*   *   *   *

While the Field Regiment of Artillery was training for their Far East adventure, a Heavy Regiment, which was a development in the northern part of the county as part of the expansion of the Territorial Force, went to France with the B.E.F. Those who got back from Dunkirk were for a long time scattered on coastal defence duty. From coastal artillery it was reconstituted as a Heavy Regiment for the Normandy invasion. It took part in the assault on the Arromanches beaches, in the subsequent attack on Mount Pincon, helped

306

Taken at Kempston Barracks less than a month after they had been called to the colours . . . in July 1939, these militiamen, many of whom were from Luton, already had a bearing of which the Army could be proud.

Locally stationed troops using the Moor as a training ground.

ABOVE: *Budding pilots of the Luton Town Centre of the Royal Air Force Volunteer Reserve taking instruction on an aircraft compass shortly before the outbreak of hostilities.*

BELOW: *Naval air cadets who later became pilots with the Fleet Air Arm received part of their training at Luton Airport. The instructor is explaining the mechanism of a machine gun.*

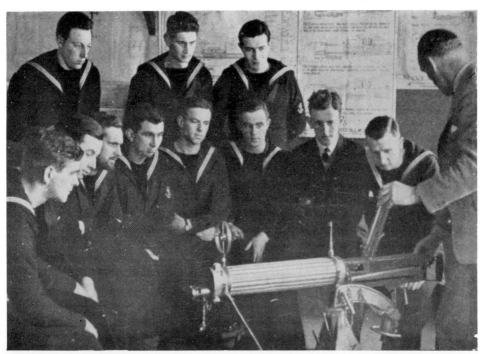

*Members of the Sergeant's Mess of the
289th Field Park Company, R.E., during
the training period in East Anglia before
the Company went to Normandy.*

*Some of the men of the 249th Field Coy.,
R.E., Luton, who became Airborne
R.E.'s for the Normandy landing.*

Officers of the 5th Batn., Bedfs. and Herts. Regiment, then under the command of Lieut. Col. A. D. Gaye, photographed at their last pre-war camp, just before the Battalion was divided in order that the 6th Batn. should be created.

to reduce Falaise, and supported the 43rd Division in the crossing of the Seine. After a period in reserve it supported the Guards' armoured push up the Nijmegen corridor in the attempt to relieve the airborne troops at Arnhem. It was said afterwards by the commander of the 1st Airborne Division that the artillery support was a deciding factor in the survival of the Division for the nine days it spent north of the Rhine.

Other big responsibilities were helping to stem Rundstedt's Ardennes offensive, participation in the 1,000-gun barrage which opened the battle of the Reichswald Forest, and the ultimate attack on the Wesel bridgehead. To take part in the attack on Bremen the regiment covered 160 miles in one day. Hamburg was due for attention, but was declared an open city soon after shelling began. Occupational duties later took the regiment to Brunswick Luneberg, where it was disbanded in April, 1946. Maybe in its reorganised form it had little more association with the county than its name and battery numbers, but it did add one more chapter to the modern history of the Bedfordshire Yeomanry.

*　　*　　*　　*

The 6th Bedfords on formation had as a nucleus the Luton and Dunstable rifle companies of the 5th Battn., and on this foundation recruited to build up a separate unit. They left Luton on November 1st, 1939, for Woodbridge, Suffolk, under their original Commanding Officer, Lieut.-Col. C. H. Miskin, M.C., who had served with the 5th Bedfords in the Gallipoli and Palestine Campaign. At Woodbridge more recruits were received, and one company went to Bawdsey to do guard duty at a big radio station.

From Woodbridge the Battalion went to Northumberland, where Col. Miskin left the unit, the first of several changes in command. The next move was to Toddington and Winchcombe, Gloucestershire; where the battalion was held as G.H.Q. reserve, preliminary to being stationed much nearer home at Aylesbury, as War Office reserve. Afterwards it was the East Anglian coast again, for coast defence and other duties. Then came a move to Caterham, where the Battalion took over the Guards' Depot for about seven months. There was still another move to come, to Beckenham, in the London District. The battalion had been brought up to a very high pitch of efficiency, and having been earmarked for independent brigade operations in connection with D-Day, at last had a prospect of going into the fray as a unit. It was therefore a cause of great disappointment to those who had been responsible for building up the battalion into a fine fighting force when a personal representative of the Commander-in-Chief came in July, 1944, with a message of regret that the battalion would have to be split up and used to strengthen battle trained units which were short of reinforcements.

As a result, when the Dorsets won fame in the thick of the fighting at Arnhem, one of their companies was actually "A" Company from the 6th Bedfords, under its original company commander, Major Grafton; but any credit they won at Arnhem will go down in regimental history as belonging to the Dorsets and not the Bedfords. Such is the fortune of war. Another company went almost in its entirety to the Seaforth Highlanders, and the rest of the battalion was split among about fifteen different units. The officers were similarly scattered, and when the battalion was finally disbanded in August, 1944, there remained only one officer who, with the exception of a period with the 2nd Herts., had been with the 6th Bedfords from beginning to end—Major G. Hickson, a Harpenden man who is with B. Laporte, Ltd., Luton, and who in pre-war days was with the Dunstable company of the 6th. At the time of disbandment he was second-in-command.

From beginning to end the battalion had only two commissioned Quartermasters, Capt. C. H. White, M.B.E., who later went in the same capacity to North Africa and Italy with the 30th Bedfords, and Lieut. C. Richards, who succeeded him. Both returned to Luton on leaving the Service, and both found a peacetime occupation with the same Luton firm.

*   *   *   *

The 249th Field Company, R.E., having shed enough of its surplus personnel to enable the 289th Field Park Company to be formed, went off under Major J. B. Smyth-Wood to Denham, Norfolk, to work on coastal defences. The C.R.E. of the companies in the group was Lieut.-Col. R. Briars, M.C., of Luton, who had previously commanded the 249th Field Company. Lt.-Col. Briars resigned owing to ill-health in 1940, and died at Luton in 1943.

At Denham five members of the company were selected to join a small force which went to Norway on a demolition job. They returned after ten days . . . " job completed."

From Denham the company went on to Morpeth and Ashington, to work on North-East coastal defences, and continued this job from winter quarters at Prudhoe. Then there was a move to Northleach, near Cheltenham, for special training, and participation in the " Bumper " and " Spartan " Army exercises, where they covered much the same ground as the 289th Field Park Company and other units in which they had an interest. They even passed through Harpenden, where they slept one night in the streets. Then they settled again for a time in East Anglia. They were stationed at Bungay, and concerned with the coastal defences of Lowestoft, Oulton Broad, and Thorpeness, where they had to clear the beaches of mines brought ashore by bad weather.

Then the company began to split up for some of the newer forms of warfare. Most of them went for training as Airborne troops. Some went to a Parachute Regiment. Others, generally those whose age was regarded as too high for those two spheres of activity went to Assault Squadrons of R.E.s.

The Airborne people went to Bulford for glider training; the Parachute troops went to Ridgeway, Yorks. to practise jumping. Glider training at Bulford went on until D-Day, when two platoons of the company, as part of the 6th Airborne Division, were the first R.E.'s down at Caen. The other platoons went by sea. They were expected to be back quite soon, to prepare for another operation. In fact, they had three months in Normandy before they came back. The men from the company who went to the parachute Regiment took part in the Arnhem adventure, and when late in 1944 the Germans attempted the Ardennes break the glider people had another job at Nijmegen and on the Maas. They eventually went on into Germany, to Brunswick and Hanover.

In the meantime there had been many other changes in the company. Major Smyth-Wood left for another appointment in 1943. Capt. Wadsworth, who had been second-in-command, left to take command of No. 556 Company at Wallingford. Ultimately the commanding officer was Major W. May, a grandson of the late Sir Walter Kent. Associated with the company from 1939, he had been second-in-command, and finally held a staff appointment in Germany.

*   *   *   *

The 289th Field Park Company, R.E., came into existence as a separate Territorial unit in Luton on September 3rd, 1939. Under the Hore-Belisha scheme for the expansion of the Territorial Army the 249th Field Company had recruited until it was almost 100 per cent. over establishment. On that morning it marched to Pope's Meadow. The 249th Field Company and 289th Field Park Company marched back to the Drill Hall. Curiously enough, it was the offshoot company which was to go through the war as a company, and the parent company which was to be broken up. The first Commanding Officer of the new company was Capt. (later Major) W. H. Wakeham, who had been a subaltern in the 249th Field Company in earlier years, had left Luton in the interim and returned when war was imminent. He was the only original officer of the company to stay until 1943, and when he left he was presented with an inscribed silver salver from all ranks.

The new company spent its first two months in Luton, getting over its teething troubles, and then went to Bury St. Edmunds, where training became more intensive and, under the watchful eye of C.S.M. Charles H. Wilmott, some of the mysteries of explosives and general field engineering were made plain.

Subsequent moves took the company all over England and Wales, and twice into Scotland. On two major Army exercises, " Bumper " and " Spartan ", the company found itself very near Luton; on other occasions they actually passed through the town, which was very tantalising to the Luton men still in the unit.

Climax to strenuous years of training came on June 6th, 1944, when the company was at Loddon, Norfolk. They had four hours' notice to move, and began a journey which did not end until, through Normandy, Belgium and Holland, they reached Arnsberg, in Germany. In Normandy, with 23rd Bridging Platoon, R.E., attached, they became the " Sappers' Shop " of the 49th (Polar Bear) Division. At the start there were few bridging problems, but after the break-out there were the rivers Vire, Dives and Toques to be crossed, and the demand for Bailey bridging material suddenly assumed enormous proportions.

During the crossing of the Antwerp-Turnhout Canal an enthusiastic " harbouring party " put down signs, " Reserved for 48 " (The company code number) in a cement factory on the far bank. Returning next day, it was discovered that overnight the Germans had re-occupied the factory and captured the unit harbour signs— an event unique in the Divisional R.E.

The advance through Roosendal to Willemstadt brought an additional problem to the Field Park Company. Besides supplying bulldozers and bridging material, numerous craters in the forward area required to be filled or by-passed, and a steady stream of tipping lorries had to be kept filled with sleepers and other material.

During a long stay in Nijmegen the Workshops Platoon did a great work in producing gadgets designed to aid " island warfare." Company records show that they also made over 5,000 signs of various kinds, while their mobile shower baths were a great boon to many units. The Stores Platoon issued 3,500 tons of R.E. stores, while the Bridging Platoon issued 6,720 feet of Bailey Bridge.

The company command had changed several times after Major Wakeham left. C.S.M. Wilmott left in 1940, and was succeeded by C.S.M. J. D. McIlroy, who was a sticker until transferred to the 2nd Army R. E. School in August, 1944. The company ceased to exist on December 20th, 1945, those not then due for demobilisation being transferred to other R.E. units. During the six years of its existence it was a happy company. Its members have many grand memories, and a record of which they can well be proud.

*　　*　　*　　*

The 534th (Ammunition) Company, R.A.S.C., was a Territorial unit which had existed but a few months when it went off from Luton to take part in the war. It was started only in March, 1939, because one of the three existing R.A.S.C. companies in the East Anglian Division which had its headquarters at Barking had been converted into an anti-aircraft unit. Bedfordshire was regarded as the best recruiting ground for the establishment of an entirely new company, Luton as the best spot in the county, and the company was largely built up of men who were in the motor industry or were competent drivers of heavy vehicles. Perhaps this was why, although it was such a new unit, so many of the men in it got into the war very quickly. While other local Territorials were combining coast defence with further training, many of the men in the new R.A.S.C. company found themselves in France with the B.E.F. The company as such became the 4th Division Ammunition Company, and retained that identity at home until the end of 1941. Then it became a Tank Transportation Company, and in this capacity did very good work in North Africa, and subsequently in Italy. Long before that, however, because of the number of drafts the company had provided, and their replacement by a general intake, it had lost practically all the Luton men who joined it on formation, but to the end of hostilities little groups of those originals were still sticking together in some company or other. Some of them will have lasting memories of leaving Dunkirk in the *Lancastria*. They got home. The *Lancastria* did not. If in later days any of the original members of the company looked for their original headquarters in Old Bedford Road, they looked in vain. Badly damaged in an air raid incident, they had to be completely demolished.

*   *   *   *

Members of the Luton Town Centre, R.A.F.V.R., received the call to service on September 1st, 1939. It was a broadcast announcement which also required Navy and Army reservists to rejoin. It was assumed that the Air Volunteers, most of whom held rank as sergeants, would be posted away almost immediately for training. It involved one important decision, to sell the remaining stock of beer in the Sergeant's Mess at 1d. a pint ! The beer was sold, but the Volunteers stayed on.

No. 29 Elementary and Reserve Training School, as it was officially known, came into existence in Luton in August, 1938. Part of a reservist training scheme announced in Parliament two years before, it was one of a number of similar schools formed at civil flying fields throughout the country. The original intention at Luton was to train 100 men. A Town Centre, opened in George Street West, was soon found inadequate, and larger premises were obtained in Bute Street, with ample room at that time for offices, lecture rooms, and a Sergeants' Mess. Most of the ground training was carried on there during the week, volunteers being expected to attend on two evenings for lectures by Service and civilian instructors, under the supervision of the Commandant, Wing-Commander Waller, of Harpenden. At week-ends they went to the Airport for flying training on Miles Magister aircraft, and later on advanced trainers of the Hawker Hart series.

After the Luton School had been open two months there were 25 pilots under training. Some had gone solo and another 40 had passed the Selection Board. Munich put a different complexion on things. During the last few months of 1938 numbers steadily rose, and early in 1939 it was announced that there were no more vacancies for pilot training.

About this time two further categories for air crew were opened, for observers and air-gunners. The Bute Street premises became overcrowded, and a factory in John Street was taken for lectures.

A little later volunteers were called for ground duties in a number of trades. Again the response was good. Week-end training for ground crews was mostly at Henlow Camp, and evening training at the Luton Centre.

In the summer of 1939 the pilots went to " practice camp " at Luton Airport for a fortnight's continuous training, but there were no facilities for other categories.

Following the call to service on September 1st, the Luton volunteers had to report daily. Amid the suspense and anticipation, there was a good deal of drilling in the L.N.E.R. station yard. Only a few of the pilots had uniforms, the rest still wore civilian clothes.

As September drew to a close the first batches were sent to training stations. Some of the pilots went to an Initial Training Wing at Hastings ; observers were posted to Staverton, between Cheltenham and Gloucester. At first the Regulars with whom they had to mix were a little disgruntled at this intrusion into their ranks, but during the testing days of 1940 many were the gaps that had to be filled by " week-end flyers." Although most of the observers, air gunners, and ground crew were rapidly posted away, some pilots had to wait for training facilities, and temporarily returned to their civilian occupations. The Town Centre was still in existence, but the spirit of the " week-end flyers " had departed.

Some of the Luton V.R. ground crew found their way to France before the year was out. They were followed later by a few observers and air gunners. One air gunner from Luton " baled out " twice from his Lysander in the few months before Dunkirk.

By the spring of 1940 a large percentage of the air crew members had joined operational squadrons, and took part directly with the fighters or indirectly with the bombers, in the Battle of Britain. Many of the " week-end flyers " paid the supreme sacrifice or were taken prisoner in this period and the years that followed. Those who were more fortunate carried on. Commissions were granted to the greater number, and a few reached senior rank. Between them they obtained quite a number of decorations.

With the war over, pre-war volunteers have met to talk over old times, but many faces are missing. Now the R.A.F.V.R. is to be born anew, and it is probable that Luton will again be a centre.

*   *   *   *

The 12th Bedfordshire Company, W.A.T.S., was mobilised on September 1st, 1939, and left Luton for Aldershot, where in time it lost its county status, and became just A.T.S. Formed about November, 1938, it was one of the earliest units of its kind—so early, in fact, that the service numbers of members were in the first thousand. When recruiting was started Mrs. R. M. Primett was appointed Junior Commander, the company was given headquarters at the Drill Hall, and for drill attached to the 249th Field Company, R.E. The N.C.O.'s of that company had the unusual job of putting the women through

The men who came back. Men of the 5th Bedfords, survivors of the Singapore calamity celebrated their return from captivity, and remembered those they had left behind, at a thanksgiving and memorial service at St. Paul's Church, Bedford, in December, 1945. Above are some of the officers.

ABOVE: *A section of the men marching to the service.*

BELOW: *Officers and men of the Bedfs. Yeomanry, 148 Field Regiment, R.A., also survivors from the Far East, at the dinner held in their honour at Dunstable Town Hall in January, 1946.*

The Corn Exchange Canteen, one of the two opened for British and Overseas troops in Luton, became a popular rendezvous for serving men and women. Here are some of the voluntary workers preparing for an invasion of hungry souls. At the extreme right is Mrs. Grace Goring, who was the controller from the day the canteen opened in 1940, until the last cup of tea was served in 1946.

their foot drills and marching exercises. Originally it was intended that it should be purely a Luton company, but later Dunstable was added to its recruiting area. When on mobilisation the company went to Aldershot it was attached for duty to the R.A.O.C., and there, in October, 1939, it had the distinction of being the first A.T.S. Company to be inspected by the King. With the expansion of the A.T.S. an increase in the establishment of companies, transfers and the normal wastage of personnel, the company largely lost its Luton associations, but there were some of the Luton originals still with the company till the end of the war.

*　　　*　　　*　　　*

The 1st Bedfords were in Cairo when the war started, but during the autumn they went back to Palestine, which they found quieter than before. There they guarded prisoners taken in General Wavell's advance, but some picked personnel went off to Abyssinia on " hush-hush " jobs. Later these were heard of at Mombasa. In March, 1941, the battalion went to occupy the island of Lemnos, near the entrance to the Dardenelles, to ensure its safety as an R.A.F. base, but with the approach of the Germans to Athens it was withdrawn to Alexandria. Orders to reinforce the Crete garrison having been cancelled just before the fall of that island, the next move was to Syria. There, the Vichy French agreeing to an armistice, they had only one accidental casualty. In October, 1941, orders were received to proceed to " an unknown destination." This proved to be Tobruk. After Tobruk it was Syria again, then India, the Arakan, and finally into the Burmese jungle behind the Japanese lines as part of the famous Chindit Force.

*　　　*　　　*　　　*

The 2nd Bedfords went to France as part of the original B.E.F. After Dunkirk they had a strenuous time training at home for they knew not what. It proved to be the landing in Tunisia. With the North African campaign successfully completed, they took part in the invasion of Italy. After the war in Europe had ended the battalion had to go to Greece to help check internal disorders, and they were still there during the Greek elections of early 1946.

*　　　*　　　*　　　*

The 30th Bedfords, a category unit which originated from the 7th Bedfords, mobilised at Ampthill, and went to North Africa in August, 1942. There they were responsible for train and dump guards. In January, 1945, they crossed to Italy for the same kind of duty, and were eventually disbanded early in 1946. They were one of 10 Bedfordshire battalions which existed during the war years, compared with 21 in the 1914-18 war.

*　　　*　　　*　　　*

The 1st Hertfords spent some time on garrison duty at Gibraltar, during the period when it was feared that the Rock might become a major object of enemy attention, and then went into the Italian campaign, taking part in some of the fiercest fighting in the Gothic Line. The 2nd Hertfords found that their way into battle lay across the Normandy beaches. They eventually reached Palestine.

*   *   *   *

During the six years of war county regiments lost much of their local association, and although men might be Bedfords when they joined as recruits there was no guarantee that they would remain Bedfords. Nor was there any guarantee that they would be Bedfords at all. It depended on what regiment happened to be most in need of new men. This accounted for the presence of a considerable number of Luton men in the Buffs at Malta throughout the blitz. Unfortunately they went afterwards to Leros, and then into captivity. A number of Luton men managed to keep together in an R.A.F. unit commanded by Sqdn.-Leader R. B. Waller, O.B.E., of Luton. With the Eighth Army in ill-fortune and good, they constituted an Air Force Park which, having had experience of moving in retreat, turned and travelled the whole length of the Desert Front, went across to Sicily, were taken from there to Italy in a landing craft which had Lieut. Rex Sanders, of Luton, as one of its two officers, and could claim to be the only Air Force Park established in front of the Army's field guns, which fired over them at Salerno. There were other instances of Luton men keeping together through long periods of service.

Newer fighting formations like the Parachute Regiment and the Commandos naturally attracted many volunteers. It was really surprising how many Luton men " dropped in " at Arnhem during the great adventure of 1944. The technical units which kept the Army moving were also very popular with those who had an engineering training, and a lot of Luton men so qualified found their way into the R.E.M.E. when this organisation was created.

*   *   *   *

One most significant change with the passing of the war years was the fading-out of conscientious objectors. They were numerous in the early stages of the war. The question was raised as to whether they ought to be retained in the service of public authorities. Sometimes their appeals against military service were heard in London, sometimes in Cambridge. A considerable number appealed successfully, although exemption from armed service was usually conditional on service in a non-combatant unit, or working on the land. It is a remarkable fact that nothing was heard of conscientious objectors among the younger classes called up in the latter stages of the war. On the other hand, cases are known of men who, after obtaining exemption, changed their minds after learning of some of the things done in the name of Nazism or Fascism, and threw in their lot with their fellows in the common struggle against these evils.

As registration of women for the Services had not come into operation in the period when the tribunals had to sit most frequently to hear claims to exemption on conscientious grounds, no women appeared before them, and there is no record of Luton having produced a woman objector of Service age.

* * * *

Unlike August, 1914 when almost as soon as the Luton Territorials marched off to their training area in East Anglia the North Midland Division descended on Luton and spread itself over the town and neighbourhood, there was no great friendly invasion of this kind in September, 1939, or afterwards. In 1914 the streets of Luton became parade grounds. Whole battalions were billeted in close proximity. There were whole streets where every house had to take in several soldiers. There were not enough open spaces for their drills. Sergeant-majors exercised their lungs in public, to the great edification, among others, of some small boys who became mascots, complete with uniform, and who in the latest war may themselves have become sergeant-majors.

But if there was no such wholesale invasion by troops who would later apply Luton place-names to trenches they dug on the battlefields of France, Luton nevertheless had some interesting Service visitors. In the early days of the war a Tank Regiment was the most notable. The men in it regarded themselves as a grade above soldiers. They were technicians. Their tanks may not have been very good, for tanks had not then become commonplace, but the men prided themselves on their job, and made many friends before they went to the Far East. Those in command exercised a thoughtfulness in one direction which might well have been shown by others, but wasn't. If a pavement had to be crossed from parking ground to highway, it was not permissible to leave the pavement muddy, no matter what the weather. The pavement was cleaned immediately, and again when the tanks had returned from an exercise. This example was not followed by other units which used Pope's Meadow, and often left that part of Old Bedford Road in a terrible mess.

Throughout the war period quite a variety of units came and went. For a long time Luton accommodated a big R.A.S.C. training school. The personnel of this were the most permanent visitors of their time. Later a Smoke Company of the Pioneer Corps stayed a long time, but with the disappearance of the smoke canisters they also disappeared. There was a considerable period when a Bomb Disposal Company went every day from Luton on their dangerous jobs. The Fleet Air Arm trained at the Airport until it was decided to transfer this activity to Cheshire, and so make the Airport available as an Air Transport Auxiliary Centre. There was a ring of searchlight batteries in and round the town, but these seemed to change periodically. Some Defiants were stationed at the Airport for a time, although it seemed a toss-up whether at night they scared off or attracted enemy planes. They moved on, as they had done several times before they came here, but even after they had gone night fighters from somewhere seemed to

321

be in the air over Luton just as quickly after the sirens had sounded. Apart from light machine guns on the roofs of some factories, that was pretty much the extent of Luton's opposition to air attack.

Usually there were one or two infantry battalions quartered in the outer areas of the town, generally using unoccupied houses as billets, the Army Fire Service had a post here for some time, and after the creation of the R.E.M.E. Luton was one of the headquarters of this new organisation. There was also an A.T.S. headquarters, one reason why, in addition to the familiar " Redcaps," one section of which kept a particular eye on the driving on military vehicles, it became a fairly common sight to see A.T.S. " Redcaps " patrolling in pairs.

The approach of D-Day, however, brought some of Luton's most interesting Service visitors. Tank transporters, all " waterproofed,' almost blocked some of the streets. Some had taken part in earlier landings. In due course most of them disappeared. They were followed by a new lot of transporters each carrying a " Buffalo "— apparently a sky-blue combination of turretless tank and paddle boat. They in turn went away, to ferry troops across the Seine, the Rhine, and many lesser rivers. Their special tracks acted as paddle wheels while waterborne, and then served to climb out of the water and advance on land, no matter how marshy the ground was.

For D-Day, also, Luton was the assembly point of the first Field General Hospital to land in Normandy. Many of the personnel had already seen service in North Africa or Italy. Their strength was made up by others to whom landing on a hostile coast was to be a new experience. The doctors were not conspicuous. The nursing sisters were, in the grey and scarlet which in the field gives place to khaki battle dress. They landed in Normandy. Later a similar party left Luton for Burma.

There were no such picturesque visitors in the streets afterwards. Small parties of troops continued to come to one or other of the technical training schools, although the Salvage Training School had vanished, and about the only distinguishing feature of uniforms subsequently seen was a black " flash " which indicated, as did their goat mascot, that the unit was one which had its normal headquarters in the Principality.

*   *   *   *

Wherever there were troops there had to be canteens. Voluntary canteens at the Electricity Showrooms and the Corn Exchange were very popular with the troops stationed in and around Luton. They were originated by the late Alderman C. C. Dillingham. In his forceful way he told some of his friends that they would help him, and relieved them of some of the necessary capital. The canteens started in a modest way, developed as time went on, and although their standard of comfort was never very luxurious, the ladies in charge at least made their patrons feel very welcome. After Ald. Dillingham's death the canteens became the responsibility of a welfare committee.

Accommodation, heat and light were provided free by the Town Council, choirs, orchestras, concert parties and individual artistes attended from time to time to entertain the troops, and things served over the counter were mostly sold at cost. Cups of tea were about the only source of a small profit, but even from this margin it was found possible to do something to improve the lot of the men and women at searchlight stations round the town.

Started in 1940, the canteen at the Electricity Showroom was originally in charge of Mrs. C. C. Dillingham, with Mrs. G. Wistow Walker as deputy. When Mrs. Dillingham retired Mrs. Walker became Controller, and, with Mr. R. Collier as deputy, carried on the canteen until it was closed at Christmas, 1945. At the Corn Exchange, Mrs. Grace Goring was Controller throughout, with Mrs. Blake as deputy, and when this canteen closed on March 31st, 1946, Mrs. Goring had not missed one night's attendance in six years.

An interesting sidelight on this canteen which was subsequently given was that takings during the six years totalled £19,000. That represented quite a lot of work by the voluntary staff, some of whom were with Mrs. Goring from start to finish. It was largely the product of serving two million cups of tea.

*   *   *   *

A welcome, though unofficial, form of welfare work was undertaken by readers of *The Luton News* through what was known as the " Warm Greetings Fund." This was started in the first winter of the war, when opposing armies looked at one another but did not fight. A Luton artillery sergeant in France wrote asking whether something could be done to make the winter a little brighter and more bearable for his men. Woollies and things like that were wanted. They were sent, and that was why it was called the " Warm Greetings Fund." In those days woollen comforts were easy to obtain. Wool was not then on coupons. Some good people quickly formed themselves into knitting circles, bought their own wool, and kept the fund supplied with pullovers, Balaclava helmets, scarves, gloves, socks, etc. Little money was necessary at that time, except to pay the postage on the parcels, but money also came along. It made possible the inclusion of other acceptable things, then also easily obtainable. They were sent not only to local men in France, but to those in the Navy, at isolated air stations, and anywhere where Luton men were known to be serving. In that first winter, too, a bulk gift was sent to France for the 2nd Bedfords. Even wireless sets, sports equipment, musical instruments, and a variety of other bulky things were sent. In those days they could be had for the asking.

Similarly, if a searchlight battery near Luton wanted something, the need had only to be mentioned. What was wanted came along or, if heavy, could be fetched. Such gifts ran to armchairs, tables, china, and even pianos.

In later days, when the North African desert was the principal scene of fighting, it was possible to send some things which would otherwise have been quite unobtainable by the recipients, or would have involved paying a fantastic price. And always, whatever else was sent, there was a demand for books. As the war dragged on and life became more austere, the character of the gifts which could be sent had to change somewhat. A repetition of the gift of thousands of cigarettes by the wholesale tobacconists of Luton as a body could not be expected. Many other things which had regularly been bought became scarce in the shops, but there were some good trade friends who saw that when the things which were most wanted were available, those responsible for running the fund had first opportunity to buy. The money was always there. Except in the early days that was never a problem. In some places there were regular collections. Some individuals sent regular monthly contributions. Towards the end it was possible to announce that, with the end actually in sight, no more money would be needed, there being ample already in hand to carry on right to the end of 1945.

In the closing stages recipients in home units generally received a money gift, to apply as they thought fit, and postage stamps. Those abroad still received a parcel of articles which were certain to be acceptable, plus a postal order. It was found that the parcels were appreciated all the more because they were unexpected. They made men feel that, although far from home, they were by no means forgotten.

In all, 5,328 men and women from Luton who were in the Services received individual gifts, quite apart from what was done for units.

The Eagle's Brood

IT was our American friends who discovered Luton as a holiday resort.

Some may question the level of intelligence which induced them to choose Luton ; but they had their reasons, and the better the type of American, the better his reasons. They came, and came again.

It began quite early. They were still a long way from the war. The day of mass raids by Liberators and Flying Fortresses had yet to come. The same camp routine, the same faces day after day, irked them. In time everybody on the camp knew everybody else. They did the same things, at work or during their leisure. They spoke the same language.

When they had 48 hours' leave, their impulse was to get clear of camp. Who first discovered Luton we shall never know, but the word must have gone round quickly that in Luton there were sociable and hospitable people. More and more came.

Take a look at three typical G.I.'s. Late one evening they arrived from the Midlands, strangers in a blacked-out town. They found hotel accommodation a problem they hadn't expected, but they dug in somewhere quickly enough to have a good time at a dance. They were at a dance the second night.

The third night they absolutely had to leave by a train about 9.30, or invite trouble at camp. Uncertain where the "Depot" was in the blackness, they hung on till practically the last minute, the most staid member of the trio keeping an anxious eye on the clock. They accepted on trust an absolute stranger's offer to deliver them at the station in time. They caught their train with a minute to spare. They left, loud in praise of the good time they had had, and full of assurances that Luton would see them again.

There were many such parties. They didn't all want London all the time. They were not all from the big cities of the West. They wanted to see something less artificial, something more representative of the real folk of this England, even if they didn't quite understand them. So they came. Not many Luton people would choose to travel such distances to spend a week-end at a strange place which to them had no more claim than Luton to be a holiday resort.

Most of our visitors, of course, belonged to the U.S. Army Air Force. Not all were flying officers or even top-sergeants. Many were just technical personnel. Some were very smart. Some, less smart, made us wonder how they managed in their own wide open spaces, with no buildings to prop up.

"Ah," we were told, "they are not the pick of the U.S. Army. They are draftees. The regulars, the really smart men, are all out in the Pacific." And that dictum we had to accept.

*   *   *   *

Some could have been put into British Service dress, and been mistaken for the real thing. Others, no matter what their dress, would still have shown that their forbears originated from Middle Europe, and that not many generations ago. Of the coloured element Luton saw little except grinning black faces and white teeth as their owners drove convoys of trucks through the town.

All G.I.'s seemed well provided with money. They would sometimes deny this, and stress that they were only allowed to draw part of their authorised pay. But they seemed able to buy everything they and their lady friends wanted if it was on sale. Perhaps they were sometimes a little too greedy and insistent, but they were a long way from home.

What was particularly noticeable was the change some of these men underwent through staying here a year or two. Of the first who arrived, many were very akin to the first American arrivals on the Continent in the previous war. Then they arrived full of assurance that they were the outfit who could finish the job in a twinkling. They were not at all pleased when they found themselves attached to British units " for instruction." They found that war as it was then being waged was a job they had to learn anew, from people who really did know.

Similarly, a good many arrived this time, full of the same assurance. They remained to realise that in this country we knew something, at least, about the job, having managed to stay in the fight quite a long time on our own. Then these particular visitors became much less vocal, and really human.

*   *   *   *

To the leave men, of course, there were added those stationed at airfields not far from the town. They rolled in at night, in fleets of buses and Service trucks. They were going to have a gayer night than camp offered.

But some of the most interesting were those who came for reasons of family sentiment.

There was the man who came from the far North, with only a few hours to spend here . . . When he got back home he wanted to be able to talk to his father about Luton. First he had to find Bute Street, and see whether the place where his father once worked still existed. If not, he wanted to be able to tell father why, and what else had happened in Bute Street. He wanted to know about other places which his father would recognise if he could re-visit the town of his birth; if they had gone, he wanted to know why, and what had taken their places.

His was a well-known Luton name, and he was told where he might find some probable relatives. But the train service did not permit. Provided with pictures of the Luton his father would remember, he went back to the North rejoicing.

*   *   *   *

The one main grouse of those able to stay awhile was that their own authorities had not provided a hostel. Eventually the American Red Cross did establish a club in George Street, with Miss Isobel Lee in charge, but this was not until June, 1944. The Donut Club became very popular—may it be suggested that it was because it was so largely staffed by Luton ladies? But it did not cater for the bed and breakfast so many wanted. Americans, in fact, often slept in the air raid tunnels when they could find no better accommodation. The club did not open until 10 a.m., and they badly felt the need of a clean-up before that. The meal question was not so difficult, if they were content with one of the many cafés which sprang up in Luton during the war years.

True, a number of people set out to cash in on this need, and some gave the Americans a very square deal. Others, if the comments of the Americans themselves were well-founded, seemed to aim at getting the most cash for the minimum they could be induced to

Mrs. R. Andrews, Luton's W. V. S. organiser, makes a presentation to Miss Van der Meid, director of the Luton American Red Cross Club, at a party at the Savoy Cinema in September, 1945. The Club staff and voluntary helpers subscribed to the present and the party was given by the American Red Cross and United States Army, as an expression of thanks to the staff, and to the people of Luton for their hospitality to American Servicemen.

LEFT: *An American host pours the lemonade at a party at the American Red Cross Club, Luton. Nearly one hundred children who had not been able to attend any party during the season were entertained.*

ABOVE: *Some of the guests enjoy a doughnut at the American Red Cross Club, Luton, when an "Open Day" was held on November 23rd, 1944 . . . America's Thanksgiving Day. In the centre of the picture is Miss Isobel Lee, the first Director, with Mrs. Venniker, in charge of local voluntary helpers, and Mrs. M. Plasom, staff assistant, on her right.*

RIGHT: *British wives of American serving men with their babies, at a Baby Show held in the Club, shortly before it closed.*

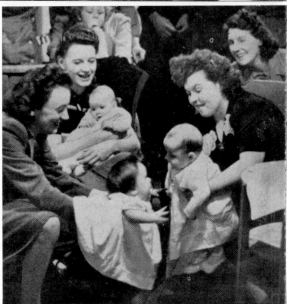

ABOVE: *Service with a smile as Miss Henrietta Christian, captain in charge, serves her first customer at the refreshment bar of the American Red Cross Club in George Street, opened in June, 1944.*

LEFT: *Cpl. Nichols L. McKay was the first customer to check in at the "Donut Dug-out," as the Club became known to the Americans. Standing behind the counter is a member of Luton W.V.S.*

BELOW: *Coffee and doughnuts for some of the first G.I.'s to make use of their club, which had recreational facilities and an information bureau.*

provide. Then the G.I.'s grouse about the lack of a hostel became really vehement.

*   *   *   *

After a few months the authorities did something about it. They provided dormitory accommodation for 50 at the Donut Club. Simultaneously they opened 46 and 48, Downs Rd., with a local lady in charge, one house accommodating 50 and the other 75. All three dormitories were used to capacity until the Americans began to move homewards ; after that, only week-ends found them in full demand.

Running such dormitories was not without incident. There was the occasion, for example, when one young man decided that to mark his 21st birthday he would get tight—very tight. He was very young and, as we would say, very " browned-off." Home was a long way away. It was all so different from what he had planned back among the bright lights before 1941. He knew no one here. What he wanted was liquor and more liquor.

They tried to dissuade him but somehow he succeeded and got past the fuddled stage. The dormitory warden somehow got him to bed, but he was restless and unpredictable. She stayed with him, sitting by the side of his bed for a long time, and she talked to him patiently. She talked to him of his family and his mother across the other side, of his friends and his home town. Eventually he fell asleep. The next morning he was a pleasant boy again and when he saw the warden he was so grateful.

*   *   *   *

The Donut Club, with Miss Van der Meid as successor to Miss Lee, continued very popular right to the end, and when, because so many of those for whom it was intended had gone home, a closing date was fixed, there was such an outcry by those still using it that sentence was suspended, but only for a few weeks. It closed its doors on November 20th, 1945.

Local ladies who gave so much voluntary service there will remember one special occasion. Determined to show their appreciation, the Americans themselves threw a party for the canteen helpers, donned aprons, served refreshments and did all the washing-up, and then proceeded to demonstrate how to make a party go.

*   *   *   *

In the latter days it was interesting to meet men who having completed or exceeded the number of operational flights which entitled them to go home, came to have a last look at Luton.

If a man came from one of the Southern States, he didn't think any more of our summer weather than we do. In fact, his primary reason for being glad of a chance to go home early, even if it was midsummer, was that at home he would at least be able to feel warm again.

But there were others not so anxious to go home in a hurry. They wanted to have a good look round, in case they could never come again.

330

They were quite content to stand aside in favour of other, and perhaps younger, men, who were to go on to the Far East after home leave.

* * * *

It was to be expected that international marriages would be fairly numerous. Prospective brides were not deterred by the warning that they did not acquire American citizenship, that they would have to wait a long time before they could go to the States, and that if and when they did arrive the conditions of the new life awaiting them might be not at all to their liking. Marriages continued to take place. Husbands went back, their brides, left behind, started agitations and formed deputations about the lack of transportation for them. They still had to wait. They formed a " Columbus Club " ; held their own baby show.

And still more marriages took place. By the end of 1945 the transportation problem seemed to have been solved, for it was announced that they would all be out of this country by the following February. Reception centres were established where, with their children, if any, the G.I. Brides assembled before being taken to Southampton and put on a boat for the States. They were on their way.

* * * *

Now we see no more of the white-belted, white-spatted, white-gloved " Snowdrops " who had their own peculiar methods of dealing with such of their countrymen as were unruly.

Nor can parties of ultra-smart Americans come to represent their country at some ceremonial parade, as they did during the war years.

But if they continue to have more money in the States than we do here, despite how much they may have lent to us, we shall see some of those Americans again. They will come, although not in uniform.

And some are certain to come to Luton.

The Rising Generation

IF little or nothing was done by the nation in the first twelve months of the war to tap the potential of the youth of Britain, it was not because the existence of these latent energies and enthusiasms was not realised. Boys and girls of what is now colloquially known as the " teen-age " classes were in 1939 an unknown factor. From 14 to 16 they were either of senior school age or had already moved into industry, which was accelerating its service to the nation. At any rate they were creatures with minds and wills of their own. From 16 until the ages when the call up operated, boys and girls had become young men and women who were productive assets to industry.

What was their reaction to war? That was not long in doubt. The teen-agers showed themselves consistent in their reasoning and persistent in their devotion to the national cause. They soaked up knowledge like sponges, docketed it, and produced it without effort. They were authorities on the most abstruse technical matters connected with the fighting services. Their enthusiasms were phenomenal and lasting. Boys of 16 fought their way into the Home Guard through a maze of regulations and by all manner of subterfuges. Once in they displayed a quick-wittedness that astounded their older comrades. No job was too menial. No job was skimped. Their physical and mental stamina was astounding.

Youth could easily have been conscripted, trained and disciplined from a very early age, but the horrid example of Hitler Youth, of children bereft of the finer human attributes, was anathema to the British mind. Youth must not be regimented, yet it must be encouraged, carefully yet vigorously, to use its tremendous energies where most needed.

So it fell out that youth was given a very definite place in activities arising out of the war, quite apart from any useful war work in which the young people who had left school were engaged during the day.

Until December, 1941, it was largely left to the young people themselves to seek membership of one or other of the existing youth organisations, but after that until the end of 1945 they had to register at the age of 16, so that information could be obtained as to their leisure-time interests. The intention was not that those who were apparently at a loose end should be *directed* into some suitable organisation. It gave an opportunity to recommend them to join an organisation.

It gave an additional impetus to recruiting for the three pre-entry training organisations, although it may be said that most of the young people who joined these, or became members of the cadet divisions of the Red Cross Society or St. John Ambulance Brigade, or the N.F.S. messenger service, did not need much guidance.

*   *   *   *

In Luton, as in other places, the war severely handicapped the older youth organisations like the Boys' Brigade, the Church Lads' Brigade, the Scouts, and Luton Boys' Club, by taking away many of their enthusiastic leaders, and in other ways by making it difficult for the remaining leaders to carry on. But it also brought other youth organisations into being, and it was natural that those which provided pre-entry training for the three Services should exercise the greatest appeal. The very fact that these youths were provided with smart uniforms which, except in size, were indistinguishable from the real thing, was an added stimulus to recruiting, if one were needed, and nothing was so heartening as the way these young people reacted to

Service discipline. They enjoyed it. They studied it, practised it with fervour. In the result, when they were eventually called to the fighting Services proper they had already learned responsibility and leadership. The doors to promotion were quickly opened to them.

*   *   *   *

It was only natural that of the pre-training organisations which came into existence during the war, the Air Training Corps should make the greatest appeal to youth. When it came into existence on February 1st, 1941, the thrilling deeds of the R.A.F. in the Battle of Britain were fresh in the public memory. Among youth there was a general ambition not only to fly in some capacity or other, but to play the same stirring part as did the Battle of Britain heroes.

In Luton the Air Training Corps inherited a valuable legacy. A Luton squadron of the pre-war Air Defence Cadet Corps had been formed in 1938 under the auspices of the Air League of the British Empire. Luton was one of the first towns in the country to form such a squadron, which was registered as No. 10 (Founder) Squadron. Mr. Frank Facer, the first Luton man ever to fly—and that was pre-1914—was in charge. He and other pioneers of the Youth Air Training Scheme did much hard work, and many members of the squadron later joined the R.A.F., and built up very creditable war records. Notable among the early entrants from the A.D.C.C., as it was known, were five lads who spent almost every moment of their spare time in making themselves proficient as wireless operators. They were completely successful, and after a special examination at an R.A.F. Station they were accepted into the R.A.F., as special-entry wireless operators some months earlier than they would otherwise have been eligible to join.

By the end of 1940 the need for aircrews had become of vital importance, and the Air Ministry decided to assume complete responsibility for all pre-entry R.A.F. training. The wisdom of this decision was more than justified by later events.

February, 1941, then, saw the birth of the Air Training Corps as an integral part of the R.A.F. The Luton response to the call for volunteers was really remarkable. An organising committee, a nucleus of officers under Mr. H. T. Rushton, with a number of civilian instructors, quickly got to work. The officers, although granted commissions in the R.A.F.V.R., worked on a purely voluntary basis, and from the earliest days gave all their spare time to the organisation and training of the cadets. The local unit took over the No. 10 (F) Squadron, A.D.C.C. as a nucleus, became the 10(F) Squadron, A.T.C., and recruiting went ahead rapidly. In a very few weeks more than 200 cadets had been enrolled, and they were augmented by many enlisted airmen who, on joining the R.A.F. proper, had been sent back temporarily to their jobs. These were " deferred service " airmen, and they reported for pre-entry training with the A.T.C. pending actual call-up. By May of that year the strength of the squadron had

333

reached 300, and it had become necessary to hold classes on every night of the week except Saturday. In the early days the instruction was confined mainly to drill, P.T., signals, air navigation and calculations, interspersed with lectures by serving R.A.F. officers. As training got under way there were also visits to airfields, mainly with a view to giving the cadets a little Service " atmosphere," and many other courses were added, such as aircraft recognition, theory of flight, engines, armament, wireless mechanics, and so on.

Numbers continued to grow, in spite of the fact that cadets were already passing into the Services, and it was inevitable that a second squadron (No. 1979) should be formed. To this end a certain number of officers and cadets were transferred from the parent squadron. Mr. H. R. Waller had by this time taken over from Mr. Rushton, who had taken a higher appointment with the A.T.C., and Mr. R. A. Gibbs went to 1979 Squadron. The two Luton squadrons then took under their wing the newly-formed Toddington Flight, and initiated a Works Flight at Vauxhall Motors, Ltd. A few months later the latter attained a strength sufficient to justify the formation of yet another Luton squadron, which became No. 2122 (Vauxhall) Squadron, under Mr. W. J. Hunter. In time Mr. C. Miller succeeded Mr. Gibbs in command of 1979 Squadron.

Until well into 1944 A.T.C. training went on without a halt. Each year saw many of the cadets go off for a week's course, which included flying in Service machines, at an R.A.F. Station. Practically everyone had already done some flying, and many had passed proficiency examinations set by the Air Ministry. Ex-members on leave, wearing wings or air crew brevets, were a frequent sight at A.T.C. headquarters at Waller Street School.

Not so common, but gradually increasing in numbers, were ex-cadets who had gained commissions, sometimes in the other fighting Services.

By mid-1944 the demand for air crews became considerably less, and many members of the local squadrons, who had devoted a lot of time to training to fit themselves for aircrew duties, found they were being called for service as R.A.F. ground staff, or for the Navy or Army, or even for the mines. There was some dissatisfaction with high policy on this matter, and the inevitable result was a falling off in numbers.

After the cessation of hostilities the incentive to train disappeared, and No. 1979 Squadron was eventually re-absorbed into No. 10 (F) Squadron which continues.

Luton may well be proud of the part its squadrons of the Air Training Corps played during the war. They passed between 600 and 700 semi-trained youths and men into the Services. Of these at least fifty were granted commissions, and it is known that at least three were awarded the Distinguished Flying Cross.

Sport was greatly favoured as part of the cadets' training, and in spite of the war the Luton A.T.C. squadrons sponsored four highly successful swimming galas. No. 10(F) Squadron also did well on the football field, winning the Eastern Command Trophy in two successive years and reaching the final in the following season.

The A.T.C. were also the first local pre-training unit to have a fully equipped band, which became in great request.

Tribute must be paid to the civilian instructors who so willingly gave, and still give, their services without stint to help the youths in the squadrons. Without their help the corps could hardly have existed. The results would certainly not have been the same. Nor would a high standard of discipline have been so quickly obtained but for the influence of Mr. Edmund Canterbury, a South African veteran who had won a Long Service award even before he went into the Gallipoli Campaign, and who saw in the A.T.C. an opportunity for still further useful service.

*   *   *   *

The Luton unit of the Sea Cadet Corps, which became a popular pre-training organisation for many boys, was really the successor of the Navy League Sea Cadet Corps, which had been in existence for many years prior to the war. Not until 1942, however, did the Admiralty take it under its wing as an official recruiting agency for the Royal Navy, and decide on a large expansion, with Luton as the centre of a unit.

Admiral Sir Lionel Halsey, who is so well known throughout the county, and who is Commodore of the Sea Cadet Corps of the whole of the British Isles, contacted the late Mr. C. C. Dillingham, and the Luton unit was formed. It was fortunate in having for its first commanding officer Lieut.-Commander T. H. Keyes, who had had long experience in the Royal Navy, and through his connection with George Kent, Ltd., was closely in touch with some of Luton's youth. Other original officers were Lieut. W. S. Hyde (No. 1), and Sub-Lieuts. G. H. Bone, E. G. Baker, T. C. Gregory, and F. Gowing (Administrative Officer). Three of the originals have now left, and the work is now carried on by Lieut. Hyde, as commanding officer, and Sub-Lieuts. Bone, Gowing and Warwick.

The unit was given an establishment of 100, and held its first parade on June 1st, 1942, at its headquarters, Beech Hill School. Cadets are trained in seamanship, signalling, squad drill, etc., and sport plays an important part in training. A football team plays in a local league, and Luton has won the swimming competition once, and the athletic competition twice, in the last two years in competition with its neighbours at Dunstable, Bedford, Hitchin, Welwyn and Biggleswade.

In 1945 the Luton unit organised a parade of ten units from Bedfordshire and Hertfordshire on the Wardown Sports Ground, where they were inspected by Admiral Sir Lionel Halsey. They afterwards marched through the town, the salute being taken at the Town Hall.

But competitions and ceremonial parades, however useful and successful they may be, are not the be-all and end-all of the movement. Its essential aim is to give boys a preliminary training for a life at sea. That it is fulfilling this primary purpose is shown by the fact that by early 1946 it had passed 44 boys into the Royal Navy, six to the Fleet Air Arm, and 15 to the Merchant Navy, while three had succeeded in gaining commissions. Letters are frequently received from ex-cadets now scattered all over the seven seas, and when on leave they always call at headquarters to renew old friendships.

Summer camps are held at Naval establishments under Service conditions and Admiralty supervision.

The Luton Sea Cadets certainly had no cause for unhappy memories of Victory Day, June 8'h, 1946. The pouring rain which spoiled the pleasure of the celebrations mattered not at all to them while they were exploring the mysteries of *H.M.S. Diadem*, the second ship adopted by Luton during the war. It was an exceptional opportunity for them. *Diadem* was lying in the Thames off Greenwich for public inspection on the two days following V-Day. The Sea Cadets had a private view on V-Day, at the invitation of Captain Knapp. They had the run of the ship—and a grand tea.

*　　*　　*　　*

The Army Cadet Force came into existence in Luton as a pre-service unit in February, 1942. The first Company was formed by Lieut. V. Russell in connection with Luton Boys' Club, Park Street. Very soon afterwards Luton Grammar School, then known as Luton Modern School, established a second unit, with Lieut. S. J. Pointing as its first commanding officer. The movement increased in popularity among the youth of Luton, and in July of the same year a further unit was formed for Leagrave and Limbury, under the command of Lieut. F. H. Rowe. Lt.-Col. R. Briars, M.C., had much to do with the organisation of the A.C.F. in Luton in its preliminary stages until persistent ill-health compelled him to relinquish the work. He died in 1943.

Like so many other organisations, the Army Cadet Force movement in Luton suffered from lack of suitable accommodation. By 1944 conditions at Park Street had become very difficult, and a move was made to Williamson Street, where the Boys' Club Section was re-formed as the Luton Town Company. With the stand down of the Home Guard, this later found its way to more spacious premises at the Drill Hall, Old Bedford Road.

Changing personnel somewhat retarded the progress of the Cadet Force until, their other duties having ceased, a number of Home Guard officers and instructors found the Cadet Force provided them with a new field of service. Through the hard work and interest of Major F. G. Harmer, M.M., an up-to-date social club for the cadets was provided at the Drill Hall and, with a committee of voluntary workers, it became a very popular place with the " young soldiers."

The Sea Cadets—training for the Royal Navy—had a strong war-time Corps in Luton. In the picture above a signals class is receiving a semaphore message.

Officers and cadets of the Luton Sea Cadet Corps photographed during the war years.

A. J. Mander inspecting Luton Army Cadets in July 1943.

ABOVE: *A squad of the Luton Grammar (then Modern) School Army Cadet Corps put in some foot-slogging in the playground.*

BELOW: *Councillor J. Burgoyne, then Mayor of Luton, pinning the first gold medal for gallantry to be awarded by the Air Defence Cadet Corps (later the A.T.C.) on to the tunic of Cadet H. G. Pyper, of No. 10 F. Squadron, for his heroism in rescuing a five-year-old boy from the River Ouse at Bedford.*

BELOW: *Six Luton Air Cadets, who, although under 18, were accepted for special entry into the R.A.F. in January, 1941, after passing a signalling test at 20 words a minute. With them is their instructor, Sgt. Day, of the Home Guard, who later became an A.T.C. officer, and assumed command of No. 10 F. Squadron in 1946.*

Air Chief Marshal Sir Robert Brooke-Popham inspecting the band of Nos. 10 F. and 1979 Squadrons, Luton A.T.C. On his right is Squadron Leader H. T. Rushton, and on his left Flight Lieutenant H. R. Waller.

Heading the parade through the town, the band of Luton A.T.C. Squadrons march through George Street, shortly after its formation at the end of 1942.

Members of the Girls' Training Corps swing past the saluting base at the Boys' Brigade Diamond Jubilee parade in June 1943.

BELOW: This bucket-swinging quintet were off to fetch the water at a week-end camp for Luton patrol leaders, guides and rangers, held in Stockwood Park in August 1943.

ABOVE: Four G.T.C. girls get down to a spell of morse practice.

During the war period very successful camps were held at Bedford and at Ampthill Park, and a series of week-end camps and courses proved very popular, while for 1946 a seaside camp was found practicable, for training under something very approaching service conditions. As compulsory service for the youth of the country is to continue, the wider training which cadets now receive should be even more valuable than that received by the earlier cadets, a large percentage of whom passed into the Services, where they found that even such A.C.F. training as they had been able to receive was very helpful in their new life.

For cadets of a technical bent special courses were arranged at the Luton R.E.M.E. School, under Capt. A. Driver, and here they were able to obtain a very practical form of instruction.

The sporting side received special attention, and District and Command finals of the A.C.F. Boxing Championships were staged at the Electrolux Canteen, through the kindness of the management of the company.

During War Savings weeks the cadets rendered very useful service, and in Youth week they provided demonstrations. Now, organised in close association with the County Regiment, the Army Cadet Force goes on, and will continue to attract lads who can appreciate the value of pre-entry training for the service to the country which they will be called on to render in due course.

*　　　*　　　*　　　*

Founded as the Whittlesey Club in the years following the first World War, Luton Boys' Club put up a record of service in the Second of which it may well be proud.

After Munich a number of senior members joined the Territorials and the R.A.F.V.R., and were mobilised immediately war was declared. The calls of Civil Defence made further inroads on the leisure of many of the older members, and parties of all ages joined in sandbagging, the provision of shelters, and the other hasty provisions of those hectic days. Evacuation also brought its problems, and London schools billeted in the area were allowed to use the club premises during part of the evenings for games for their boys. The Air Training Corps, in its earliest days, also used part of the club as temporary headquarters. The first Army Cadet Force unit in Luton was also formed at the club, and was an immediate success. Later it was absorbed into a local battalion and moved to the Drill Hall.

Meanwhile more and more members had been conscripted with their age groups, and as far as can be ascertained the total reached over 250. Others, although on war work, gave a vast amount of time to all branches of Civil Defence. The bombing incidents in the Park Street district cost the club considerable damage to property and equipment. At these times it was used by the police and Civil Defence as an information post.

All through these difficult times the club remained open and active.

Leaders and Old Boys were all serving in one cause or another, yet time was found to keep the flag flying. Games and other activities were naturally not anywhere near pre-war standard, but members on leave found the place a mine of information about old friends, where they were, and what they were doing. News, good and bad, arrived and filtered out.

War casualties cost the club many popular lads, for 23 gave their lives, two with the Navy, seven in the Army, and 14 with the R.A.F., while two came back each minus a leg. The ending of the war in the Far East brought the return of a number who had been prisoners, but some who did not return have found their last resting place many thousands of miles from home.

*   *   *   *

Some 100 officers and boys of the Luton and District Battalion, Boys' Brigade, were called to the Colours, and five made the supreme sacrifice. In spite of the loss of officers to the Services, and the fact that the remaining leaders were on shift work, doing overtime, or engaging in some other phase of the national effort, membership almost trebled during the war years. This would not have been possible without the fine work of the senior boys.

The boys of the companies rendered valuable service in many ways. When the L.D.V. was started, they made up a rota of members to attend at L.D.V. headquarters from early evening till late at night, taking out urgent messages to members of the L.D.V. who were wanted for duty out of their turn because some others had to put overtime or Sunday work on urgent jobs even before their L.D.V. duty. Messenger work for the police and the N.F.S. was also undertaken throughout the war.

Headquarters instituted a National Service badge. To qualify for this, boys had to render at least 100 hours of voluntary, unpaid service. Besides messenger duty, many did fire-watch in their streets or at their school; some did organised work in the Dig-for-Victory Campaign, or systematic collecting for the Red Cross. First aid is always part of B.B. training, but during the war larger numbers than ever attended classes. Now it is quite common to see the National Service badge among the badges worn within the battalion.

*   *   *   *

The Church Lads' Brigade, like many other organisations, suffered considerably in Luton through the effects of war. During 1939 and 1940 many of its officers and instructors volunteered for the Services. Then came the greatest difficulty of all—the problem of uniforms and equipment. Supplies became very short, and the senior section of the local unit found it impossible to carry on. Biscot, the parent company in Luton, closed down for the time being, but Leagrave and Stopsley bravely kept their junior sections going, in spite of the drawbacks of the blackout and raid warnings, and the fact that most of the church premises were heavily taxed by the needs of the Services or the local authority. Now, with the return of many old members, the release of equipment, and supplies of uniforms in prospect, it is hoped that the C.L.B. will rise again, and take a prominent place among Luton's youth organisations.

*   *   *   *

" Carry on, but Forward," was the Girls' Life Brigade motto during the war years, and the Luton and District Battalion can be proud of their endeavours to fulfil this motto. Like other organisations, they had many difficulties. Officers and other prospective leaders were called to the Women's Services or became nurses in hospitals, and although their G.L.B. training in discipline, home nursing, etc., served them well, their departure made things harder for those left to carry on. They had to spend much time which would normally have been devoted to Brigade activities at work on munitions, driving ambulances, firewatch, etc.

Moreover, halls used for Brigade meetings were commandeered, with the result that some companies had to close down temporarily or meet in very inadequate premises. The introduction of clothing coupons was also a blow, making " uniform " a trying problem, and one which long after the cessation of hostilities was a continuing problem.

In spite of these handicaps the Battalion grew in size. Six new companies, including three which now form part of the new Dunstable and District Battalion, were affiliated, increasing the number of active companies to twelve. This increase cannot be attributed to the registration of young people for guidance into youth groups, as the majority of members recruited were under fourteen. This was mainly due to the fact that lack of officers precluded the running of Pioneer Sections (girls of sixteen and over) in many companies. It was also found that girls in the higher teens, with no previous Brigade experience, preferred mixed clubs.

In view of the greatly increased interest in youth activities during the last five years, however, it is certain that had helpers been available the work of the Girls' Life Brigade, with its four-square programme— spiritual, physical, educational and social—would have been greatly extended in spite of prevailing difficulties. But much was done, and is being done, by the Luton Battalion. Ordinary activities were continued in spite of raid warnings. Keen competition was roused between the companies by the introduction of P.T., general efficiency, and other competitions. Interest in First-Aid lectures, which pre-war had been regarded as " rather boring," resulted in the institution of a First-Aid competition, and incidentally led to many members joining First-Aid units. Many knitting badges were won by knitting for the Forces, and, later, for China's children. Money was raised for deserving causes by displays, collections, etc. Members helped farmers, looked after evacuee children, hemmed bandages, searched for moths in stored clothing for bombed-out families, and did not let the "good

343

work " cease with hostilities. Under the G.L.B. post-war reconstruction scheme, members raised money to help European countries. Bibles for Norway, groats for French babies, funds for the reconstruction of Continental Sunday Schools, were provided.

*　　*　　*　　*

Luton Boy Scouts' Association, which now includes Sea Scouts and Air Scouts, lost 136 members to the Services. Of these, 12 gained commissions, 11 were killed, 10 wounded, and one listed as " missing." Scoutmaster Alec Brown was subsequently awarded the Medal of Merit for the way he carried on his Scouting life " under the most terrible conditions " while in the hands of the Japanese at the Changi Prison Camp.

The Civil Defence Services claimed 88 members, of whom two were killed. The George Medal was awarded to the Scoutmaster of the St. Peter's Troop, Section Officer S.A. Wright, N.F.S., for bravery during the blitz on Thames Haven.

Younger Scouts collected 35 tons of salvage, erected 85 air raid shelters for other people, and put in 4,040 hours on harvesting and other farm work, 1,030 hours for the emergency medical service, 351 hours on Home Guard duties, and also found time to assist with evacuees.

*　　*　　*　　*

Some Luton girls found an opportunity to " do their bit " when in May, 1942, the Luton Girls' Service Company, affiliated to the Luton High School Company of Service, was formed. A year later it became the Girls' Training Corps, with Mrs. Evans, a High School mistress, as commandant. Service ranks were instituted.

The G.T.C., though termed a youth organisation, was more than that. Many of its members filled important posts as N.F.S. and W.V.S. messengers in connection with raid incidents, did secretarial work for the Luton Army Cadet Force, and assisted in the Youth Headquarters' canteen.

They studied a variety of subjects which were of much use to those who afterwards joined the women's Services. Drills and parades were naturally held, other subjects including A.R.P. lectures, aircraft recognition, morse, first aid, hygiene and crafts. Dr. F. Grundy, Luton's Medical Officer, himself gave a series of lectures on health.

The social side of the organisation was not neglected, and the girls held dramatics, sports, hikes and socials. Talks on current events were also given.

Membership of the G.T.C. naturally varied, but the peak was about 80 girls. The closure of the women's Services on certain occasions throughout the war, and the declaration of peace, affected members, but 775 Corps of the G.T.C. still carries on in Luton.

*　　*　　*　　*

But as the war progressed there were still numbers of boys and girls who remained outside these organisations. Their leisure was a pretty

344

ABOVE: *Luton Sea Scouts being inspected by Lt. Col. D. C. Part at a church parade in July,* 1945.

BELOW: *The President of the Luton Battalion of the Boys' Brigade, Mr. A. E. Harris, carries out an inspection of one of the Luton companies.*

ABOVE: *Cheers from some Luton Boy Scouts who were taking part in District Competitions in March,* 1945.

*Members of Beech Hill Youth Centre in
a physical training demonstration at an
open evening in May, 1941.*

*Some of the leaders and members of the
High Town Youth Centre photographed
in May, 1942.*

aimless thing. To induce them to apply it a little more beneficially, if only to themselves, Youth Centres were opened. They were financed and controlled by the County Education authority, acting through an area committee, which had Mr. H. O. Crouch as secretary. The Centre Leaders did not have an easy job, but they got down to it, activities were arranged to be interesting as well as instructive, and in time a useful work developed.

The centres and their leaders were :—High Town (at Hitchin Road Girls' School), Miss K. V. Wilson ; Beech Hill, Mr. A. D. McMullen ; Chapel Street, Mr. R. Eling ; Stopsley, Mr. A. C. Benson.

The High Town Centre, with 520 members, was by far the largest. Beech Hill and Chapel Street were less well attended, but ran one another very close in membership. Stopsley Centre, catering for a district where the population is much more scattered, could be excused for attracting the smallest attendance.

The work of the centres was not planned on a rigid programme which had to apply equally to each. The programme was variable according to the reasonable wishes of members, but in general the activities covered physical training, cookery, domestic science, music and the drama, and discussions, with cricket, football, rambling, and social gatherings encouraged according to the season.

It cannot be said that the older public's first impressions of the centres were altogether favourable. It was not easy to make the young people realise that the movement was intended to have a more serious background than just some additional provision for their entertainment. But that stage passed, and as some of the young people began to indicate a growing sense of responsibility they were encouraged to express their views through their own Youth Council, although this could not be more than an advisory body.

The Youth Council came into existence in July, 1942. It held its inaugural meeting in the Council Chamber at the Town Hall, and received some good advice from the Mayor. Urging the young people not to go through life just as fault-finders and grousers, he said :— " Don't wait until you have a more prominent place in this Chamber. Find yourself a job, satisfy yourself it is your job, equip yourself well, and cultivate some of the grace and courtesy which is said to be disappearing from our society."

The idea of a Youth Council was undoubtedly good, but events suggested that it was put into operation rather prematurely. There were weak points in this provision for the leisure of youth. Only registration was compulsory. There was no compulsion to join any organisation, and outside the pre-service organisations, little power to discipline any who, after joining, were inclined to be unruly. It also became clear, after central Youth Headquarters were established in Guildford Street, that there were still a good many members of youth centres still holding the view that they ought to have still more of the entertainment to which they seemed to think they were entitled, and that they were under no obligation to regard membership as a lead to any more serious application of their leisure.

Because of this, the Guildford Street headquarters, intended as a connecting link not only for the Youth Centres but for all youth organisations, came in for considerable criticism at one period. In fact, at a meeting of the County Council a Luton member alleged that the County Service of Youth was turning young people into jitterbugs instead of forming characters which would make the young people good citizens. This was not wholly admitted, but it was not denied that the crowds which gathered at Guildford Street showed that the place was not being used strictly as contemplated.

Guildford Street Headquarters had been intended for use for joint function of youth organisations and to provide facilities for occasional central meetings of voluntary clubs and organisations, but because of the free entertainment and social life that quickly developed there, it became so overcrowded at week-ends and so many were seeking admittance on Sundays, that two " houses " had to be run.

A music and dancing licence was sought but it was refused, and although one member of the responsible committee seemed to regard this as a setback, those familiar with the building realised that it was the only decision which could be reached.

There had to be a change. It was arrived at in a very amicable way. The Area Committee asked the Youth Council Executive Committee and its own executive committee to meet separately to go into the matter. They did so, published independent reports, found afterwards that they were almost of like opinion, and soon reached an agreed policy on the use of the Headquarters. Main principles were that the building should be maintained as headquarters, and not used as a club ; the premises to be available for use by any bona-fide youth organisation from Mondays to Fridays, for the purposes originally contemplated ; organised activities of at least 45 minutes per session to be arranged for Saturdays and Sundays, the Sunday evening programme to end on a serious note ; admission to be by a special card.

Although over 1,000 membership cards were ultimately issued, the average nightly attendance fell to about 150, and gradually the Headquarters reverted to its original purpose.

An additional step early in 1946 was the appointment of Mr. J. Leyshon as full-time warden. As he had been a school-master and then a warrant officer in the Army, it was reasonable to anticipate that he would be able to maintain a rather higher standard of discipline. Steps were also being taken to secure more suitable premises for head-quarters. When Guildford Street was opened, it was a case of taking what could be had, and had the Co-operative Society not been helpful it might have been necessary to wait a long time before any place could be found. Future activities will centre at what was Waller Street School.

It was fitting that the youth organisations of Luton should celebrate their war effort by combining in an Empire Youth Pageant at Wardown in May, 1946. Two thousand young people, representing every Luton youth organisation took part in a march through the town. The parade was a fitting demonstration of the services given by youth to the war effort. Youth has shown that it can rise to responsibilities, that it is developing qualities of leadership and that the future of Britain will be in capable and enterprising hands.

Social Survey

THE outbreak of war had an immediate and stunning impact on the social life and habits of Luton people. Social life in general can be divided roughly into two sections, that which revolves round public or commercially provided facilities, and that which has its foundation in the good neighbourliness of little circles of people, largely families who live and move and have their being in close domestic proximity.

Theatre, cinema and publicly provided entertainment bulk largely in people's lives at all times. Their commercial development up to 1939 had led the public to place so much reliance on the excellence of their fare, that some few thoughtful people interested in sociology had wondered whether we were not in danger of losing the art of entertaining ourselves, of becoming shallow-minded, and incapable of constructive and thoughtful argument; in short, whether we were not likely to lose some of the social virtues that sweeten the activities of the human mind.

The tempo of life had increased with the years; the telephone, the car, the aeroplane, the stop press and the radio had stepped up the speed of human activity so that more could be got through in less time. Big business had found the remedy for a permanent mental fatigue It found that it could sell, and the public would buy, escapism at 3s. 6d., 2s. 9d., 2s., 1s. 3d. a time. The halls of glamour were filled with young and old of both sexes.

*   *   *   *

When war came, theatre and cinema alike were closed to the public from the Monday in that fateful week of early September, 1939. What the days and nights were to bring was in the lap of the gods, but it was obviously unwise to allow people still to crowd into such places of entertainment. The Government therefore imposed the ban.

There was no immediate bombing. On the Saturday of the first week of war the ban was lifted, but a closing time of 10 p.m. was fixed. The ban was not re-imposed in the worst of the blitz periods. Even when Luton was being bombed all that was done was to advise people to go to the pictures or the theatre as early in the week as possible, and so even out the attendances. At the same time a limit was imposed on the attendance at some dances, to make dispersal easier in emergency.

The 10 p.m. limit for cinemas sealed the fate of one pre-war cinema custom, but probably even those most directly affected could not readily name it. Gone is the afternoon performance when 6d. secured a seat in the stalls, and a little more the freedom of the house. Housewives were the chief patrons, but the bargain price held good for all who entered before 4 p.m., so here is a reminiscent comment by a mere man—" When I had a free afternoon I could bring the wife in by bus, go to the cinema with her, take her home by bus, and all on eighteenpence. Now, for a single seat alone . . . "

The principal performances had to start earlier; the 6d. afternoons had to go and join other things belonging to the good old days.

However, if the war took away some possibilities of entertainment for those who must be entertained, war or no war, it provided others. To the screen came some things which would not otherwise have had a place. There were times in years gone by when the exhibition of a film which was of purely educational or interest value was a sure way of clearing the house of those who had seen the main part of the continuous programme. The war caused people to look on many a non-fictional film from a new angle. The documentary film often held their interest quite as much as one of purely entertainment value. Sometimes the documentary and the entertaining were cleverly combined.

Desert Victory was purely documentary, but it drew big audiences because so many had a personal interest in the men who won this victory. The official record on the screen showed them things which were beyond their imagining—things they could not build into a whole from the scrappy letters of relatives out there. *Coastal Command*, *Ships With Wings* and *The Big Blockade* were others in the same category. Pictures like *Went the Day Well?*, *Next of Kin*, *Millions Like Us*, and *The Moon is Down*, although primarily entertainment, all had a lesson for thoughtful patrons.

The documentary film brought war propaganda to a fine art. Its purpose was to maintain and enhance the morale of the people. It did not need to be fictional, though it often was, but it had to be technically and histrionically perfect. It had to be a vivid narrative. It had to show the starkness of war but Allied courage and perseverance in face of odds must always triumph and point the moral and the right and the magnitude of the issues at stake.

49th Parallel was a wonderful way to put across the lesson that the people of two enormous countries, Canada and United States, can live as peaceful neighbours without the necessity of any fortifications along the longest international frontier in the world, when fortified frontiers had failed to save many other countries from being overrun by an enemy. *In Which We Serve* told in a very graphic way the things which go to make a warship an efficient fighting unit. *Way to the Stars* was a notable tribute to the relationships of the R.A.F. and the U.S.A.A.F. *This Happy Breed* was another outstanding story.

The task of the Navy in safeguarding *The Western Approaches* was well brought home by this film, and people did not find it any the less interesting because it came within the strictly documentary class. *The Great Day* was another. *Sergeant York* used a true story of the 1914-18 war to drive home a great lesson, *Mrs. Miniver* had Greer Garson in the title role. It was the picture of the average middle class British mother's reaction to the dark days of 1940. Many cinemagoers hold that it was the outstanding picture of the six years of war. *The First of the Few* was another big drama. It told of the birth of the Spitfire and the Battle of Britain.

Thirty Seconds over Tokio and *I Live in Grosvenor Square* brought some of the American aspects of war to the screen.

True Glory and *Burma Victory* were other notable documentary films.

At all cinemas, of course, the news reels reached exceptional heights of interest. The risks run by the cameramen to get their pictures would have provided a documentary in themselves.

In addition to those mentioned, readers will recall that these other films also contributed much to the morale of the people and the war effort.

1939 : *The Lion has Wings.*

1940 : *For Freedom* (the story of the Battle of the River Plate and the Altmark rescue).

1941 : Chaplin's *The Great Dictator* ; *Target for To-night* (the story of a bombing raid on Germany) ; *Atlantic Ferry* ; Quentin Reynolds *One Day in Soviet Russia.*

1942 : *The Defeat of the Germans at Moscow* ; *Unpublished Story* (the London Blitz) ; *One of Our Aircraft is Missing* (the escape of a R.A.F. crew who baled out over occupied Holland) ; *Secret Mission* (about the British Secret Service).

1943 : *Nine Men* (a Libyan Desert story) ; *The Silver Fleet* (anti-Nazi sabotage in occupied Holland) ; *Immortal Sergeant* ; *The Story of Stalingrad* ; *Commandos Strike at Dawn* ; Leslie Howard's *The Gentle Sex* (life in the A.T.S.) ; *We Dive at Dawn* (the submarine service) ; Mr. Joseph Davies' *Mission to Moscow* ; *Convoy* ; *The Battle of Britain* ; Disney's *Victory Through Air Power.*

1944 : *San Demetrio, London* (the story of a torpedoed petrol tanker) ; Irving Berlin's *This is the Army* ; *Tunisian Victory* ; *The Nelson Touch* ; *The Way Ahead* with David Niven (the infantryman in training and at war) ; *A Canterbury Tale* ; *The White Cliffs of Dover.*

There were other films too, which, though they had no war interest, nevertheless will be remembered. In 1939 there was *Goodbye Mr. Chips.* Arthur Askey's *Band Waggon* and Will Hay in *The Ghost of St. Michael's* came in 1940 and early 1941 and later that year Leslie Howard starred in *Pimpernel Smith.* Shaw's *Major Barbara* and Ronald

Colman in *The Prisoner of Zenda* also came that year and there was a succession of Walt Disney films *Pinnocchio, Bambi, Dumbo* and *Fantasia* which were remarkable. October, 1942, brought that longest of all films *Gone With the Wind* the showing of which lasted four hours. *Happidrome* was a welcome visitor in 1943 as was *Random Harvest* with Ronald Colman and Greer Garson. 1944 was notable for *Madame Curie* and *The Song of Bernadette*.

· The limitations of the stage do not debar it from competing on level terms with the screen as the medium for telling a fine story. This was shown at the Grand Theatre when *Flare Path* was presented.

*　　*　　*　　*

In quite another field, that of music, the war also brought to Luton audiences some entertainment they otherwise would not have been able to enjoy. The B.B.C. settled at Bedford. It was comparatively easy for Stanford Robinson to bring the B.B.C. Theatre Orchestra to Luton and, having received a great welcome, to bring it again. Luton people certainly appreciated that combination and the music they put over, perhaps not highbrow enough for some, but definitely the right programmes for those for whom they were planned. In other ways, too, and not always confined to matters musical, Luton benefited by the wartime proximity of the B.B.C.

But if the B.B.C. Theatre Orchestra brought popular music, others brought something more serious, and gave Luton a chance to demonstrate that it has an audience for the Symphony concert. Orchestras normally heard only in London had for a time to look elsewhere for supporters, people being justifiably disinclined to assemble in London to hear them, even if their normal places of performance were still intact. So the orchestras came out into the country to their audiences. Often they were accompanied by some outstanding vocal or instrumental soloist. Even if such visits were only intermittent, they gave people who wanted something other than light music their chance. They did much to make Sunday concerts an established thing.

Visits of famous orchestras and artistes were not confined to events open to the public. There were many visits that went unheralded and unchronicled. Security demanded that no reference should be made in the Press to visits of conductors, orchestras, bands and variety, theatrical, and cinema personalities to big works engaged on war production. The names of these visitors were household words. In normal times their presence in Luton would have been accompanied by surging crowds of fans and packed houses. The war cloaked them with secrecy, yet in works canteens, where Ensa brought them to entertain the workers, nothing was more appreciated than the relief they brought to tired minds and bodies that had been toiling to provide the weapons of war. And it is significant that Ensa did not send only variety and theatrical stars. World-famous orchestras, conductors, pianists and violinists whose art interpreted to perfection the music of the masters, were welcomed as fervently as the cross talk comedians.

LEFT: "The Great Dictator" studies a globe of the world. Charlie Chaplin's film, which came to Luton in 1941, brought a short spell of light relief for war-weary nerves.

BELOW: A poignant scene from "Mrs. Miniver," starring Greer Garson. The family wait anxiously in their shelter as enemy aircraft thunder overhead.

The B.B.C. Symphony Orchestra were evacuated to Bedford, and became frequent visitors to Luton. Sir Adrian Boult is seen conducting during one of their concerts at the Odeon Cinema.

Mr. Arthur Davies conducting Luton Choral Society during one of their war-time performances at Luton Parish Church.

Gracie Fields . . . the ever popular "Lass from Lancashire" . . . at the microphone when she visited Vauxhall Motors Ltd., in September, 1943. Part of the large audience of workers in the canteen who saw and heard her are shown below.

Two Electrolux workers join Jack Buchanan at the microphone at the recording of a "Workers' Playtime" broadcast in November, 1942.

"Is that the meater? I want some butch!" **Mrs. Feather (Jeanne de Casalis) is in trouble** *again as she* **records** *a "Workers' Playtime" from the Skefko Works. Luton.*

Concurrently Luton Choral Society developed its activities considerably. They could not continue to perform, as for half a century before, in one hall or another not primarily built with regard to acoustics. They could and did, transfer some of their concerts to more modern surroundings; again it had to be on Sundays. They made another departure. They gave performances in the fine setting of Luton's old Parish Church, and in an atmosphere ideal for some choral works. There, also, orchestral concerts were a wartime departure from precedent.

There were many forms of locally organised entertainment that served the war effort—and served it well. Outstanding among them was the Luton Girls' Choir, founded and developed by Mr. Arthur E. Davies, who was also playing a prominent part in the Luton Choral Society. The choir had been in existence before the war, and had already raised large sums for charity. It continued during the war, and towards the end it attracted the notice of the B.B.C. and began to acquire a national fame. To-day the Luton Girls' Choir, whose harmony is " like birds singing," and the Luton Choral Society are two of Luton's most valuable goodwill exports.

*   *   *   *

From the first week of the war many other forms of social activity had to suffer a war dim out ; some a total black out. A primary cause was the military requisitioning of many halls where the smaller social events were normally held. Concerts, dances, whist drives and the like, all suffered.

Annual banquets, less pretentious annual dinners, and some very cheerful annual reunions, were all abandoned at the start of the war. It was felt to be not the thing to continue them in the circumstances of the time. Later, their resumption was made difficult by rationing and by the price restrictions on public meals.

Some people may have considered this a blessing in disguise. No longer had they to suffer those speeches which were inevitably on the toast list because so-and-so had to be given the opportunity to say a few words, thus detracting from the real entertainment and conviviality of those gathered round the fleshpots.

With so many of the smaller halls not available, there was also no longer a Winter Assembly Hall for the larger gatherings. Through the war winters it continued in its summer guise of a swimming bath. It was kept as a static water tank—though it was never drawn on. It took a General Election after the end of the war in Europe, and the presumed need of a big hall where political eloquence could be let loose, to bring it back into use as an Assembly Hall. Now it will presumably alternate seasonally, as in pre-September, 1939, offering hospitality to swimmers in summer, and catering for other recreations and " letting off steam " in winter.

The closing of so many halls emphasised the inadequacy of the Assembly Hall at the Town Hall.

When the Town Hall was built, Whitehall ruled that the ratepayers of that time could not afford the fine concert and assembly hall that was part of the plan and was badly wanted by the town.

The small hall under the Council Chamber became therefore the Assembly Hall at the Town Hall but it was quite inadequate and from time to time there have been bitter complaints that " The Town Council have failed in their duty, etc." It is Whitehall that is to blame.

The site for the big Concert and Assembly Hall adjoins the Town Hall, but what the cost will be and when it can be done no one yet knows.

*   *   *   *

The black-out, the earlier closing of shops, the suspension of late buses, all combined in developing a habit of earlier home-going. So did the sirens, after Luton had been bombed. Then attendance at clubs and other places where men foregather of an evening quickly thinned out when a warning sounded. Men went home to reassure their womenfolk, and did not return. For aliens, however friendly, earlier homegoing became compulsory. They needed a permit to be out after the prescribed hour, but, if residents of old standing, did not find obtaining a permit too difficult.

If the war affected some forms of public entertainment and also public hospitality, what of its effect on private hospitality? It suffered considerably, and particularly among the many who had no canteen facilities to supplement their rations, and could not afford those off-ration extras which might have helped. But, despite these limitations, a good many people managed to extend some private hospitality to Service people, and particularly to men from overseas. It could not compare with that extended to our own men in South Africa, Canada, or the States, where life was not so austere, and the number of visitors small in proportion to the population. It was only a tithe of what would have been offered if larders had been better stocked. As one family man said—" My boy, when he comes on leave, usually brings another with him. If it's only for one meal it's not so bad, but if it's for a weekend . . . they forget we don't get Army rations . . they can eat . . . whole loaves and cakes vanish . . . we'd like to do more, but things just don't run to it in a small household."

The household was very much a self-contained unit. There was something symbolical about drawing the black-out curtains and so shutting out the dark world without and the terror by night. The eerie wail of the siren brought to all hearts an unexpressed but anxious feeling of expectancy. Many families went naturally to their own Anderson shelters. Others made a point of joining forces, a habit that subconsciously, at any rate, did serve to bolster up personal morale.

Books played a great part in the isolated, blacked-out life of the home. The war brought a spate of reading matter, some good, some indifferent in quality, but in the main it brought not only more reading but more good reading. The Library service in Luton, not only the Public Libraries but the subscription libraries, have always found a ready patronage, and they did much during the war by the maintenance of that service to help the public mind forget the hazards of everyday life. The Public Libraries experienced a phenomenal demand. During the last year of the war, according to the Borough Librarian, Mr. Frank M. Gardner, over a million books were issued. The total for 1939 was 460,000. Mr. Gardner recorded that, in the same year, over 200,000 non-fiction works were issued compared with under 100,000 in 1939. Classical authors were in much greater demand, too, Trollope, Jane Austen and Dickens enjoying a definite revival.

*   *   *   *

When public shelters were completed there developed among those who used them a queer form of communal life. They were the troglodytes, and wherever two or three families met regularly in the dark but safe world of the underground, there, without fail, was found someone who, as shelter-marshal, devoted himself to the entertainment and social intercourse of his group of shelterers. Never was better work done. While Heinkels and Dorniers ranged the skies and circled the town, the tunnel-shelter life of the townsfolk became almost an eagerly-anticipated nightly feature.

Another aspect of the neighbourly visits between families was that it was found to result in a useful economy. Fuel and light had to be watched so that no waste occurred. To share one's light and warmth and even cooking became a pleasurable duty. Many an erstwhile shy and retiring housewife became a good solo player and learnt to throw a pretty dart.

Looking back on the experiences of those six years, it may have imposed many handicaps on social life, but it has introduced much that would otherwise have been slow in coming. People generally became better mixers. Their voluntary war work was a great leveller. Truly " the colonel's lady and Judy O'Grady were sisters under the skin '

Sport during War

SPORT was one of the first of our social activities to feel the full effect of war. From the day war was declared there was a temporary blackout of sport as complete as that ordered to defeat enemy bombers. The fundamental cause was the possibility that, if the expected bombing materialised, the gathering of large crowds for League football or other major sporting events would intensify the danger. The simplest way to eliminate this danger was to ban all such assemblies for the time being, and this the Government decreed.

As with the contemporary ban on cinemas, etc., it was relaxed after a time, but as a safety precaution some attendance limits were substituted. Many sporting activities were then resumed. Their scale became more and more restricted as time went on and as more and more players went into the Services. But, on some scale or other, sport had to continue, if only for its beneficial effect on nerves frayed by other impacts of war on the life of the individual. Travel restrictions, loss of star players, problems in obtaining or renewing kit, coupons for such sport clothes as had to be bought, could not stop it entirely, and if matches with time-honoured opponents had to be suspended, there were often good Service teams eager to take the field.

In one of the early summers of the war, in fact, it was not unusual to see four Service teams playing cricket on Wardown Sports Ground, and playing some jolly good cricket, too, though, with the players in their khaki on a dull afternoon much of the atmosphere of cricket seemed to be missing.

*   *   *   *

FOOTBALL

On September 5th, 1939, all professional players' contracts were suspended, all League competitions were cancelled, and all football under the auspices of the Football Association was temporarily suspended pending further instructions. Thus the first Saturday of the war, September 9th, was completely blank from the sport viewpoint.

However, the ban on football was quickly relaxed, and clubs were permitted to arrange friendly matches, except in prohibited areas, and subject to attendance limitations. Luton was not a prohibited area, so matches were resumed. For a considerable period spectators had a grim reminder that there were more serious things than football afoot. Mounted above the grandstand, as on other buildings in Luton were machine guns manned in the expectation of air attack.

Some of the Luton Town players left the district immediately the suspension of contracts took effect, but the Town were able to field a pretty representative side in their first friendly match, which was against Brentford at Kenilworth Road on September 16th.

Players who did not leave the district found work of national importance locally, but gradually, one after the other, they went into the Services, and their record during the war bears favourable comparison with that of any other club in the country.

Four lost their lives on active service. Best known of these was Joe Coen, the first team goalkeeper for several seasons, who was killed in an air crash. Charlie Clark, a sergeant in the Army, was killed in Tunisia. Jock Gillespie was one of the many who gave their

After fixtures for the Football League, Division II, had been suspended in September, 1939, there was an interval of a few weeks and then the game went on. Supporters, however, were few and far between as our picture shows when Fred Roberts led out the Town team for a Southern Section match.

It's a goal! No, the goalkeeper has deflected the ball round the post. An incident in a war-time game on the Town Ground, when Nottingham Forest were the visitors.

ABOVE: *With a number of their younger players in the Services, Luton Town Cricket Club had a thin time during the war years. But the game went on. Arthur Fryer is seen above leading out his team to meet Welwyn in the first game of the 1945 season.*

BELOW: *The Australian XI which visited Wardown in August, 1942 to meet a combined Luton Town and Vauxhall team. In three-and-a-half hours the visitors had dismissed the Luton team for 99 runs, and scored 100 for 3 wickets to score an easy victory.*

Luton Borough Police were the visitors when this picture was taken at Luton Town Bowling Club in July, 1941.

Organisers and visitors at a darts match at Castle Street Hall, Luton, in April, 1945, when a Luton team entertained the "News of the World" champions.

ABOVE: *Outdoor boxing on the Luton Town Football Ground was a feature of the town's "Holidays at Home" programme. This picture was taken at a six-contest tournament on July 25th, 1942.*

BELOW: *Waiting for the pistol at the start of the 100 yards at a triangular athletic contest between Luton Grammar (then Modern) School, the Old Boys and an R.A.S.C. team. £50 was raised for the British Red Cross Society.*

lives at Dunkirk. C. J. Ladd, a full-back of much promise, joined the Navy, and was killed in H.M.S. Hood.

Another player, Doug. Gardiner, was a prisoner of war for some years after being shot down over Germany, but was freed when Germany was overrun, and resumed the Town colours with credit. Others who joined the Services quite early on, including Billington, the centre-forward, were retained in the Services so long that they could only make very occasional appearances for the Town even after the end of hostilities, and it was almost the end of the 1945-46 season before the Town could regularly field a side which could be anything like a regular team. Even when that season ended there were still many players on the Town books who could not be seen on the Town ground because they were in the Services.

Friendly matches had only a short spell, and then gave place to Regional Leagues. Luton Town were in the Midland Section, with the Wolves, Northampton, Birmingham, Walsall, Coventry City, Leicester City, and West Bromwich Albion. Each club played the other four times, but while these matches aroused a certain amount of interest among supporters, it was far below that of normal times, and at Luton, at any rate, did not create any need for an attendance limitation.

As time went on the player position became increasingly difficult, and the Town were forced to follow the example of other clubs and utilise " guest " players, a system which permitted a player to appear for a club other than his own, always provided his own club gave permission. Among those who played for Luton under these circumstances was Eddie Hapgood, English International and Arsenal star. It was not unknown at an away match to have to borrow a man from the home club. Local youngsters also got a chance and, with an eye to the future, Luton began to take a greater interest than ever in rising talent in the immediate neighbourhood.

Conditions became even more trying as the years went on. Added to the shortage of players were the difficulties of travel and the shortage of playing kits and footballs. One thing which also caused the Town management many headaches was the almost impossible job of obtaining gatemen. Gates generally were considerably lower than pre-war, but as players' wages dropped, most clubs managed to avoid adding to their liabilities, and some even made modest profits.

In the 1940-41 season Luton were included in the Football League South Region, but when the London clubs broke away and formed a competition of their own the Town got together with such clubs as Portsmouth, Watford, Brighton and Cardiff, and the League South "C" was formed. There was also the Midland Cup Competition and the Football League Cup. In the following season the London clubs extended their league, but Luton remained under the Football League, in a competition in which clubs arranged their own matches.

The London clubs returned to the fold for the 1942-43 season, and Luton was included with them to form the Football League South, an arrangement which continued for the two following seasons. On the whole this Regional football filled the gap well. It was the best that could be done while travelling difficulties were so great. Making cup ties a matter of home and away matches, and depending on the goal aggregates of the two meetings, was also a wartime innovation.

The Luton District and South Beds. League shared the fate of all other competitions and closed down, but the Executive Committee began a subsidiary competition of three divisions as soon as permission was given for competitive football to be resumed. The League managed to continue throughout the war, and had much to do with maintaining a high standard in local junior football. The Minor League also ran successfully. The Bedfordshire F.A. saw to it that the clubs had cup competitions, and the pre-war competitions were maintained right throughout the war. Amateur clubs, of course, had all sorts of wartime worries and troubles, and it was only enthusiasm, fine team spirit, and hard work by the officials, that enabled many of them to survive the disadvantages of the time.

Both the leading local amateur clubs, Vauxhall Motors and Luton Amateur, joined the Herts. and Beds. Combination which was formed shortly after the beginning of the war. This competition was ill-starred, and fell through at the beginning of 1941, mainly owing to the inadequate number of clubs and the travel restrictions. After that, both teams played friendly matches for charity. They also ran teams in the subsidiary competition of the Luton District and South Beds. League.

In the latter war years some important Service matches were seen on the Town Ground, but their appeal was largely confined to Service supporters.

*   *   *   *

CRICKET

In the 1940 season Luton Town C.C. cut down the number of teams fielded each Saturday from four to two, and on this limited basis had quite a good season. In later years, in common with all other sports clubs, they experienced such difficulties in finding players that they considered themselves fortunate if able to field one strong side a week. They had other difficulties. The pavilion was taken over as an A.R.P. post, and players had to change on the verandah. The opposing players could not have their time-honoured social interval over tea, for the provision of tea became impossible, and players who wanted tea had to take it with them in a flask.

Equipment became very scarce, any replacement of boots or flannels or sweaters involved surrendering precious coupons, and road transport was next to impossible. But even under these conditions the game went on, chiefly through the efforts of a handful of club stalwarts who simply would not give give it up even temporarily.

Vauxhall Motors kept their first XI and their Sunday XI going throughout the war years. During that period many notable cricketers visited the Vauxhall ground with Service teams. They included the Rev. E. T. Killick, England and Middlesex; Leslie Todd, Kent; L. G. Berry, Leicestershire; F. Buse, Somerset; and Spencer, Kent. The first attempt by the club to arrange a two-day match was in June, 1943, when the Royal Australian Air Force Overseas H.Q. brought down a strong XI. The match was notable for high scoring. Vauxhall made 412 for four wickets, T. Clark and R. Hills each contributing a century, and there was a first wicket stand of 183. The Australians improved on this, running up 265 for the first wicket. Workman and Sheidow each reached three figures, and the side's total was 361 for seven wickets. In all, three two-day matches were played against the Australians, and it was not until 1945 that the visitors were able to claim a victory.

Another match that caused much interest, and produced a big sum for charity was when a British Empire XI came to play a strong side chosen by Mr. J. E. D. Moysey. It was staged on the excellent ground of Kent's Athletic. But such matches were the exception, interesting as they were. The really local " derbies " of the war years were the matches played between the Town Club and Vauxhall on Whit Monday and August Bank Holiday in each year. These matches were arranged as part of the Holidays at Home programme.

Many of the smaller clubs in the town carried on gallantly in spite of their many handicaps, and it can be said that local cricket came through its greatest testing time with credit.

*   *   *   *

BOWLS

Luton Town Bowling Club, like the Town Cricket Club, had their pavilion invaded, only in this case the invaders were the Army. For a long time it was used as a sergeants' mess, and club members had to be content with the use of one odd corner. Even the small building on the opposite side of the green was taken over by the Army, for use as a food store. The other clubs with private greens escaped any such requisitioning.

County competitions and inter-County matches had to lapse during the war years, but all the local clubs managed to remain active and to continue club competitions and reasonable match lists, although some old fixtures had to be dropped because of travel difficulties. Keeping the greens in condition was by no means easy, but, whatever the drawbacks, bowlers continued to trundle the wood, and at times to put the Red Cross and other organisations in their debt.

*   *   *   *

HOCKEY

After the first few weeks of war Luton Town Hockey Club was able to function more or less normally for the rest of that season, but the number of players leaving to join the Services forced clubs generally to do some hard thinking about the future. Accordingly, in the 1940-41 season Luton Town, Old Dunstablians, and Kent's joined forces

367

and pooled their playing resources. The combination was named The Remnants, the moving spirit being the late Mr. J. J. Payne. After his unfortunate death much of the work of the club devolved on the shoulders of Mr. J. A. R. Oliver, who also captained the side.

The Remnants were able to put an excellent team into the field, and can point with pride to their record of not once having had to cancel a match. They were honoured, too, by a visit to their ground at Wardown by a Hockey Association XI, an occasion which provided a big day for local hockey enthusiasts.

Vauxhall Motors were able to carry on independently, and gained much success.

* * * *

RUGBY

Luton Rugby F.C. managed to complete the 1939-40 season, but then found the difficulties facing them were overwhelming, and suspended activities until the 1945-46 season.

Vauxhall Motors, better placed as regards availability of players, carried on and fielded one team regularly throughout the war years. Most of their matches were against Service teams, chiefly from neighbouring R.A.F. Stations. Apart from this, local rugby was definitely pushed into the background by the war.

* * * *

GOLF

Both golf clubs catering for Luton players had to manage without a professional during the greater part of the war, and to maintain their courses as best they could with the minimum of ground staff. Loss of members to the Services, and transport restrictions, meant that county championship meetings and inter-club matches had to be abandoned; major trophy competitions were discontinued for a time, and the Luton and District Banks and the Vauxhall Golfing Societies ceased to function.

South Beds, having spent thousands on preparations to transfer part of the course to new land, on seeding it and constructing new greens, had this land requisitioned for agriculture; but, unlike 1914-18, when a large part of the then course became a rifle range, members were able to continue playing over 18 holes. Dunstable Downs had to shorten their course somewhat, but with the expert assistance of a farmer member, made quite a good profit out of farming their spare land.

Ball shortage was the greatest handicap in the closing stages of the war. There were no new balls, but those who could scrape up a dozen old ones could send them away, and expect to receive nine playable " remakes " in return. The life of a " remake " had no guarantee. Sometimes, in fact, it was very short. But with these most players had to be content, while as to buying new clubs, the best thing to do was to wait.

However, despite all handicaps, members managed to keep the

clubs going, to offer hospitality to players in the Services, and to raise considerable sums for war and other charities ; and 1946 opened with prospects so good that South Beds. felt warranted in increasing the subscription to meet rising costs, and to reimpose an entrance fee, while Dunstable Downs membership was so full that there was a waiting list.

*   *   *   *

GREYHOUND RACING

Greyhound racing is dependent on artificial lighting for evening meetings. That, of course, was out of the question. For three weeks there were no meetings at Luton Stadium. Then the management began to stage meetings on Monday afternoons. Later, meetings were also held on Friday afternoons, but in 1942, the Government stopped mid-week meetings because it was felt workers might be tempted to lose precious hours from vital jobs, and for the rest of the war greyhound racing at Luton Stadium was on Saturday afternoons only. Despite staffing difficulties and transport restrictions, which prevented owners from bringing dogs long distances, racing continued successfully on a one meeting a week basis until conditions had so changed that an evening meeting could be added.

*   *   *   *

DARTS

Darts played a big part in the indoor recreational life of Luton during the war, and the Luton Clubs' League made rapid strides. The Licensed Victuallers' League, finding their clubs could not raise teams during the early part of the war, discontinued activities until 1944, which was a bumper year. Members of both Leagues raised large sums for war charities, and an open competition in aid of comforts for the troops was a big success. Darts was probably the most popular of all war-time recreations. Wherever there was a Home Guard post, an A.R.P. post, a firewatcher's room, there one could always find a darts board occupying an honoured place on a pitted wall. In pubs and clubs, in the kitchens and the halls of thousands of homes, there was the darts board.

*   *   *   *

BILLIARDS

The war caused a break in the Luton Billiards League's long run of successful seasons. Those concerned with the League decided to suspend activities for the first winter of the war. In fact, it remained dormant until the autumn of 1945, when activities were resumed on much the same lines as in pre-war years, the only notable difference being that the teams were reduced from six to four players.

In the various clubs the cup competitions which were a feature of the winter season were also suspended, but it was found possible to arrange exhibitions by notable professionals and amateurs for various war charities, and the demonstrations given by some lady experts were

369

particularly good, not only with the cue, but in the way they relieved spectators of charity money.

*   *   *   *

BOXING

In the amateur field some really good performances were put up during the war years by members of the Boxing Sections of the Vauxhall and Electrolux Recreation Clubs, and members of these clubs won honours in national championships. At both places facilities were also provided for interesting Service displays, and for these local support was always forthcoming, but professional boxing as staged in Luton during that period was by no means the popular venture it is in some towns.

New Brooms

TIRED of Coalition politics after the 1914-18 war, Luton, a traditional Liberal seat, swung over to Conservative representation. During the ensuing years it wobbled from time to time between Liberalism and Conservatism and then settled down as a National Liberal constituency. But during the inter-war years Labour as a political force had been growing and out of the 1945 elections, Luton emerged with its first Labour M.P.

The 1945 Elections were a landslide ; the biggest political landslide since 1906. When places like Bedford, Hitchin and St. Albans, regarded as essentially safe Conservative seats, went Labour in keeping with the general trend of things, who could be surprised to find that an industrial town like Luton had also voted Labour ? And particularly so when regard is paid to the fact that the electorate had been swelled in the latter pre-war years by large numbers of people from the North, Clydeside and Wales ; from many places where for long Labour had been the dominant political party. It is reasonable to assume that many of the younger men who had reached electoral age while in the Services also voted Labour, in the belief that Labour might advance the country one stage nearer the Utopia which has been promised for years. They believed that the time was ripe for a change of Government, and certainly, they thought, such a change could not make things worse ; it might make them better.

*   *   *   *

From the beginning of the war party politics were nominally in suspense. Towards the end of 1944, however, portents of victory

370

became more marked, and attention began to centre on domestic issues which would revive party divisions. Mr. E. L. Burgin had been Luton's M.P. since 1929. He was elected as a Liberal. The succeeding brief Labour administration resulted in some party ties going to the melting pot. In the 1931 election, with no Conservative opponent, he was re-elected as a Liberal National, with a 24,000 majority over Labour. From then onwards he retained the support of Conservatives, and in 1935 was again re-elected. His Labour opponent on that occasion, Mr. F. L. Kerran, succeeded in reducing Mr. Burgin's majority to about 13,000, the first sign of the political change which was taking place.

Mr. Burgin had an eventful career at Westminster. First a Charity Commissioner, then Parliamentary Secretary to the Board of Trade, and then Minister of Transport, in 1939 he was appointed the first Minister of Supply. It was a somewhat thankless job at that period, for the productive capacity of the nation had still to be developed. In office he had many critics, and when, in the dark days of 1940, Mr. Churchill became Prime Minister and re-shuffled the Government, Mr. Burgin joined the ranks of the ex-Ministers. Nevertheless, as an eminent international lawyer, his specialist help was much in demand by the Government during the war years, but by early 1945 his health was causing concern. At the time of the election in July he was gravely ill and could not have contested the seat. He died in August at the age of 58.

Labour had been looking for a new candidate since 1944 and in December of that year they fixed on Mr. William N. Warbey, who since 1941 had been Chief English Press Officer to the Norwegian Government in its exile in this country. Mr. Warbey wasted little time. Early in the New Year he launched his campaign.

The Labour campaign was working all through the early months of 1945, but it was late May before it was known to the Liberal and Conservative Co-ordinating Committee that they also would have to find another candidate. The General Election had already been fixed for July 5th. Barely a month remained for campaigning when Lieut.-Col. Leonard Graham Brown, M.D., F.R.C.S., was announced as a National Candidate. Senior ear, nose, and throat specialist at Charing Cross Hospital, and winner of the M.C. in the 1914-18 war, he was new to the political platform. Against highly expert opponents, quick to seize on everything which would react to the advantage of the Labour campaign, he found himself at a great disadvantage, a disadvantage which persisted throughout the campaign. Labour was all out for social legislation of the kind which has since hit the country almost as a tidal wave. Against this Dr. Graham Brown could do little beyond declare himself an opponent of Socialism, and urge electors to back Mr. Churchill.

Both sides introduced some big names for their chief meetings in the Winter Assembly Hall. Lord Teviot, Lord Simon and Mr. A.

T. Lennox-Boyd, a Conservative who successfully defended his own seat in Mid-Beds., came in support of Dr. Graham Brown. Mr. Warbey's advocates included Hannen Swaffer and Professor Harold Laski.

Polling took place on July 5th, 1945, on a register hastily prepared for the election, and far from satisfactory. Many people had failed to take precaution to ensure that they were included, and both sides complained bitterly of anomalies, such as children's names appearing and parents' being omitted. One result was that a revised and much more accurate register was prepared for the subsequent municipal elections.

For the result of the election there was a wait of nearly three weeks, to ensure that the votes of people in the Services overseas arrived.

Ballot boxes were kept in police custody until July 25th, and then taken to the Winter Assembly Hall, where most of one day was occupied by a preliminary check to ensure that no Service voter had voted both by post and by proxy. Next day Labour optimism was justified. Mr. Warbey was Luton's first Labour M.P. His majority was 7,421. Actual voting was :—Warbey, 39,335 ; Brown, 31,914. 74.9 per cent. of those entitled to had voted. That evening Labour had a big celebration at the Winter Assembly Hall. Ward Associations followed with Victory Socials.

*　　*　　*　　*

Success in the General Election stimulated the Labour party throughout the country to go all out in an effort to secure control of municipal authorities in the following November. At Luton, although the Labour Co-operative group on the Town Council was small in 1939, and any casual vacancies which occurred while elections were suspended during the war years had been filled on the basis of maintaining the *status quo*, Labour considered that there were distinct prospects of their obtaining a majority for the first time. It was anticipated that, as after the end of the 1914-1918 war, a number of the senior members of the Council would retire. It was known that some would have done earlier had there been no war. Room for fresh blood was therefore certain. In addition, those who by being co-opted during the war had found the road to municipal honours easy had all to seek electoral approval of their continued membership. This meant 14 vacancies in the nine wards to be filled on November 1st.

The constitution of the Council was : Liberal 14, Conservative 12, Labour Co-operative Group 9, Independent 1. Four Liberal or Conservative aldermen out of the nine, including Lady Keens, the Mayor, were due to retire on November 9th. Of the retiring councillors, 12 were in the Liberal-Conservative group, one was a co-opted Labour member, and one the Independent.

As early as February the Labour party had announced two prospective candidates, and others were introduced at later ward meetings. The naming of the first Liberal-Conservative candidate in April was

LEFT: *Dr. Graham Brown, Liberal National candidate for Luton in the General Election of July 1945, chats to stallholders in Luton market.*

RIGHT: *Luton Labour supporters give a cheer. Front centre is Mr. W. N. Warbey, newly elected M.P. for Luton, with Mrs. Warbey.*

BELOW: *The scene at the counting of the votes inside the Winter Assembly Hall.*

followed by a Ratepayers' Association declaration that they also intended running candidates, and when the Communists also began to talk about entering the field there was prospect of a free-for-all. Labour made it clear that they were going into the fight on strict party lines. Individualism would count less than ever, they declared. The Liberal-Conservative group, declaring that the ratepayers were only concerned with efficient service, pooled their resources and called their nominees " People's Candidates." The announced candidates of the Ratepayers' Association did not all materialise, while the one announced Communist candidate, instead of handing in nomination papers by 5 p.m. on the appointed day, discovered that 9 a.m. next day was too late.

Even so there were 32 candidates. Labour put forward 14—one for every vacancy ; Liberals, 7 ; Conservatives, 5 ; Ratepayers' Association, 4 ; and there were two Independents. The use of the Parliamentary register gave the vote to many who had never before voted in municipal elections because they were not rated occupiers of property, and equally so to all who had newly come of electoral age. Altogether some 20,000 more were eligible to vote.

Labour gained six seats, Independents, two. The Ratepayers' Association nominees were all defeated. 48 per cent. of the electorate voted.

*   *   *   *

Labour now had 15 councillors out of 27 . . . not a majority of the whole Council, but a majority of councillors, and councillors were the only members entitled to vote in the election of aldermen. To get an absolute majority they could either elect four Labour aldermen from their councillors and rely on winning the resultant by-elections, or they could adopt an easier course. The Local Government Act enables aldermen to be chosen from outside the Council. Labour could do this, gain their objective, and avoid the expense and possible risk of defeat in by-elections. There were few instances on record of such a course having been adopted, but the opportunity was there, and they took it. The Labour-Co-operative group, with their councillors in majority, elected Councillor W. G. Roberts as Luton's first Labour Mayor, voted off the Council Lady Keens, who had just completed her term as Mayor, and also Alderman A. E. Ansell, the other two aldermen due to retire having intimated that they did not desire re-election. They then elected as aldermen four non-members of the Council of whom two had been unsuccessful at the polls eight days earlier. This was a point not overlooked by many critics of this method of securing political control. The strong feeling aroused, however, found no reflection in the voting when two by-elections were held within a few weeks, following the resignation of Councillor T. H. Knight, a Co-operative member, and Councillor A. W. Gregory, Conservative. Labour nominees won both seats. They increased their majority on the Council to four.

When County Council elections followed in March, 1946, Labour did better in Luton than anywhere else in the county. There were 18 Luton seats to fill, and only four retiring members seeking re-election. Labour put forward 18 candidates. Luton's one previous Labour member was re-elected, two secured seats without opposition, and six others were successful at the poll, against an opposition again largely composed of " People's Candidates."

The one Communist candidate failed.

Final Victory

VICTORY in Europe gave to Luton its first taste of one of the four great freedoms that the Atlantic Charter envisaged— Freedom from Fear.

From the announcement on September 3rd, 1939, that this country was again at war with Germany, the town had known many fears— the fear of invasion and all that it implied ; the fear that a loved one in the armed forces would find torture or death in a far-off land ; the fear that a home painstakingly put together would be shattered in an instant, and the fear that German bombing would snatch from its homes the children for whom the future was planned.

But from the beginning of 1945 there surged strongly in every heart the hope and expectation that the end was near. The Armies of Liberation had swept across France almost to the Rhine, the last Nazi counter-offensive in the Ardennes had proved abortive, the V. sites had been overrun, the Russians had liberated Budapest and stood at the gates of Warsaw. Surely, surely, only a few more months remained.

And it was natural that thoughts should turn to the most fitting manner in which the return of peace to Europe should be celebrated. When it was first announced that the Town Council proposed to spend up to £2,000 in providing entertainment a storm of protest was raised. Recalling that many soldiers had returned as cripples, that others still languished in Japanese prison camps, and that more were still fighting in the Far East, there were many who thought Luton should " weep rather than sing." They derided the suggestion that people should dance in the streets, and felt that rejoicing should be delayed until the entire world had returned to peace and sanity.

Others argued that the occasion should not pass unrecognised, and their opinion was the view of the majority. They acknowledged the devastation the war had caused in many homes ; the grief occasioned by personal loss; and the sorrow that came with remembrance of thousands still in the hands of the Japanese, whose torture of prisoners had revolted the civilised world.

The voice of the majority grew louder and reached its culmination in the utterance of a woman who asked, " Shall I weep on V-Day because I no longer need to listen for the siren, no longer need to dash downstairs with my children to the shelter ?

" Shall I weep when I find the worry and strain of the war with the Germans over at last, and my children and other children can look forward to the normal existence I had as a child ?

" No, I shall not, unless they are tears of joy. I hope I shall sing and dance, whether in George Street or in my own home. My first thoughts will be to thank God, and everything I do will be in thanks to God and our dear boys who will have made this wonderful thing possible.

" Must we make our boys who have lost their lives or limbs ashamed of us by being miserable on the glorious day, or can we show them that what they have done has been worth while ?

" Let us all, when V-Day comes laugh, sing and be happy, and wipe out the bitterness of the last five years.

" For many it will not be easy, but with prayers and courage in our hearts, songs and smiles on our lips, it can be done."

* * * *

On May 7th, 1945, came the news that Germany had surrendered unconditionally. Momentarily the town stood still. Its people had waited so long for that news, and too often had their soaring hopes of its imminent arrival been dashed. They hesitated to accept its full portent. They had expected the first news of Germany's defeat to come from the Prime Minister, but when a late announcement declared that the following day was to be VE-Day and that the Prime Minister would broadcast, then all doubts vanished, and Luton had its first night free from fear.

Varied emotions surged through the minds of all. Memories of those who gave their lives so that the town might enjoy that day temprred the celebrations in many homes, but the thought that a father or son who had helped to carry retribution right into the heart of Germany might soon return added to the happiness of many more. The conflict between sorrow and joy, however, was submerged by the wave of thankfulness and relief that arose from every heart.

This was the dominant note of all celebrations—celebrations which were rightly regarded as but an intermediate stage on the road to complete and final victory. It was the end of a major task, however, and Ltuon in common with the rest of the country found time to count its blessings and snatch a few brief hours from the dreary task of making war.

The town did not await the dawn of VE-Day to begin its celebrations of the overthrow of Nazi oppression and tyranny. No sooner was it made known that the next day—May 8th—was to be the day of national thanksgiving than the drab, grey streets of war-time became avenues of colour in profuse array, enriched in darkness by beams of light from countless windows and the flickering flames of many bonfires. It was the end of more than five years of war-darkened streets, the end of the fear and havoc of the then seemingly unceasing nightly terror raids. No longer was it necessary for mothers to rouse their sleeping children and dash for safety to the cold and cheerless shelters. They could retire for the night and sleep until a natural awakening. It was the occasion to celebrate—the winning of a dearly bought victory.

Luton's first big cheer for victory was heard at the Town Hall, from which the news that hostilities in Europe had ceased was relayed. It was the spontaneous outburst of pent-up emotions—feelings that had long lain dormant and subdued under the staid exterior of the so-called prosaic and unimaginative Britisher. But that night, Luton gave the lie to the phrase. It celebrated as a victor should, and though outwardly carefree it remembered those who had suffered, with a deep and abiding respect that has outlived those transitory outbursts of joy.

The cheer that greeted the victory report was momentarily hushed while the then Mayor, Lady Keens, announced that the celebrations next day would commence with a service of thanksgiving which she and members of the Town Council would attend.

Afterwards bonfires were lighted, and the people danced and sang in the streets. Music was hastily improvised, one householder going so far as to drag a piano from his home and play for a jubilant crowd of neighbours.

Greatest scenes of animation, however, were in the immediate vicinity of the Town Hall—the nerve centre of the town throughout the war. Complete strangers joined hands to dance in the Palais Glide, British and American troops mingled with carefree camaraderie among the jostling and cheering throng. It was the climax of hope frustrated for many years, and the merriment continued until VE-Day was born.

The slightest incident that night was made the occasion of good-humoured banter and cheers. The majesty of the law was forgotten by more than one of the milling crowd. Two policemen had a lively chase before they could recover helmets snatched from their heads by revellers and quickly hand-passed through a scrum of several hundreds. They seemed to relish the chase, though another of their comrades wore a slightly embarrassed look when two light-hearted maids, evidently appreciative of the temporary waiving of dignity, implanted their over-elaborately painted lips on his blushing cheeks. A soldier was similarly decorated, rather more willingly, and had a V-sign in lipstick drawn on his forehead.

Luton awakened slowly from its unexpected outburst of cheer. It was rather forcibly reminded that though Germany had bowed the knee, some war-time restrictions must remain.

Housewives were early afoot, queueing for bread and other perishable goods before shops put up their shutters for days of long-awaited rejoicing. Earlier still, however, were the thousands of workers, who, confused by the unexpected method of the peace announcement, caught their usual bus to make sure that they really had the day off. At Vauxhall Motors, Ltd., more than 1,000 reported for work. The firm, appreciating that they had turned up to honour arrangements announced on notices throughout the works, decided to grant them an extra day's holiday with pay. Eventually all Luton appreciated that VE-Day was a reality, and that a holiday had been declared.

*　　*　　*　　*

The official opening of the borough's celebrations was at the Parish Church, where hundreds, unable to get inside, waited in the churchyard in a downpour of rain to join in a service relayed through loudspeakers. Inside, the Mayor and Corporation, who had walked in procession from the Town Hall, sat in the crowded Church, where both before and after the service, the bells rang joyous peals proclaiming victory.

It was a proud occasion for the many mothers, wives and sweethearts, most of whom wore red, white and blue rosettes, with regimental and other service badges, as they heard the Vicar, Canon W. Davison, R.D., voice the thanks of all for the victory of righteousness over the forces of evil.

" Let us," the Vicar said, " not relax our efforts now, and let us resist temptation to become cynical and despairing.

" This hour of victory, this day of rejoicing, will be an empty spectacle, a mere piece of emotional satisfaction, unless it spurs us on to greater efforts.

" Let it also be a day of rededication as we bow our heads in memory of the gallant dead.

" Then let us go on in the same spirit as we have continued the struggle, with courage undiminished and with strength renewed, to the still greater tasks that lie ahead."

Later in the day services were held in Chapel Street Methodist Church and at the Sports' Ground, where several thousands, led by Luton Band, raised their voices in the singing of " Abide with Me."

Speaking after the morning service, the Mayor, from the bandstand at the Town Hall, said the day had given her the proudest moment of her life, adding, " We are full of thanksgiving to God for having brought us through to victory. We grieve for our friends who have lost loved ones, but we rejoice with those whose loved ones are returning.

" We have seen the powers of darkness put to flight. We have seen the morning break."

Later, Lady Keens wrote, " Our first thought must be one of thank-

378

*Peace in Europe . . . The scene in George Street, look-
ing towards the floodlit Town Hall on the night of VE
plus* 1.

ABOVE: *Luton Parish Church was filled to capacity for the V.E. Thanksgiving Service.*

BELOW: *Many who were unable to gain admission listened in to the loudspeakers which relayed the service in the church-yard*

ABOVE: *Hundreds of people packed George Street on V.E. Day to listen to the band, and generally air their feelings.*

LEFT: *Waitresses from a nearby restaurant join in the dancing in George Street.*

BELOW: *V.J. Day, too, brought the revellers to the town centre, where rejoicing went on through the evening, and into the night.*

Lady Keens, Mayor of Luton, is in the centre of this happy group at the Blundell Road V.E. Party . . . one of the many street parties held in the town.

Bonfires in the streets marked the end of a happy day on V.J. Day . . . let the tar melt, who cares!

fulness to God that we have been granted the victory for which we have striven so hard and so long.

" The people of Luton have played a proud part in this struggle— on the field of battle, in the air, on and under the sea, in the factories and in the home. I have seen at first-hand some of the immense amount of voluntary service which has ungrudgingly been given by men, women—yes, and children, too. A common danger united us, a common aim bound us all together as never before.

" In this hour of triumph we remember those who have fallen, and those who are sick in mind and body. I hope our actions in the coming years will show that this remembrance is not mere lip-service, but a real and living thing.

" With the end of the war in Europe one great cloud has been lifted from our town and our country. I wish I could say that all the clouds had been lifted. There remains the war in the Far East, with all the anxieties it must bring to those households in Luton which have, or will have, men fighting out there. And there are those, always in our thoughts, whose men have been the prisoners of the Japanese since 1942.

" We must back up our men in the Far East as we have backed up their comrades from the dark days of Dunkirk until the day of victory.

" I am sure Luton will do it. There is the fine tradition of these last five and a half years to guide us—a tradition of hard work, of splendid voluntary service, of willingness to do the little extra in the larger cause.

" And when the war in the Far East is over, when we can celebrate the total victory and turn all our energies to solving the problems of reconstruction, I hope we shall retain a large measure of the good neighbourliness and understanding that carried us through times the like of which we hope never to see again."

*　　　*　　　*　　　*

The lighter side of Victory celebrations was continued with unabated vigour—dancing in the streets was resumed, with joyous voices continually raised in song and light-hearted banter. The gaily decorated streets presented a scene unparalleled in the history of the town.

Elderly women with ribbons in their hair vied with younger women in a colourful array of dress, while small children wore flag-fashioned frocks.

There were also scenes of incongruity that brought smiles to the straightest face—a man wearing a boiler suit and top hat being escorted home by his wife brought the biggest laugh, though a soldier wearing a straw boater ran him close as a mirth-producer.

In the dazzling glare of peace-time lighting the celebrations again continued until a late hour. The Town Hall tower was floodlit, coloured lights twinkled in the trees in New Bedford Road and V-signs etched in electric bulbs could be seen all over the town.

Traffic was diverted from the main streets, and from George Street to Wardown Park thousands jostled, danced, sang and whistled, while bells, rattles and a few fireworks made a varied contribution of sound and vigorously contested the right to be heard with the music of bands and recordings relayed from the Town Hall.

As the night advanced, bonfires were again lighted in all quarters of the town, and in no small number of them Hitler's effigy came to an appropriate end.

In the Selborne Road district there was no doubt as to the residents' idea of Hitler's " last territorial claim." A scaffold was erected and the execution of Der Fuehrer carried out, while an effigy of Goering swung from a near-by lamp-post, lighted up by the rays of the lamp he had helped to keep extinguished so long. In other districts, Mussolini met a similar fate.

Even after midnight the revelry continued unabated in the vicinity of the Town Hall, where many, well-nigh exhausted, sat on the steps and watched those who had still the energy to sing and dance.

Greatest memory of the day, however, was the hush that fell on the rejoicings when the King and the Prime Minister broadcast. When Mr. Churchill ended, the huge crowd spontaneously sang " There'll always be an England." It was a grand and moving spectacle.

The scenes on VE-Day were renewed with no less exuberance on the following day, and that night the whole front of the Town Hall was floodlit and the rejoicings continued.

Though extensions of licences had been granted to public houses throughout the town, the supply was not equal to the demand, and many had closed their doors at a very early hour. In the circumstances a sailor who paraded Williamson Street with a bucket of beer and dispensed it by the cupful was a cheering sight.

That night searchlights raked the sky, and passing aircraft flashed the V-sign to the jubilant townspeople.

The days did not pass without some casualties, but though nineteen persons were taken to the Luton and Dunstable Hospital no one was seriously injured. Indeed, so well did Luton behave that the Chief Constable, Mr. Ronald Alderson, publicly thanked the people through the Press.

" I am grateful to everyone," he said. " It was a credit to the town. The people enjoyed themselves well, and did so in a manner that considerably lightened the police duties on such an occasion."

*   *   *   *

Eight babies were born in Luton on VE-Day, which was commemorated in the names of two. One, whose surname begins with E, was christened Vivienne and the second was called Veronica Edith.

Nor were the children forgotten in the greater realisation by their parents of what the day meant to all. Streets all over the town became banqueting halls where, at flower-decked trestle tables, thousands of children were entertained. Nothing was spared to give them the day of their lives.

They were visited by the Mayor, who was greeted with tumultuous cheers and the singing of " For she's a jolly good fellow," as she made a tour of the parties to speak, and cheerfully sign autographs.

The children also had fancy-dress parades, sports, entertainments, and at night out-lasted their parents in revels around bonfires as fireworks crackled and sparkled to seemingly unending cries of delight.

Accompanying the Mayor was the Chief Constable, who remarked, " This is the sort of thing we want our children to remember, not the experiences they have undergone in the past five years."

Luton's love of children, shown in pre-war days by the number of parties given for them, was re-born in the dawn of peace in Europe.

*　　*　　*　　*

Seven bands took part in Luton's victory parade and thanksgiving service on the following Sunday, when the Town was given an inspiring picture in perspective of its war effort.

It was a proper perspective too, for Luton was not pushing herself to the fore. As a tribute to the United States, American soldiers, with the Stars and Stripes and their regimental colours, headed the procession, led by the Luton Band.

Next came British troops with a golden-horned goat mascot, followed by the A.T.S. and the R.A.F.

Then the procession assumed its more intimate local aspect—all sections of the Civil Defence organisations were there, with the Home Guard and N.F.S. Special Constables paraded with the police and the War Reserve force, together with the Women Auxiliaries.

The great share women had taken was symbolised by their sections of the Civil Defence, the Red Cross, St. John Ambulance and kindred contingents. Besides the Women's Voluntary Services there was also the Women's Land Army and the Women's Section of the British Legion, with women war workers in their overalls.

There were the pre-Service units too, and older organisations for girls and boys, trade union and guild representatives.

The parade took half-an-hour to march past. Cheer upon cheer came from the crowds along the route from the Manor Road Recreation ground to the Town football ground. Many in the crowds wore medals or medal ribbons, but it was in the procession that medals were most conspicuous, though some wore only ribbons.

Two policemen who were Old Contemptibles led the procession, while many more were included in its ranks.

Reminders of Luton's bombing ordeals were two Luton George Medallists—Supt. Sear at the head of the police, and Major J. C. Cunningham, D.S.O., with the Home Guard.

The Luton Band played for the march past the Mayor, who was

385

z

accompanied by most members of the Council. The service was conducted by the Rev. G. H. Woodham, president of Luton Free Church Council, the Vicar of Luton, Canon Wm. Davison, R.D., giving the address.

The celebrations gradually drew to a close, though children's parties continued for many days, and controversy, so loud when the planning for victory was taking place, stilled completely when the Town Council announced that the celebrations cost only £440 out of the £2,000 allowed.

*   *   *   *

Luton again went back to work to win, this time, world peace, and three months and a week later stopped to celebrate again the achievement of its aspirations—It was VJ-Day, August 15th.

Once again the Town celebrated a great and joyous occasion in a thoroughly decent way, and though there was again plenty of noise and quite a few bonfires and fireworks, there were no excesses.

Thousands of people, in exuberant mood, thronged the streets by night and day, but there was not a single incident requiring police attention.

Luton fittingly began its celebrations of world peace with a service of thanksgiving in the Parish Church, to which the Mayor and Corporation in their robes marched in procession through streets once more beflagged.

In the church, which was again inadequate for the many who wished to participate in the service, seats were specially reserved for Forces' personnel and for relatives of men killed in the Far East or prisoners in Japanese hands.

The Vicar, Canon Davison, struck a note of hope and expectation in his address, when he commented, " Our hearts are full of thanksgiving that this time of suspense, this nightmare of agony, has at last passed, and that our loved ones in the Far East will soon be released."

" World peace can be effected by men of resolution working towards that end. The idea of isolationism must now be shattered for ever."

After a morning of drizzling rain the sun came out, and crowds again filled the main streets to sing, dance and make merry. The celebrations continued in the same strain as on VE-Day, bonfires glowed red against the night sky, and the flashing and sparkling of fireworks mingled with the brilliance of floodlighting as the people brought to a reluctant close the first of their two VJ holidays.

The rejoicings were again hushed to hear the King's speech broadcast from the Town Hall, and the crowd joined lustily in singing the National Anthem, before they resumed their laughter and making cheer.

During the speech the Mayor, Lady Keens, stood in the Town Hall balcony with Mr. W. N. Warbey, M.P. for Luton, who travelled from the opening session of the new Parliament to join in the town's celebrations. He also attended several children's parties, which were again a feature of the town's rejoicing.

So well did the people enjoy themselves on the first VJ-Day, however, that the remaining celebrations were tame by comparison. The tempo of events increased only in the late afternoon of the following day, and again revelry ruled to a late hour.

But the first flush of Victory had gone, and while children's parties continued to hold daily sway, a feeling of sober relief and thankfulness seemed to pervade the thoughts of adults. It was as though Luton had said, " We have won the war, now let us make sure that we win the peace." Her eyes seemed to peer deeply into the future in search of the day—

> " *When the war-drums beat no longer,*
> *And the battle-flags are furled ;*
> *In the Parliament of man,*
> *The Federation of the world.*"

> *Men, women and children are among the names in Luton's Roll of Honour. Some did not live here, yet they were our townsfolk, for Luton sheltered them in their callings. All were sons and daughters of Luton. Their graves are in foreign lands and in the deep waters. They lie, too, here in their home-town. None will be forgotten.*

The Roll of Honour

ABEL, SIDNEY, 4, St. Paul's Road, Luton. Sgt.-Pilot, R.A.F. Killed on active service, May 1st, 1943.

ABBOTT, LESLIE CHARLES, 134, Turners Road, Luton. Pte., 4th Royal Norfolks. Killed in action, Paula Uban Island, Singapore, February 8th, 1942.

ABBOTT, ROBERT, 17, Corncastle Road, Luton. Spr., R.E. Died on active service, Cairn Ryan, Scotland, March 25th, 1942.

ABRAHAMS, ROBERT CHARLES, 8, Cumberland Street, Luton. Rfmn., K.R.R. Died of wounds, Sangro, Italy, May 13th, 1944.

ADAMS, RONALD BERTRAM THOMAS, 212, Dunstable Road, Luton. Pilot Officer, 174th (Rocket Typhoon) Squadron, R.A.F. Presumed killed on operations, Osnabruck, Germany, February 24th, 1945.

ADDISON, ERNEST, 1, Dunstable Close, Luton. Chief Cook, M.V. *San Vittorio* (Tanker). Lost at sea, May 16th, 1942.

AINSWORTH, STANLEY, 15, Villa Road, Luton. F/Sgt., 51st Squadron, R.A.F. Killed on operations over Leipzig, Germany, December 4th, 1943.

AITCHISON, JOHN FREDERICK, 4, Ferndale Road, Luton. Cabin Boy, Merchant Navy. Died as P.O.W., Japanese prison camp, after sinking of SS. *Kirkpool*. Place and date of death unknown.

AITKEN, JAMES McLAUGHLIN, 41, Solway Road, Luton. Spr., R.E. Accidentally killed on active service, Newcastle-on-Tyne, June 15th, 1940.

ALLEN, CLIFFORD CHAS., 54, Cambridge Street, Luton. Gnr., 133/41st Light A.A. Regt., R.A. Killed in action, Middle East, October 17th, 1943.

ALLEN, CYRIL, 16, Vernon Road, Luton. Cpl., 8th Royal Warwicks. Regt. Died on active service, October 27th, 1942.

ALLEN, DONALD BERTIE, 178, North Street, Luton. Boy (First Class), R.N. Lost at sea, Crete, May 22nd, 1941.

ALLEN, JONATHAN WILLIAM, 29, Drury Lane, Houghton Regis, and B. Laporte, Ltd., Luton. Bdr., R.A. Died as Prisoner-of-War, Japanese Prison Camp, 1944.

ALLEN, OLIVER JAMES, 54, Windsor Street, Luton. Cpl., 2nd Battn. Bedfs. and Herts. Regt. Killed in action, Cessena, Italy, November 21st, 1944.

ALLEN, RONALD WILLIAM, 25, Collingdon Street, Luton. Tpr., Reconnaissance Corps. Killed on active service, November 12th, 1942.

ANSELL, GLADYS, 58, Old Bedford Road, Luton. Killed by enemy action, at Luton, October 14th, 1940.

ANSELL, HORACE GEORGE, 2a, Dordans Road, Luton. Sgt., R.A.F. Missing, presumed killed, France, August 17-18th, 1943.

ANSTEE, JACK, 111, Ashburnham Road, Luton. F/Officer, R.A.F. Missing, presumed killed, night operations over Germany, January, 1944.

APPLEBY, FREDERICK WILLIAM, 109, Cambridge Street, Luton. Spr., R.E. Killed in action, Italy, April 1st, 1944.

ARCHER, Harry, 16, Leicester Road, Luton. Killed by enemy action, at Vauxhall Motors, Ltd., Luton, August 30th, 1940.

ARDLEY, Guy, 52, Lemsford Road, St. Albans, and Hayward-Tyler & Co., Ltd., Luton. F/Officer, R.A.F. Missing on operations, September, 1944.

ARLIDGE, Frank, 25, Rondini Avenue, Luton. Killed by enemy action at De Havillands, Hatfield, October 3rd, 1940.

ARMITAGE, Harold William, 8, Hayes Close, Stopsley, Luton. Able Seaman, R.N., H.M.S. *Cornwall*. Died of wounds, Bay of Bengal, April 5th, 1942.

ARMSTRONG, Percy, 1, Hayes Close, Luton. Gnr., R.A. Lost at sea while prisoner of Japanese, November 18th, 1942.

ARNOLD, Edward Fred, 9, Overstone Road, Luton. Died of injuries caused by enemy action at Vauxhall Motors, Ltd., August 30th, 1940.

ARNOLD, Sidney Allen, 90, Ash Road, Luton. Pte., Suffolk Regt. Died as prisoner of Japanese, No. 4 Camp, Siam, July 16th, 1943.

ASHDOWN, Cecil Joseph, 18, High Street, Houghton Regis, and Home Counties Newspapers, Ltd., Luton. Died as prisoner of Japanese while working on Burma-Siam Railway, July 23rd, 1943.

ATKIN, Aubrey Cyril William, 2, St. Paul's Road, Luton. Dvr., R.E. Killed in action, Singapore, February 13th, 1942.

ATTFIELD, Alfred James. Killed by enemy action at Vauxhall Motors, Ltd., Luton, August 30th, 1940.

ATTWOOD, Harold Ernest Edward, 21, Faringdon Road, Luton. Flt/Sgt., R.A.F., att. No. 423 R.C.A.F. Squadron, Coastal Command. Killed on operations, North Sea, November 13th, 1943.

AUSTIN, John Prescott, 216, Cutenhoe Road, Luton. F/Officer, Bomber Command, R.A.F. Killed in action, Northern France, August 18th, 1944.

AXBY, Leslie Frederick, 77, Milton Road, Luton. Sgt./Pilot, No. 466 Squadron, R.A.A.F. Missing, presumed killed, January 30th, 1943.

BACON, Leslie Bernard, 16, Chaul End Lane, Luton. Pte., Suffolk Regt. Died as prisoner of Japanese in Siam, November 1st, 1943.

BACON, Leslie William, 64, Leicester Road, Luton. Sgt. Obsvr., R.A.F. Killed on active service, air operations, 1941.

BADRICK, Cyril Ezra, 20, Maidenhall Road, Luton. Stoker, First-Class, R.N., H.M.S. *Dulverton*. Lost at sea, November 17th, 1941.

BADRICK, Robert Edward, 26, Tower Road, Luton. A/Seaman, R.N. Killed on active service, Normandy Beaches, June 8th, 1944.

BAILEY, George Alfred, 93, Trent Road, Luton. Pte., Suffolk Regt. Died as prisoner of Japanese, Sonkrai, Siam, August 7th, 1943.

BAKER, Frederick William, 34, Denbigh Road, Luton. Royal Corps of Signals. Killed on active service, Palestine, May 26th, 1946.

BAKER, Norman John, 194, Strathmore Avenue, Luton. Spr., 288th Field Coy., R.E. Killed whilst laying land-mines, September 22nd, 1940.

BALL, Sidney A., 126, Hartley Road, Luton. Gnr., Commandoes. Killed in action, December, 1942.

BARFORD, Sidney William, 30, Edward Street, Luton. Pte., Cambs. Reg. Died as prisoner of Japanese, August 15th, 1943.

BARFORD, W., 10, Derwent Road, Luton. Able Seaman, R.N. Killed in action, 1940.

BARKER, Leslie, 40, Windermere Crescent, Luton. Paratrooper, Parachute Regt. Parachuted behind German lines in Normandy before D-Day. Died of wounds, June 28th, 1944.

BARKER, Marcus Edgar, 44, London Road, Luton. Flt/Sgt., 221st Squadron, R.A.F. Missing after operations off coast of Italy, February 2nd, 1943.

BARNES, Arthur Charles Jack, 50, Turners Road, Luton. Lt., Loyal Regt. and 1st Somerset L.I. Died on active service, Burma, March 4th, 1944.

BARNES, Henry Charles, 14, Gillam Street, Luton. Gnr., R.A. Died on active service, January, 1940.

BARNES, William Henry, 46, Linden Road, Luton. Cpl., R.E. Killed in action, Boulogne, France, September 17th, 1944.

BARRETT, John James, 46, Charmouth Road, St. Albans, and B. Laporte, Ltd., Luton. Lt., R.E. Killed in action, North Africa, 1943.

BARTON, Norman Richard, 170, Cutenhoe Road, Luton. Gnr., 148th Field Regt., R.A. Killed as result of air operations while prisoner of Japanese, Indo-China, April 9th, 1945.

BATCHELOR, William, 15, Alder Crescent, Luton. Pte., 6th Battn. Bedfs. and Herts. Regt. Died on active service, India, April, 1942.

BATES, Arthur F., 16, The Crescent, Toddington, and Luton Co-operative Society, Ltd. Tpr., 53rd Reconnaissance Regt. Died of wounds, Normandy, August 18th, 1944.

BATES, Francis Robert, 18, Strathmore Avenue, Luton. Sgt., R.A.S.C. Died of wounds, Middle East, February 18th, 1942.

BAVISTER, Joseph, 74, Dumfries Street, Luton. Gnr., 412th Batty., 148th Field Regt., R.A. Lost at sea while prisoner of Japanese, September 12th, 1944.

BAXTER, George, 14, Portland Road, Luton. Pte., Cambs. Regt. Died as prisoner of Japanese, Siam, June 18th, 1943.

BAYNHAM, Mrs., 83, Biscot Road, Luton. Killed by enemy action at Luton, November 6th, 1944.

BEALES, Rex, 7, Abingdon Road, Luton. Sgt./Pilot, R.A.F. Died on active service, August 2nd, 1940.

BERRESFORD, Benjamin, 44, Conway Road, Luton. O/Seaman, R.N., H.M.S. *Martin*. Lost at sea, presumed killed in North Africa landings, November 11th, 1942.

BETTS, Alan Victor, 64, Bramingham Road, Luton. Stoker (First Class), R.N. Lost at sea, off French Coast, July 20th, 1944.

BILEY, Jack, 139, New Town Street, Luton. L/Cpl. Died as prisoner of Japanese, No. 2 Camp, Siam, June, 1943.

BIRD, Alfred Henry, 82, Cobden Street, Luton. Pte., R. Norfolk Regt. Missing, presumed killed, Dunkirk, May, 1940.

BIRD, Kenneth Sydney, 94, St. Peter's Road, Luton. F/Officer, R.A.F. Killed on air operations over France, April 17th, 1943.

BIRD, Sidney Frederick, 124, Langley Street, Luton. Cpl., 1st Battn. Royal Norfolk Regt. Killed in action, Caen, July 8th, 1944.

BLACK, Archibald William, 93, Russell Rise, Luton. P/Officer, R.A.F., No. 91 (Spitfire) Squadron. Missing on air operations south-west of Boulogne, November 17th, 1941.

BLACKWELL, William Alfred, 27, Whitecroft Road, Luton. Sgt. W/Op. A.G., R.A.F. Killed on operations over Germany, May 27th, 1943.

BLATCHFORD, J., 256, Biscot Road, Luton. Sgt./Pilot, R.A.F. Killed on active service, December, 1940.

BLIGH, Rex William, Icknield Way, Luton. Flt./Sgt., R.A.F. Died on active service, India, January, 1944.

BLINDELL, David, 25, Talbot Road, Luton. Flt./Mech., R.A.F., Bomber Command. Killed in flying accident in Canada, August 11th, 1943.

BLOW, Kenneth Leslie Owen, D.F.C., 390, Dunstable Road, Luton. W/Officer, R.A.F. Killed on operations, Holland, December 10th, 1943.

BLOWER, Douglas Roger, 293, High Town Road, Luton. Pte., Queen's Royal Regt. Died of wounds, El Alamein, October 24th, 1942.

BLOY, Charles Robert. Killed by enemy action, at Vauxhall Motors, Ltd., Luton, August 30th, 1940.

BLYTHE, Thomas Francis, 135, Harcourt Street, Luton. Sgt. W/Op. A.G., R.A.F. Killed in action, November 27th, 1942.

BOND, Victor Cyril, 100, Castle Street, Luton. Sgt., 203rd Squadron, R.A. Died from injuries and burns received on active service, Egypt, October 9th, 1942.

BONE, James Reginald, 9, Woodland Avenue, Luton. Pte., R.A.M.C. Died on active service, February, 1946.

BONNER, Maurice Norman, 61, Bury Park Road, Luton. L/Cpl., R. Norfolk Regt. Died as prisoner of Japanese, Thanbyuzayat, Burma, September 17th, 1943.

BONNER, Reginald William, 7, Willow Way, Luton. Gnr., Heavy A.A. Regt., R.A. Killed in action, Italy, January 21st, 1944.

BONNICK, Reginald George, 102, Cambridge Street, Luton. Died September 2nd, 1940, as result of enemy action at Luton, August 30th, 1940.

BORLAND, Isabel, 15, Highbury Road, Luton. Killed by enemy action, at Luton, October 14th, 1940.

BOSS, Kenneth, M.C., 117, Farley Avenue, Luton. Capt., R.A. Died of wounds, N.W. Europe, July, 1945.

BOSTON, Brian James, 58, Clarendon Road, Luton. F/Officer, R.A.F., Bomber Command. Killed during operations over Germany, August 26th, 1944.

BOURNES, Arthur Bowland, 44, Brunswick Street, Luton. Fatally injured while on fire watch, Luton and Dunstable Hospital, November 2nd, 1941.

BOWERS, Donald, 24, Sherwood Road, Luton. Airborne Unit. Killed in action, Normandy, July, 1944.

BRACEWELL, Jim E., 118, Bishopscote Road, Luton. Gnr., 420th Battery, R.A. Died as prisoner in Japanese hands, Pratchai, Kirakan, Siam.

BRANSOM, Lewis Egbert, 37, Whitefield Avenue, Sundon Park Estate, Luton. Stoker i/c. R.N., H.M.S. *Harvester*. Lost at sea, Mid-Atlantic, March 11th, 1943.

BRAY, Ronald, Gresham Assurance Coy., Luton. Sgt.W/Op., A.G., R.A.F. Killed in raid on Brest, 1941.

BREEZE, Evan John, 88, Chester Avenue, Luton. Killed by enemy action, at Vauxhall Motors, Ltd., Luton, August 30th, 1940.

BRIARS, Ronald Albert, 458, New Bedford Road, Luton. L/Cpl., Cambs. Regt. Died as prisoner of Japanese, Malaya, June 29th, 1943.

BRIGHT, Sidney J., 54, Park Street, Luton. L/Cpl., Corps of Military Police. Killed in action, Italy, December 17th, 1944.

BROWN, Donald H., 1, Ridgway Road, Luton. Sgt./Obs., R.A.F. Killed on active service, air operations, Far East, September, 1942.

BROWN, Douglas, 248, Dunstable Road, Luton. Lt., Bedfs. & Herts. Regt., att. Royal Warwicks. Regt. Killed in action, Western Front, October, 1944.

BROWN, Harold, 153, Dallow Road, Luton. Sgt., R.A.F. Killed in action, Far East, January 26th, 1942.

BROWN, Peter Charles, 22, Newark Road, Luton. Sgt. W/Op. A.G., R.A.F., Coastal Command. Killed in action, air operations, March, 1944.

BRYANT, Frank Dennis Widdows, 107, Shelley Road, Luton. Second Officer, Merchant Navy, S.S. *Whitford Point*. Lost at sea, Irish Sea, October 20th, 1940.

BUGG, Eric John, 65, Lincoln Road, Luton. Pte., 1st Battn. Northants. Regt. Killed in action, Dangyin, Burma, April 20th, 1945.

BURCHMORE, William Robert, 97, Harcourt Street, Luton. Killed by enemy action, at Luton, August 30th, 1940.

BURNS, Kenneth J., 57, Durham Road, Luton. Sergt., No. 211 Squadron, R.A.F. Died as prisoner of Japanese, Moena Island (Celebes), November 1st, 1944.

BURR, William Henry, 172, Blundell Road, Luton. Volunteer, 4th Bedfs. Battn. Home Guard. Killed on exercises, June 15th, 1941.

BURROWS, George, 16, Midland Road, Luton. Killed by enemy action, at Luton, September 5th, 1942.

BUSHBY, Stanley G., 46, Conway Road, Luton. Killed by enemy action, at Luton, October 14th, 1940.

BUSSEREAU, Victor Roque, 120, Leagrave Road, Luton. Lt., R.C.N.V.R. Missing, presumed killed, H.M.S. *Rajputana*, May, 1941.

BUTCHER, Thomas Derrick, 14, Inkerman Street, Luton. W/Officer, No. 24 Squadron, R.A.F. Killed in air accident, Llanfair, nr. Ruthin, Wales, July 17th, 1942.

BUTLER, Thomas Walter, 11, Applecroft Road, Luton. Cpl., K.R.R. Killed in Egypt, August, 1941.

BUTTERFIELD, Ronald Alfred, 33, Cambridge Street, Luton. Pte., Bedfs. and Herts. Regt. Killed in action, Italy, June 28th, 1944.

BUXTON, Cyril Charles William, 8, North Street, Luton. Pte., Oxon. and Bucks. Light Infantry. Died of wounds, Hamilkein, Germany, March 24th, 1945.

CAFFELL, Gordon W. J., 26, St. Margaret's Avenue, Luton. L/Bdr., 148th Field Regt., R.A. Died as prisoner of Japanese, Siam, January 31st, 1944.

CAIN, Anthony Richard, 20, The Close, Kinsbourne Green, and Vauxhall Motors, Ltd., Luton. Sgt./Navigator, R.A.F. Killed in action, June, 1941.

CAIN, Leslie, 81, Ashcroft Road, Luton. Tpr., 142nd Regt., R.A.C. Died of wounds, Algiers, July 2nd, 1943.

CAIN, Robert William, 5, Hart Lane, Luton. Cfm., R.E.M.E. Killed on active service in Irak, August 15th, 1944.

CANHAM, Rex, 18, Rothesay Road, Luton. Gnr., Light A.A. Battery, R.A. Died as prisoner of Japanese, Kuomoto Camp, Japan, January 16th, 1943.

CARD, Francis Austin William, 506, Hitchin Road, Luton. Sick Berth Attendant, R.N., H.M.S. *Curacoa*. Lost at sea, October 2nd, 1942.

CARR, Robert, 30, Kingsley Road, Luton. Pte., 2nd Battn. Duke of Wellington's Regt. Killed in action, Burma, June 4th, 1944.

CARTER, Beryl, 77, Biscot Road, Luton. Killed by enemy action, at Luton, November 6th, 1944.

CARTER, Clifford Jack, 24, Montrose Avenue, Luton. Able Seaman, Merchant Navy. Lost at sea through enemy action, March, 1941.

CARTER, Edward George, 16, Kingsway, Luton. Cpl., Royal Signals (Paratrooper). Killed at Bosnia, Yugo-Slavia, August 15th, 1944.

CARTER, George, 1, Preston Path, Luton. Gnr., R.A. Missing from Japanese transport after fall of Singapore, 1942.

CARTER, Harry G., 24, Medina Road, Luton. Killed by enemy action, at Luton, October 14th, 1940.

CARTER, Reginald A., 37, St. Peter's Road, Luton. Gnr., R.A. Killed on active service, August, 1941.

CASE, Norman, 72, Selbourne Road, Luton. Able Seaman, R.N. Died, August 27th, 1943.

CASTLETON, Alexander Gordon, 28, Lyndhurst Road, Luton. Sergt., Royal Corps of Signals. Died on active service, May 14th, 1946.

CATLIN, Herbert Edward, 113, Beechwood Road, Luton. Pte., Pioneer Corps. Lost at sea with S.S. *Lancastria* during evacuation from Dunkirk, June 17th, 1940.

CATO, Cyril George, 178, Dallow Road, Luton. Sergt., 289th Field Park Coy., R.E. Died after invaliding from Germany, July 15th, 1946.

CATO, Frederick George Bert, 289, Dallow Road, Luton. Pte., 5th Battn. Bedfs. and Herts. Regt. Lost at sea on board the *Hofoko Maru* as prisoner of Japanese, September 21st, 1944.

CHALKLEY, Horace Frederick, 49, Lyndhurst Road, Luton. Sgt., 148th Field Regt., R.A. Lost at sea in the Pacific as prisoner of Japanese, September 12th, 1944.

CHALKLEY, John, 52, Mayne Avenue, Luton. Sgt.-W/O., R.A.F. Missing on operations, Berlin, August 23rd-24th, 1943.

CHAMBERLAIN, Ernest John, 31, Cannon Lane, Stopsley, Luton. Pte., 5th Battn. Bedfs. and Herts. Regt. Lost at sea as prisoner of Japanese, September 21st, 1944.

CHAMBERLAIN, Gladys, 3, Hitchin Road, Luton. Killed by enemy action, at Luton, October 14th, 1940.

CHAMBERLAIN, Marion A., "Sarina," Turners Road, Luton. Killed by enemy action, at Luton, October 14th, 1940.

CHAMBERS, Alfred George, 101, Milton Road, Luton. Cpl., R. Norfolk Regt. Killed in action, Battle of the Imphal Road, Burma, June 9th, 1944.

CHAMBERS, Frank H., 48, Avondale Road, Luton. Killed by U.S. bomb lorry explosion, Offley, January 8th, 1945.

CHAMBERS, George Harry. Killed by enemy action, at Vauxhall Motors, Ltd., Luton, August 30th, 1940.

CHAMPKIN, Douglas George, 42, Lincoln Road, Luton. Sgt.-F/Engr., 460th Squadron, R.A.F. Killed on operations ; buried at Lahr, Baden, Germany, April 27th-28th, 1944.

CHANCE, Philip James, 74, Durham Road, Luton. Gnr., Light A.A. Batty., R.A. Died at sea while prisoner of Japanese, November 13th, 1942.

CHAPPELL, Peter C., 5, Oakley Road, Luton. P/Officer, R.A.F., Bomber Command. Killed on operations, Abingdon, July 28th, 1941.

CHERRY, Harold Arthur, 3, Douglas Road, Luton. Lieut., R.A., att. Tactical Air Force. Killed in Italy, February 26th, 1945.

CHERRY, Kenneth Edwin, 48, Castle Hill Road, Totternhoe, and Percival Aircraft, Ltd., Luton. L/Cpl. Died of wounds, Greece, December 27th, 1944.

CHESHAM, Amelia, 4, Mountfield Road, Luton. Killed by enemy action, at Luton, October 14th, 1940.

CHESHIRE, Sidney James, 32, Harcourt Street, Luton. Tpr., Reconnaissance Regt. Killed on active service, April 24th, 1942.

CHOTE, Arthur Haydn Frederick, 38, Marston Gardens, Luton. F/Sgt. 14th Squadron, R.A.F. Killed on active service, near Chester, August 3rd, 1942'.

CHURCH, Frederick James, 89, Putteridge Road, Luton. A/Seaman, H.M.S. *Isis*, R.N. Died on war service from exposure at sea, July 20th, 1944.

CLARIDGE, Albert Edward, 62, Talbot Road, Luton. F/Officer, R.A.F. Died, May 31st, 1944.

CLARIDGE, Cyril Charles, 5, Alfred Street, Luton. Pte., 4th Battn. Suffolk Regt. Killed in action, Singapore, April 22nd, 1942.

CLARIDGE, Sidney George James, 31, Brooms Road, Luton. Pte., Suffolk Regt. Died as prisoner of Japanese, Japan, February 3rd, 1944.

CLARINGBOLD, Leon Jack, 2, Crescent Road, Luton. A/Seaman, R.N. Lost at sea, May 23rd, 1941.

CLARK, David, 15, Derwent Road, Luton. Sgt. (O), R.A.F. Killed on active service, Scotland, December 10th, 1941.

CLARK, William Henry, 10, Tower Road, Luton. F/Sgt., Security Police, R.A.F. Accidentally killed on active service, Burton-on-Trent, February 18th, 1945.

CLARKE, Brian Edward, 56, Lyndhurst Road, Luton. Sgt. W/Op.-A.G., 576th Squadron, R.A.F. Killed on operations, Kollerbecke, near Detmold, Germany, January 14th, 1944.

CLARK, David, 29, Montrose Avenue, Luton. Sgt./Observer, R.A.F. Bomber Command. Killed on active service, December 10th, 1941.

CLARK, John F. S., 41, Cavendish Road, Luton. Died, India, 1941.

CLARK, Ronald Ernest, 79, St. Augustine's Avenue, Luton. Pte., Royal Scots. Killed on active service, May, 1945.

CLEARY, Albert Edward, 35, Chester Avenue, Luton. Sgt., R.A.F. Missing, presumed killed, South Atlantic, August 17th, 1941.

CLINTON, Basil, 251, New Bedford Road, Luton. P/Officer, R.A.F. Killed on active service near Cape Hotham, Australia, July 31st, 1945.

CLOUGH, R. A. Died as result of enemy action at Vauxhall Motors, Ltd., Luton, August 30th, 1940.

COCKS, WALTER HENRY. Killed by enemy action, at Vauxhall Motors, Ltd., Luton, August 30th, 1940.

COEN, JOSEPH LEO, Beechwood Road, Luton. Sgt., R.A.F. Killed on active service, October 15th, 1941.

COKER, J. W., 28, Curzon Road, Luton. Spr., R.E. Died as prisoner of war in Japanese Camp, Siam, 1943.

COLE, HENRY WILLIAM, 175, Biscot Road, Luton. Gnr./Dvr., 217th Batty., R.A. Killed in action near Bremen, Germany, May 1st, 1945.

COLE, ROBERT ARNOLD, 38, Reginald Street, Luton. F/Sgt., R.A.F. Killed on operations over Leverkusen-Wesdorf, Germany, July 30th-31st, 1943.

COLEMAN, EWART REGINALD, 23, St. Michael's Crescent, Luton. Gnr., R.A. Died of injuries on active service, May 16th, 1944.

COLEMAN, HENRY, 130, Wenlock Street, Luton. Pioneer Corps. Killed on active service, December, 1940.

COLEMAN, JOHN, 47, Whitecroft Road, Luton. Pte., The Buffs. Died as prisoner of war, Germany, July 24th, 1944.

COLEY, JOHN WILSON, 47, Russell Rise, Luton. L/Sgt., R.E. Killed in action, N.W. Europe, November 8th, 1944.

COLLINGS, DONALD HERBERT, 93, Russell Rise, Luton. Sgt./Pilot, 6th (P) Adv. Fighter Unit, R.A.F. Killed on active service, September 18th, 1943.

CONISBEE, GORDON H. C., Sgt. (N), R.A.F. Killed on active service, Walney Island, Barrow-in-Furness, September 30th, 1944.

CONLEY, CECIL VERNON, " Hazelmere," Icknield Way, Luton. Sapper, R.E. Died on active service, Basra, Irak, June 19th, 1942.

COOK, ALFRED, 40, Belmont Road, Luton. Pte., 5th Battn. Bedfs. and Herts. Regt. Died as prisoner of Japanese, Krian-Krai, September 10th, 1943.

COOMBES, HARRY, 73, Latimer Road, Luton. Pte., R. Berks. Regt. Died of wounds, C.M.F., February 14th, 1944.

COOP, GEORGE, 122, Fourth Avenue, Sundon, Luton. Killed by enemy action, at Luton, November 6th, 1944.

COOPER, CHARLES SAMUEL, 58, Cobden Street, Luton. Killed in action, Italy, November 4th, 1943.

COOPER, GEORGE WILLIAM, 1, Ferndale Road, Luton. O/Seaman, R.N. Lost with H.M.S. *Boadicea* off Normandy, June 13th, 1944.

COOPER, JAMES EMERTON, 9, Beech Road, Luton. Sgt./Pilot, R.A.F. Killed in action, September, 1941.

COOPER, LESLIE WILLIAM, 122, Beechwood Road, Luton. Gnr., R.A. Died as prisoner of Japanese, Malaya, October 26th, 1943.

COOPER, NORMAN F., 7, Wenlock Street, Luton. Sgt./Pilot, R.A.F. Killed on active service, July 27th, 1940.

COOPER, RUSSELL C., 55, Arundel Road, Luton. Cpl., R.A.S.C. Invalided out died July 30th, 1943.

COOTE, BERT GEORGE, 71, Bury Park Road, Luton. Tpr., North Irish Horse R.A.C. Died of wounds, Italy, August 5th, 1944.

CORKE, JOHN FREDERICK, 92, Somerset Avenue, Luton. L.A.C., R.A.F. Killed on active service, Middle East, August, 1941.

CORNISH, ALFRED JOHN, 15, St. Catherine's Avenue, Luton. L/Bdr., R.A. Killed in action, May 27th, 1940.

COULTISH, GEORGE WILLIAM, 16, Devon Road, Luton. Pte., 1/5th Battn. Welch Regt. Killed in action, Germany, March 3rd, 1945.

COWLEY, RONALD, 29, Cavendish Road, Luton. Tpr., Royal Tank Regt. Killed in action, Southern Tunisia, April 25th, 1943.

COX, FRANK, 182, Biscot Road, Luton. Pte., R. West Kent Regt. Killed in action, Italy, November 30th, 1943.

COX, RALPH, Vauxhall Motors, Ltd., Luton. R.A.F. Killed in action, 1940.

CRABTREE, JACK COLIN, 13, St. Margaret's Avenue, Luton. Lieut., Green Howards. Killed in action, Arnhem, April 21st, 1945.

CRAWLEY, ALBERT EDWARD, 20, Whitecroft Road, Luton. Pte., 5th Battn. Bedfs. and Herts. Regt. Lost on board the *Hofoku Maru* as prisoner of Japanese, September 21st, 1944.

CRAWLEY, EDWARD ALBERT. Killed by enemy action, at Vauxhall Motors, Ltd., Luton, August 30th, 1940.

CREW, CHARLES, 155, Park Street, Luton. Killed by enemy action, at Luton, September 22nd, 1940.

CREW, GLADYS, 155, Park Street, Luton. Killed by enemy action, at Luton, September 22nd, 1940.

CREW, LOUISA, 155, Park Street, Luton. Killed by enemy action, at Luton, September 22nd, 1940.

CREW, REUBEN, 149, Park Street, Luton. Killed by enemy action, at Luton, September 22nd, 1940.

CRUISE, ARTHUR, 180, Wellington Street, Luton. Sgt./Pilot, R.A.F. Died of wounds, December 22nd, 1940.

CULBERTSON, GEORGE ANDREW YPRES, 48, Dudley Street, Luton. Died as result of enemy action, at Luton, September 2nd, 1940.

CUNNINGHAM, RICHARD FULTON, 71, Wellington Street, Luton. O/Seaman, R.N., H.M.S. *Hood*. Killed in Action, North Atlantic, May 24th, 1941.

CURRANT, P. NORMAN, 9, Elliswick Road, Harpenden, and Currant & Creak, Ltd., Bute Street, Luton. Major, Seaforth Highlanders. Killed in action, Western Front, September, 1944.

CURCHIN, R. T., Gibraltar Cottages, London Road, Luton. L/Stoker, R.N. Missing, presumed killed, March, 1942.

CURTIS, CLIFFORD SIDNEY, 42, Stanford Road, Luton. Killed by enemy action, at Vauxhall Motors, Ltd., Luton, August 30th, 1940.

DANIELS, LAURENCE RUFUS, 9, Ashton Road, Luton. L/Bdr. R.A. Died as prisoner of Japanese, Siam, October 23rd 1943.

DARBY, KENNETH ROY, 62, Pondwicks Road, Luton. Dvr., R.A.S.C., att. 87th H.A.A. Regt., R.A. Died on active service, Habbaniya, Irak, December 2nd, 1941.

DAVENPORT, HAROLD, 5, Roman Road, Luton. L/Cpl., Royal Corps of Signals. Died of wounds, Burma, March, 1944.

DAVIES, EDWARD WHELAN, 50, Naseby Road, Luton. Sgt., R.A.F. Killed on operations over Paris, December 12th, 1944.

DAVIES, HENRY GEORGE, 88, Chapel Street, Luton. Gnr., Light A.A. Batty., R.A. Died as prisoner of Japanese, Singapore, March 5th, 1943.

DAVIES, REGINALD THOMAS, 53, Windmill Road, Luton. Gnr., 79th (Scottish Horse) Med. Regt., R.A. Died of wounds, January 20th, 1944.

DAVIS, CLIFFORD FRANCIS CHARLES, 38, Belmont Road, Luton. F/Sgt. Engr., R.A.F. Killed on operations, Nuremberg, March 31st, 1944; buried at Schweinfurt.

DAY, ALFRED, formerly of Claremont Road, Luton. F/O., R.A.F. Missing, presumed killed, in operations over Stettin, Germany, January 5th-6th, 1944.

DE GRENIER-SMITH, ELVIN HENRY, 110, Oakley Road, Luton. Able Seaman, Merchant Navy. Lost at sea, June 29th, 1941.

DEAN, ALFRED JAMES, 12, Warren Road, Luton. Killed by enemy action at Vauxhall Motors, Ltd., Luton, August 30th, 1940.

DEARMAN, DERICK ROY, D.F.C., 93, Putteridge Road, Luton. P/Officer, R.A.F. Killed on operations, Paris, April 21st, 1944.

DENTON, AUBREY RONALD, 55, Tavistock Street, Luton. Gnr., 148th Field Regt., R.A. Died as prisoner of Japanese, Torsao, Siam, July 6th, 1943.

DENTON, JAMES, 7, Argyll Avenue, Luton. Tpr., 4th Reconnaissance Regt., R.A.C. Died of wounds, Italy, July 13th, 1944.

DEPLEDGE, DENNIS SYDNEY, 77, Roman Road, Luton. Petty Officer, R.N. Killed in action and buried at sea in Gibraltar Bay, January 30th, 1943.

DEWAR, JACK, 45, Talbot Road, Luton. Sgt., R.A.F. Killed on active service March 13th, 1941.

DICKENS, CHARLES FREDERICK, 51, Chase Street, Luton. Gnr., R.A. Killed in action at sea, off Greece, April 28th-29th, 1941.

DIGGINES, ALBERT E., 84, Pondwicks Road, Luton. Cpl., 2nd K.R.R.C. Killed in action, Western Front, March, 1945.

DILLINGHAM, HORACE CHARLES, 52, Chandos Road, Luton. P/Officer, R.A.F. Killed on operations over Menden, Germany, July 4th, 1943.

DIMMOCK, LESLIE CHARLES, 10, Bury Park Road, Luton. Pte., Bedfs. and Herts. Regt. Died on active service, India, May 20th, 1942.

DIXON, ERIC C., 37, Clifton Road, Luton. Dvr., R.E. Missing, presumed killed by enemy bombing, Alexandra Hospital, Singapore, February, 1942.

DIXON, MAURICE, 37, Clifton Road, Luton. Killed in action at Tobruk.

DOBBS, GEORGE, 22, Beaumont Road, Luton. S/Sergt., R.E.M.E. Died in Middle East, May 17th, 1944. Buried at Tel-el-Kebir.

DRAKE, ANTHONY GERARD, 88, Hartley Road, Luton. Gunner, R.A. Died from injuries on active service, July 4th, 1941.

DRAPER, ALEC VERNON, 31, Grange Avenue, Luton. Driver, Royal Corps of Signals. Killed in action, El Alamein, August 31st, 1942.

DRAPER, CHARLES WALTER, 31, Grange Avenue, Luton. Tpr., Queen's Bays. Killed in action, France, May 27th, 1940.

DUMPLETON, JOHN STEPHEN, 45, Waller Avenue, Luton. L/Cpl., 2nd Cambs. Regt. Killed in action, Malaya, January 26th, 1942.

DYNE, CHARLES FORBES, 63, Marlborough Road, Luton, and Santa Cruz, Teneriffe. Cpl., R.E. Died as prisoner of Japanese, in Japan, June, 1943.

EAMES, WILLIAM JOHN, 97, Kent Road, Luton. Pte., Bedfs. and Herts. Regt. Died after repatriation from German prison camp, March 6th, 1944.

EAST, DERRICK ARTHUR, 13, Roman Road, Luton. Radio-Telegraphist, R.N. Killed by enemy action, North Atlantic, November 1st, 1944.

EDWARDS, ROBERT, 23, Chesford Road, Luton. Pte. Died in Burma, May 22nd, 1944.

EDWARDS, RONALD, 308, Dunstable Road, Luton. Lieut., 1st Battn. Hampshire Regt. Killed in action, Catania, Sicily, July 26th, 1943.

EDWIN, EDWARD FRANCIS, 131, Turners Road, Luton. Sgt./Pilot, R.A.F. Died on active service, November 15th, 1940.

EICHEN, H., 48, Castle Street, Luton. Pte., 7th Suffolk Regt. Killed in action, Western Front, February 15th, 1945.

ELLIS, ALBERT WALTER, formerly 31, Roman Road, Luton. Pte. Killed in action, North Africa, April 13th, 1943.

ELLIS, JAMES, 68, Chester Avenue, Luton. Sgt., R.A.F. Died on active service, June, 1943.

ENDERBY, HAROLD FREDERICK, 187, Dunstable Road, Luton. Pte., Essex Regt. Died as prisoner in Germany, on or after October 26th, 1942.

ENGLEDOW, WILLIAM GEORGE VERDUN, 46, Maidenhall Road, Luton. Cpl., 1st Parachute Regt. Killed in action, N. Africa, February 3rd, 1943.

ENGLISH, ERIC DONALD, 56, Cowper Street, Luton. LAC. (M.T.), R.A.F. Lost at sea, November 7th, 1944.

EVANS, ANDREW, Vauxhall Motors, Ltd. Flt./Sgt., R.A.F. Killed on active service, March, 1941.

FAGE, RONALD THOMAS, 55, Rutland Crescent, Luton. Sgt., 15th Operational Training Unit. Killed on operations over Bremen, Germany; buried in Holland, June 25th, 1942.

FAIREY, LEONARD ROBERT, 63, St. Martin's Avenue, Luton. Killed by enemy action, at Vauxhall Motors, Ltd., Luton, August 30th, 1940.

FARMER, THOMAS CYRIL, 19, Bolton Road, Luton. Pte., Duke of Wellington's Regt. Killed in action, France, June 21st, 1944.

FARR, GEORGE HERBERT, 31, Argyll Avenue, Luton. Sigm., Royal Corps of Signals. Died on active service, Altrincham, June 16th, 1940.

FARR, Vernon Clifford, 31, Argyll Avenue, Luton. Sigm., Royal Corps of Signals. Died as prisoner of Japanese, Siam, August 10th, 1943.

FARROW, Frank, 42, Inkerman Street, Luton. Pte., 1st Suffolk Regt. Died of wounds, Falaise Gap, Normandy, August 23rd, 1944.

FAUNCH, William Gerald, 173, Cutenhoe Road, Luton. Died after being flown home from Italy, April 1st, 1946.

FELTON, Fernley George. Killed by enemy action, at Vauxhall Motors, Ltd., Luton, August 30th, 1940.

FENSOME, George, 39, Chobham Street, Luton. Fusilier, R.F. Killed in action, France, August 9th, 1944.

FENSOME, Harold Victor, 58, Lyndhurst Road, Luton. Gnr., R.A. Died as prisoner of Japanese.

FENSOME, John Stanley, 102, Bishopscote Road, Luton. Sgt., R.A.F. Killed on active service, January, 1941.

FICKEN, Norman J., 27, Windsor Street, Luton. LAC., R.A.F. Killed off Prince Edward Island, November, 1941.

FIELD, Reginald, 27, Elmore Road, Luton. Gnr., R.A. (Searchlights). Died on active service, September 14th, 1944.

FISH, William J., 10, Albion Road, Luton. Pte., R.A.S.C. Died in Calcutta Hospital following service in Burma, June, 1945.

FISHER, James Gordon, 3, Moat Lane, Luton. Stoker First Class, H.M.S. *Laforey*, R.N. Killed at sea, March 30th, 1944.

FISHER, Julia, 157, Park Street, Luton. Killed by enemy action, at Luton, September 22nd, 1940.

FLANIGAN, Michael Joseph, 65, Gardenia Avenue, Luton. Dvr., R.E. Field Company. Died as prisoner of Japanese, Changi Camp, May 16th, 1942.

FLINT, Ronald Renshaw, 2, Bishopscote Road, Luton. P/Officer, R.A.F. Killed on active service, March 24th, 1942.

FLITTON, Arthur, 14, Princess Street, Luton. Pte., R.A.M.C. Died in India, April 26th, 1942.

FLITTON, Derek Noel, 40, Stratford Road, Luton. Flt./Sgt., 408 Squadron, R.A.F. Killed on operations over enemy territory, June 8th, 1944.

FORSTER, Robert, 30, Tower Road, Luton. Tpr., 13th Reconnaisance Regt., R.A.C. Killed in action, Le Mesnil Patry, Nr. Caen, France, July 17th, 1945.

FOUNTAIN, Jack Heath, 68, Connaught Road, Luton. Cpl., R.A.F. (Dental Branch). Died on active service, October 26th, 1941.

FOWLER, Arthur, 19, Oakley Road, Luton. C.S.M., Pioneer Corps. Died in Germany after being injured by mine explosion, May 23rd, 1945.

FRANCIS, Ernest George, 41, Avondale Road, Luton. P/Officer, R.A.F. Killed on operations, Holland, April, 1944.

FRASER, Kenneth, 14, St. Margaret's Avenue, Luton. L/Seaman, R.N. Missing at sea, presumed killed, February 5th, 1944.

FREAK, Roy, 96, Oakley Road, Luton. Sergt., R.A.F. Killed on operations, April, 1942.

FREEMAN, Alfred George, 110a, Bury Park Road, Luton. Sgt., R.A. Died on active service in Germany, July 10th, 1945.

FREEMAN, George Edward, 1, Beaumont Road, Luton. Pte., 1st Battn. Suffolk Regt. Killed in action, Normandy, July 4th, 1944.

FRENCH, Douglas, 124, Leagrave Road, Luton. Cfm., R.E.M.E. Killed in action, Tunisia, April 6th, 1943.

FROST, Leslie Harold, 36, Broad Mead, Luton. Gnr., 148th Field Regt., R.A. Died as prisoner of Japanese, Singapore, November, 1943.

FULLER, Harry William, 74, Elmwood Crescent, Luton. F/Officer, 170th Squadron, R.A.F. Killed on operations, near Brunswick, Germany, March 7-8th, 1945.

FULLER, Jim, 18, Mansfield Road, Luton. Pte., R.A.S.C. Missing, presumed killed, Singapore, February, 1942.

GALE, Leonard, 79, Albert Road, Luton. Pte., Army Fire Service. Killed in action, Western Front, April, 1945.

GANDERTON, Robert, 47, St. Paul's Road, Luton. L/Stoker (Submarine), R.N.V.R. Killed on war service in H.M.S. *Oxley*, off Norway, September 10th, 1939.

GARRETT, Leonard V., 13, Guildford Street, Luton. Pte., Queen's Royal Regt. Killed in action, Italy, December 4th, 1943.

GATWARD, Derrick George, 110, Westmorland Avenue, Luton. LAC., R.A.F. Died on active service, New Delhi, August 11th, 1945.

GAYE, A. D., Lieut.-Col., formerly commanding 5th Battn. Bedfs. and Herts. Regt., Luton. Died, December 2nd, 1941.

GAUNTLETT, Glyndwr, 29, Weatherby Road, Luton. Gnr., R.A. Died as prisoner of Japanese, 1943.

GEE, Elizabeth Ethel, 159, Wellington Street, Luton. Killed by enemy action, at Luton, August 30th, 1940.

GEORGE, Ernest Walter, 33, Cambridge Street, Luton. Sigmn., Royal Corps of Signals. Died of wounds, North Africa, January 2nd, 1943.

GEORGE, Frederick, 36, Baker Street, Luton. Cpl., 5th Bedfs. and Herts. Regt. Died as prisoner of Japanese, Singapore, May 22nd, 1942.

GEORGE, W. F., 134, New Town Street, Luton. Cpl., Bedfs. and Herts. Regt. Died as prisoner of Japanese, Singapore, May 22nd, 1942.

GIBBONS, Samuel, 82, Church Street, Luton. Cpl., R.A.F. Died in hospital, India, March 18th, 1941.

GIBSON, William Maurice, 543, Hitchin Road, Luton. Sgt. Rear Gunner, R.A.F. Killed in action while returning from operations over Nuremberg, Germany, March 3rd, 1944.

GIDDINGS, Gertrude E., 17, William Street, Luton. Killed by enemy action, at Luton, October 14th, 1940.

GILBERT, Frederick Charles, 66, Wigmore Lane, Luton. Killed by enemy action, at Vauxhall Motors, Ltd., Luton, August 30th, 1940.

GILL, James V., 54, Weatherby Road, Luton. Sgt., 115th Squadron, R.A.F. Killed on operations, Germany, July 2nd, 1941.

GILLESPIE, James, 25, Rothesay Road, Luton. Killed in action, Belgium, June, 1940.

GILLETT, Arthur James, 100, Trinity Road, Luton. Pte., 5th Battn. Bedfs. and Herts. Regt. Died in hospital, Warwick, after return from Japanese prison camp, April 6th, 1946.

GLANCY, John Charles, 60, Bradgers Hill Road, Luton. Sgt., R.A.F. Missing, presumed killed, on operations, July 6-7th, 1944.

GLENISTER, Rex Brian, 58, Salisbury Road, Luton. Killed by enemy action, at Luton, November 6th, 1944.

GLOVER-PRICE, Leonard John, formerly of Luton. Sgt., R.A.F. Killed on operations, Dusseldorf, June, 1943.

GOODE, Leslie George, 77, Leagrave Road, Luton. Pte., 5th Battn. Bedfs. and Herts. Regt. Died as prisoner of Japanese, Malaya, August, 1943.

GOODMAN, Jack Lionel, 25, Tower Road, Luton. Able Seaman, R.N. Lost at sea, December 11th, 1944.

GOODWIN, John Anthony, 270, Old Bedford Road, Luton. Paymaster Sub-Lieut., R.N.V.R. Died on active service, Bombay, November, 1940.

GOSLING, Paul John Betts, 6, Austin Road, Luton. Tpr., 13/18th Royal Hussars, R.A.C. Killed in action, Bray et Lu, France, August 29th, 1944.

GRAVES, Cyril, C. C., 161, High Town Road, Luton. Yeoman of Signals, R.N. Lost with H.M.S. *Fleur-de-Lys*, October 14th, 1941.

GRAVES, Thomas Allan, 26, Bailey Street, Luton. Tpr., 7th Royal Tank Regt., R.A.C. Died on active service, October 25th, 1943.

GRAY, Victor, 191, Runley Road, Luton. Able Seaman Gnr., R.N. Lost in action at sea, June 19th, 1944.

GREEN, ALBERT EDWARD. Killed by enemy action, at Vauxhall Motors, Ltd., Luton, August 30th, 1940.

GREENWOOD, G. E., 124, Argyll Avenue, Luton. Sgt. (Flt./Engr.), R.A.F. Killed on operations over Berlin, January 27-28th, 1943.

GREGORY, HARRY GOODE, 58, Old Bedford Road, Luton. Killed by enemy action, at Luton, October 14th, 1940.

GRESTY, WILLIAM JOHN, 157, Connaught Road, Luton. Killed by enemy action, at Vauxhall Motors, Ltd., Luton, August 30th, 1940.

GRIGG, GEORGE STANLEY, 20, Rothesay Road, Luton. L/Sgt., R.A. Died of wounds, Far East, February 14th, 1942.

GROTRIAN, CHARLES HERBERT BRENT. Major, R.A., formerly commanding 420th Field Battery, R.A., Luton. Killed in action, Burma, May, 1944.

GUNN, ARTHUR ERNEST, 9, Mount Pleasant Road, Luton. Sgt., R.A. Killed in action, France, June 25th, 1944.

GUY, JENNIE, 45, Seymour Road, Luton. Killed by enemy action, at Luton, August 30th, 1940.

HACKSLEY, HERBERT HORACE, 18, Bailey Street, Luton, and Oxford. LAC., R.A.F. Died on active service, Kansas City, U.S.A., August 31st, 1942.

HADAWAY, NORMAN JACK, 38, Ryecroft Way, Stopsley, Luton. Pte., Bedfs. and Herts. Regt. Died, December 30th, 1939.

HALES, SIDNEY JAMES, 56, Cutenhoe Road, Luton. Killed by enemy action, at Vauxhall Motors, Ltd., Luton, August 30th, 1940.

HALFPENNY, ARTHUR CHARLES, 13, Vicarage Street, Luton. Pte., R. West Kent Regt. Killed in action, El Alamein, September 3rd, 1942.

HALL, JOHN GEORGE, 168, Wellington Street, Luton. Lieut., Pioneer Corps. Killed in action, Western Europe, January 27th, 1945.

HALSEY, RONALD WILLIAM, 63, Russell Rise, Luton. Able Seaman, R.N. Drowned while on active service, November, 1942.

HANCOCK, CHARLES, 38, River Way, Luton. Killed by enemy action, at Luton, November 6th, 1944.

HARDEN, MICHAEL LANGLEY, 135, New Bedford Road, Luton. Sub-Lt. (A), Fleet Air Arm. Killed on active service, October, 1942.

HARDING, HAROLD RONALD, 35, Brooms Road, Luton. Pte., Queen's Royal Regt. Killed in action, El Alamein, October 24th, 1942.

HARP, ALBERT FRANK EDWIN, 2, Farley Avenue, Luton. Cpl., 3rd Battn. Grenadier Guards. Killed on active service, and buried at Cesena, Italy, April 15th, 1945.

HARPER, JACK ABRAHAM, 56, Grove Road, Luton. Killed by enemy action, at Vauxhall Motors, Ltd., Luton, August 30th, 1940.

HARRIS, Ex-Sgt. THOMAS JAMES, D.C.M., 62, Dane Road, Luton. Killed by enemy action, at Vauxhall Motors, Ltd., Luton, August 30th, 1940.

HARRISON, CHRISTOPHER BASIL, 236, Old Bedford Road, Luton. Sgt./Pilot, R.A.F. Killed in action, Brest, September 30th, 1941.

HARRISON, GEORGE, 3, Browning Road, Luton. Pte., 1/4th Battn. Essex Regt. Killed in action, Forli-Rimini, Italy, November 8th, 1944.

HARROWER, ALEX AITKEN, 244, Beechwood Road, Luton. Killed by enemy action, at Vauxhall Motors, Ltd., Luton, August 30th, 1940.

HART, ERNEST HERBERT, 77, Butlin Road, Luton. Cpl., 5th Battn. Suffolk Regt. Died as prisoner of the Japanese, August 1st, 1943.

HARTUP, ARTHUR, 157, Park Street, Luton. Killed by enemy action, at Luton, September 22nd, 1940.

HARTUP, FLORENCE EMILY, 157, Park Street, Luton. Killed by enemy action, at Luton, September 22nd, 1940.

HASWELL, JAMES, 69, Turners Road, Luton. Killed by enemy action, at Luton, November 16th, 1940.

HATHAWAY, ARTHUR WILLIAM, 46, St. Lawrence's Avenue, Luton. Sgt.-Flt. Engineer, R.A.F., Bomber Command. Missing, presumed killed, on operations, Nuremberg, March 16-17th, 1945.

HATTON, Ronald Charles, 134, Leagrave Road, Luton. L Cpl., R.E. Lost at sea while prisoner of Japanese, September 12th, 1944.

HAUGHTON, Derek Basil, 1, Cannon Lane, Stopsley, Luton. Pte., 5th Battn. Bedfs. and Herts. Regt. Died as prisoner of Japanese, No. 2 Camp, Siam, August 13th, 1943.

HAWKES, Arthur Bert, 146, North Street, Luton. Sgt., R.A.S.C. Killed by enemy action, Casalbordino, Italy, November 24th, 1943.

HAWKES, Tom Bailey, 21, Shirley Road, Luton. Sgt., R.A.F. Killed in action, December 17th, 1943.

HAWKINS, Cyril Kenneth, 80, Maple Road, Luton. Able Seaman, R.N. Lost at sea, Simonstown, South Africa, on V-J Day, August 15th, 1945.

HAWKINS, Frederick Charles, 78, Icknield Road, Luton. P Officer, R.A.F. Killed on operations over Germany, October 7th, 1944.

HAWTHORN, John, 18, Hartley Road, Luton. L/Cpl., Coldstream Guards. Missing, later reported killed, Dunkirk, 1940.

HAYLEY, Douglas Andrew Ross, 7, Liscomb Road, Dunstable, and formerly of Luton. Sgt., R.A.F. Killed by enemy action, Singapore, February 12th, 1942.

HAYWARD, Alfred Harold, 64, Westbourne Road, Luton. Sgt., R.E.M.E. Died on active service, Central Mediterranean Forces, 1944.

HAYWARD, Edward, 10, Brache Street, Luton. Pte., Sussex Regt. Died as prisoner of war, Germany.

HEARN, Charles Edmund, 32, Wellington Street, Luton. Gdsm., Grenadier Guards. Killed in action, Italy, January 22nd, 1944.

HEASLEY, Alexander, 45, Farley Avenue, Luton. S/Sgt., R. Scots Fusiliers. Died of wounds, Italy, December 17th, 1943 ; buried at Sangro River Cemetery.

HIBBERT, Keith, 144, Argyll Avenue, Luton. Flt./Sgt., Pathfinder Force, R.A.F. Missing, presumed killed, over Kiel, Germany, July 24th, 1944.

HIGGINS, Albert Marshall, 58, Cavendish Road, Luton. Tpr., 59th Training Regt., R.A.C. Died on active service, October 19th, 1941.

HIGGINS, A. R., 40, South Road, Luton. Sgt., Bedfs. and Herts. Regt. Died on active service, July, 1942.

HIGGINS, Walter, 40, South Road, Luton. O/Seaman, R.N. Missing on Convoy duties, October, 1942.

HILL, Harold Denis, 120, Oak Road, Luton. Pte., 5th Battn. Wiltshire Regt. Killed in action, Mont Pincon, France, August 7th, 1944.

HILL, Lewis Albert, 452, Hitchin Road, Luton. Flt./Sgt., R.A.F. Killed on active service, October 18th, 1941.

HILL, Richard Dockrill, 70, Boyle Street, Luton. Lieut., Herts. Regt. Killed in action, Italy, September 29th, 1944.

HILLMAN, William Major, of Tredegar, and 10, Fitzroy Avenue, Luton. Gnr., 420th Field Battery, R.A. Died as prisoner of Japanese, Siam, 1943.

HINDS, William Victor, 9, Edward Street, Luton. W/Officer, R.A.F. Missing, presumed killed, S.E. Asia, April, 1942.

HOBBS, Frederick William, 76, Russell Rise, Luton. Cpl., H.Q. Staff, R.A.F. Died as prisoner of Japanese, Sandakan Camp, Borneo, May 23rd, 1945.

HOLLINSHEAD, Sidney, 54, St. Ethelbert's Avenue, Luton. Bdr., 51st Light A.A. Regt., R.A. Killed in action, Italy, July 13th, 1944.

HOLMES, Rex Alec, formerly of Stuart Street, Luton. 2/Lt., 4th Battn. Suffolk Regt. Killed in action, Singapore, February 14th, 1942.

HOLT, Herbert Thomas, 11, East Avenue, Luton. O/Seaman, R.N., H.M.S. *Barham*. Lost at sea, Mediterranean, November 25th, 1942.

HOLTON, Ralph, 43, Newcombe Road, Luton. Driver, R.A.S.C. Died on active service, Italy, July 16th, 1945.

HORN, Jack, 34, Ivy Road, Luton. Gunner, att. Yorks and Lancs. Regt. Killed in action, Burma, July 3rd, 1944.

HORTON, John William, 13, Welbeck Road, Luton. Gnr., R.A. Killed in action.

HOSKINS, Trevor, 398, Dunstable Road, Luton. Midshipman, R.N., H.M.S. *Waterwitch*. Died on active service, February, 1946.

HOUGH, Iris Olive, 176, Selbourne Road, Luton. Killed by enemy action, at Vauxhall Motors, Ltd., Luton, August 30th, 1940.

HOUGHTON, Albert E., 88, Albert Road, Luton. Pte., Cambs. Regt. Lost at sea as prisoner of Japanese.

HOUGHTON, Wilfred, 43, Saxon Road, Luton. Tpr., R.A.C. Killed in action, Italy, May 22nd, 1944.

HOUSDEN, Phyllis, 24, Applecroft Road, Luton. Pte., A.T.S. Died on active service, July 14th, 1945.

HOUSLEY, Constance Mary, of Doncaster. Killed by enemy action, at Luton, September 5th, 1942.

HOWARTH, James, 15, Newcombe Road, Luton. Sgt. Killed on active service, November, 1940.

HOWELLS, Emrys George, 43, Arundel Road, Luton. Cpl., 110th Squadron, R.A.F. Killed in action, Wattisham, Suffolk, November 1st, 1940.

HUBBLE, James Claude, 1, Windmill Road, Luton. P/Officer, R.A.F. Died on active service, Tern Hill, Shropshire, October 12th, 1944.

HUGHES, John Eynon Wynne, 56, Seymour Road, Luton. Died of wounds caused by enemy action, at Luton, August 30th, 1940.

HUME, Frederick Calvin, 85, Somerset Avenue, Luton. Pte., 6th Battn. Bedfs. and Herts. Regt. Died on active service, Indian theatre of war, December 24th, 1942.

HUMFREY, Robert Albert, 107, Neville Road, Luton. Gnr., R.A. Lost at sea while prisoner of Japanese, September 12th, 1944.

HUNT, Arthur George, 39, Wenlock Street, Luton. B.Q.M.S., 148th Field Regt., R.A. Died as prisoner of Japanese, July 3rd, 1943.

HURVID, Clifford W., 86, Highbury Road, Luton. Fusilier, 9th Battn. R.F. Died of wounds, Salerno, Italy, September 9th, 1943.

HUTCHINS, John, 26, Midland Road, Luton. Killed by enemy action, at Luton, September 5th, 1942.

HYNE, William Taylor, 25, Alexandra Avenue, Luton. Assistant C.E. to Admiralty at Simonstown, South Africa. Lost at sea by enemy action en route Liverpool-Cape Town, December 6th-7th, 1942.

IMPEY, Ronald Cecil. Killed by enemy action, at Vauxhall Motors, Ltd., Luton, August 30th, 1940.

INGREY, William Edward, 94, Argyll Avenue, Luton. Cpl., Oxf. and Bucks. L.I. Killed in action, Normandy, August 13th, 1944.

IRESON, Frank Lewis Thomas, 63, Ferndale Road, Luton. Sgt., R.A.F. Killed on operations, Holland, July 25th, 1941.

ISAAC, Ronald, 190, Leagrave Road, Luton. C.S.M., 249th Field Coy., R.E. (Airborne). Died of wounds, Normandy, June 10th, 1944.

ISAACS, William Henry, 85, Whitefield Road, Sundon, and Felt & Fibre Co., Ltd., Luton. Gnr., R.A. Died as prisoner of Japanese, Tarsao, Siam, March 17th, 1944.

JACKSON, Francis Charles, D.F.M., 23, Felstead Way, Luton. Sgt./Flt. Eng., R.A.F. Killed on active service, December, 1942.

JACKSON, Leslie Horace, 806, Dunstable Road, Luton. Killed by enemy action, at Vauxhall Motors, Ltd., Luton, August 30th, 1940.

JACKSON, William, 97, Blundell Road, Luton. Killed in action, May 22nd, 1940.

JAMES, Dennis Nelson, 13, Stratford Road, Luton. Stoker First Class, R.N. Killed in action at sea, October 1st, 1944.

JAMES, William Douglas, 37, Saxon Road, Luton. Flt./Sgt., 61 Squadron, R.A.F. Killed in action in raid on Magdeburg, Germany, January 21st, 1944.

JANES, CLIFFORD LLOYD BROWN, " Green Hills," New Bedford Road, Luton. Sgt./Pilot, R.A.F.   Killed in action, Middle East, 1943.

JANES, FREDERICK WILLIAM, 17, Pondwicks Road, Luton.   P/Officer, R.A.F., att. R.C.A.F.   Killed on air operations, believed at Ahrenfelde, near Berlin, February 14th-15th, 1944.

JARVIS, FRANK, 57, Langley Street, Luton.   Sgt.   Died in India, August, 1943.

JEFFERISS, JAMES LESLIE, 34, Lyndhurst Road, Luton.   AC2, R.A.F.   Died following road accident, 96th General Hospital, North Africa, September 13th, 1943.

JEFFS, KENNETH FRANK, 13, Lincoln Road, Luton.   Lieut., R. Norfolk Regt. Killed in action, Malaya, February, 1942.

JEFFS, PHILIP JOHN, 13, Lincoln Road, Luton.   Sgt./Flt. Eng., R.A.F.   Killed on air operations, Germany, May 25th, 1944.

JENKINS, EDWARD BERTRAM DOUGLAS, 68, Hampton Road, Luton.   Sgt./Pilot., R.A.F.   Killed on active service, December 28th, 1940.

JENNINGS, E. RALPH, 38, Sundridge Avenue, Luton.   Pte., Suffolk Regt. Died in Burma, July 16th, 1944.

JESTY, RAYMOND GEORGE, 98, Richmond Hill, Luton.   W/Officer, R.A.F. Killed on active service, August 27th, 1943.

JONES, ANTHONY, 65, Ivy Road, Luton.   Pte., Suffolk Regt.   Died of wounds, Middle East, December 9th, 1941.

JONES, ELIZABETH, 79, Biscot Road, Luton.   Killed by enemy action, at Luton, November 6th, 1944.

JONES, H. A. M., 15, Brooms Road, Luton.   Pte., South Wales Borderers. Died of wounds, Indian theatre of war, August 10th, 1944.

JONES, HENRY, 63, Chester Avenue, Luton.   Pte., 2nd Border Regt.   Died of wounds, Burma, February 3rd, 1945.

JONES, JAMES JULIUS, 31, Burr Street, Luton.   Pte., Queen's Royal Regt.   Killed in action, Italy, September 28th, 1944.

JONES, JOHN FLOOD, 67, Clarendon Road, Luton.   L/Seaman, R.N.R., i/c naval guns, s.s. *Beaverbrook*, Merchant Navy.   Missing, presumed killed, April 1st, 1941, Battle of the Atlantic.

JONES, ROBERT J., 15, Brooms Road, Luton, 6th Battn. South Wales Borderers. Died of wounds, Burma, March 10th, 1944.

KAY, GEORGE, 100, Alder Crescent, Luton.   Sgt., 1st Airborne Reconnaissance Squadron, R.A.C.   Killed on active service, Norway, June 3rd, 1945.

KEAST, STANLEY GEORGE, 2, Lincoln Road, Luton.   L/Sgt., 2nd Battn. Bedfs. and Herts. Regt.   Killed in action, Italy, June 30th, 1944.

KEATES, CHARLES FRANCIS, 3, Warwick Road, Luton.   LAC., R.A.F.   Died on active service, Persia, December 14th, 1942.

KEECH, WILLIAM FREDERICK.   Killed by enemy action, at Vauxhall Motors, Ltd., Luton, August 30th, 1940.

KEELY, MARY JULIA, 24, Avondale Road, Luton.   Killed by enemy action, at Luton, November 4th, 1940.

KEEN, JOYCE, 26, Shirley Road, Luton.   Killed by enemy action, at Luton, October 14th, 1940.

KEMP, SIDNEY, 147, High Town Road, Luton.   Pte., Durham L.I.   Killed in action, N.W. Europe, August 9th, 1944.

KENT, LESLIE GEORGE, 3, Gardenia Avenue, Luton.   Gnr., R.A.   Died on active service, April, 1940.

KENYON, REDVERS, 16, Milton Road, Luton.   Sgt. A.G., 50th Squadron, R.A.F.   Lost on operations over Norway, October 28th-29th, 1944.

KIGHTLEY, ERNEST JOHN, 113, Boyle Street, Luton.   Cpl., 6th Battn. R. Welch Fusiliers.   Killed in action, Hertogenbosch, Holland, October 24th, 1944.

KIGHTLEY, HERBERT, 118, Dunstable Road, Luton.   LAC Armourer, R.A.F. Died on service, March 19th, 1946.

KILBY, JOHN ANDREW, 64, Crawley Green Road, Luton.   Killed by enemy action, at Vauxhall Motors, Ltd., Luton, August 30th, 1940.

KILBY, JOHN CHARLES, 85, Clarendon Road, Luton.   Sgt./Pilot, R.A.F.   Killed on active service, Addo, nr. Port Elizabeth, S. Africa, January 14th, 1945.

KILBY, PERCY EWART, 3, Stockwood Crescent, Luton.   Sick Berth Attendant, Motor Rescue Launch, R.N.   Lost at sea on active service off Isle of Lewis, Hebrides, February 7th, 1943.

KIMBER, WALTER DAUNT, Bishops Stortford, and London Road, Luton. Sgt./Pilot, R.A.F.   Killed on active service, February, 1941.

KING, ALEC PERCY, 80, Wenlock Street, Luton.   Flt./Sgt., 274 Squadron, R.A.F. Killed on active service, August 26th, 1943.

KING, CECIL ROBERT, 73, Clarendon Road, Luton.   R.A.M.C.   Died after return from B.A.O.R., February 10th, 1946.

KING, CHARLES HENRY.   Killed by enemy action, at Vauxhall Motors, Ltd., Luton, August 30th, 1940.

KING, CHARLES WILLIAM, 30, Church Street, Luton.   Sgt., 7th Battn. Hampshire Regt.   Killed in action, Holland, September 25th, 1944.

KING, ROBERT JOSEPH, 18, Lincoln Road, Luton.   Gunner, Field Regt., R.A. Killed on active service, July 31st, 1941.

KING, SIDNEY, 152, Selbourne Road, Luton.   L/Bdr., R.A.   Killed after escaping from German prison camp near Dresden, May 11th, 1945.

KINGHAM, ERNEST ARTHUR, Gladstone Avenue, Luton.   P/Officer, R.A.F Killed on operations over enemy-occupied territory, June, 1944.

KINGSNORTH, FRANK WILLIAM, 28, Pomfret Avenue, Luton.   L/Sgt., Anti-Tank Regt., R.A.   Lost at sea while prisoner of Japanese, December 9th, 1944.

KNOWLES, IAN, 3, Ludlow Avenue, Luton.   Rfm., R. Inniskilling Fusiliers. Killed on active service, May, 1944.

LACEY, ALEXANDER WILLIAM, 8, Lansdowne Road, Luton.   F/Lt., R.A.F. Killed on active service, December 21st, 1941.

LACEY, RALPH, 157, Graham Gardens, Luton.   Killed by enemy action, at Vauxhall Motors, Ltd., Luton, August 30th, 1940.

LAMB, CYRIL EDWARD, 6, Latimer Road, Luton.   Spr., R.E.   Died as prisoner of Japanese, Siam, June 21st, 1943.

LAND, HERBERT JOHN, 74, Wenlock Street, Luton.   Pte., 5th Battn. R. Norfolk Regt.   Killed in action, Singapore, February 14th, 1942.

LANE, RONALD ERNEST, 230, Marsh Road, Luton.   Spr., R.E.   Died of wounds, Anzio Beach Head, Italy, February 26th, 1944.

LANG, JACK, 1, Latimer Road, Luton.   Pte., 6th Airborne Division (Parachutist). Died on active service, Palestine, December 29th, 1945.

LARGE, HORACE WILLIAM, 25, Dorset Street, Luton.   Dvr., R.A.S.C.   Died on active service, Middle East, May 31st, 1942.

LARGE, LESLIE WILLIAM, 88, Stapleford Road, Luton.   First Class Stoker, R.N. Killed by enemy action, Northern Waters, November 13th, 1944.

LAW, HAROLD JOHN, 8, Kent Road, Luton.   L/Sgt., 419th Batty. 148th Field Regt., R.A.   Lost at sea as prisoner of Japanese, September 12th, 1944.

LAWRENCE, DEREK, 10, Northview Road, Luton.   AC., R.A.F.   Died at sea, April, 1941.

LAWRENCE, JAMES, 246, Biscot Road, Luton.   L/Bdr., R.A.   Died as prisoner of Japanese, Siam, September 6th, 1943.

LAZELL, OLIVER JOHN, 61, Solway Road, Luton.   Killed by enemy action, at Luton, August 30th, 1940.

LEMMON, DOUGLAS JAMES WILLIAM, 74, Ferndale Road, Luton.   Pte., 5th Battn. Bedfs. and Herts. Regt.   Lost at sea as prisoner of Japanese, September 21st, 1944.

LETTING, BERNARD, 23, Fitzroy Avenue, Luton.   137 Squadron, R.A.F.   Died on active service off Kastrup, Copenhagen, June 14th, 1945.

LEWIS, Ivor Rees, 36, Tennyson Road, Luton. P/Officer, R.A.F. Killed on operations over the Baltic, August, 1943.

LITTLE, John Frederick, 427, Dunstable Road, Luton. W/Officer-Pilot, R.A.F. Presumed killed on operations over Dusseldorf, Germany, August 29th, 1943.

LOCKEY, Roy Cecil Sale, 3, Finsbury Road, Luton. L/Cpl., Suffolk Regt. Killed in Burma, June, 1944.

LONG, Ronald, 14, Adelaide Street, Luton. Gnr., R.A. Presumed died of wounds, Singapore, February, 1942.

LONG, Sidney James, 49, Whitecroft Road, Luton. Died as result of enemy action at Luton, August 31st, 1940.

LOVELOCK, Maurice, 114, Bishopscote Road, Luton. Pte., 1st Battn. Worcester Regt. Killed in action, Cleve, Germany, February 17th, 1945.

LUBBOCK, Cecil Alfred, 437, Dunstable Road, Luton. Tpr., 3rd Dragoon Guards, R.A.C. Killed in action, Burma, May 8th, 1944.

LUSTY, Arthur David, 66, St. Ethelbert's Avenue, Luton. Cpl., 1/7th Queen's Royal Regt. Killed in action, El Alamein, October 24th, 1942.

McALLISTER, James, 8, Bolton Road, Luton. Gnr., R.A. Died of wounds, Singapore, February 15th, 1942.

McCAULEY, Ronald James, 110, Kingsway, Luton. AC.2, 656 Squadron, R.A.F. Killed on active service, Ramrae Island, Burma, January 25th, 1944.

McCRACKEN, James, 23, Whitefield Avenue, Sundon, and Adamant Engineering Co., Ltd., Luton. L/Bdr., R.A. Died as prisoner of Japanese, Kanburi, Siam, December 12th, 1943.

McDADE, Edward Albert, 59, St. Peter's Road, Luton. Cpl., R.E. Died as prisoner of Japanese, Siam, January 21st, 1944.

McGEORGE, John Sydney, 52, Montrose Avenue, Luton. Driver, R.A.S.C., att. R.A. Killed by Allied bombing while war prisoner, Stalag XVIIIa, Wolfsberg, Austria, December 18th, 1944.

McMANUS, Patrick, 77, Church Street, Luton. Sgt., R.E. Died on active service, Middle East, November, 1943.

MANLEY, Ralph, 35, Wellington Street, Luton. Cfm., R.E.M.E. Died of wounds, Germany, April 30th, 1945.

MANN, Richard Stephen, 11, Farley Avenue, Luton. Killed by enemy action, at Vauxhall Motors, Ltd., Luton, August 30th, 1940.

MANT, Kenneth Victor, 102, Westmorland Avenue, Luton. Sgt. W/O., R.A.F. Missing on operations, May 12th-13th, 1944.

MARSHALL, Frederick E. W., 39, Corncastle Road, Luton. Driver, R.E. Killed in action, Italy, October 26th, 1943.

MARSHALL, William Charles, 65, Fountains Road, Luton. Sgt. W/Op. A.G., 18th Squadron, R.A.F. Missing on operations, Malta, December 26th, 1941.

MATHESON, David Black, 218, Ashcroft Road, Luton. Pte., R.A.S.C. Lost at sea with the *Ceramic*, Atlantic, December 6th, 1942.

MAUGHAN, John, 10, Roman Road, Luton. Gnr., R.A. Killed in action, Italy, October 22nd, 1944.

MEAD, Ernest, Luton. Gnr., R.A. Died on active service, January 31st, 1945.

MEDCRAFT, Cyril, 110, Lea Road, Luton. Pte., 1/4th K.O.Y.L.I. Killed in action, N.W. Europe, June 25th, 1944.

MELDRUM, Bernard Richard, "Dawnaday," Taunton Avenue, Luton. Cpl., R.A.S.C., att. 16/2nd H.A.A. Batty. R.A. Missing, presumed killed, Greece, April 28th, 1941.

MERCER, John, 5, Seymour Road, Luton. L/Cpl. Killed in action, Burma, February 2nd, 1945.

MERCER, Wilfred, 89, Summerfield Road, Luton. Pte., Suffolk Regt. Died as prisoner of Japanese, Burma, September, 1943.

MILES, Henry William, 7, Gloucester Road, Luton. Killed by enemy action, at Luton, August 30th, 1940.

MITCHELL, Samuel, 75, Kent Road, Luton. Bedfs. and Herts. Regt. Died on active service in Germany.

MITCHENER, Charles, "Westlea," Walcot Avenue, Luton. F/Officer, R.A.F. Missing, presumed killed, in operations over Hamburg, July 26th-27th, 1942.

MOCK, Charles Albert, 28, Tower Road, Luton. Leading Telegraphist, R.N. Lost at sea as prisoner of the Japanese, June 26th, 1944.

MOORE, Norman James, 27, Court Road, Luton. Killed by enemy action, at Luton, November 6th, 1944.

MORGAN, William, 7, Dunstable Close, Luton. Stoker, 2nd Class, R.N., H.M. Corvette *Bluebell*. Lost at sea, homeward bound from Russia, February 17th, 1945.

MORRIS, Reginald Francis, 67, Hazelbury Crescent, Luton. Chief Petty Officer, R.N. Killed in action, Far East, December, 1942.

MORRISON, Margaret Jean, 93, Harcourt Street, Luton. Killed by enemy action, at Luton, August 30th, 1940.

MORSLEY, Richard William, Birmingham, and formerly Crescent Rise, Luton. Killed by enemy action, April, 1941.

MORTLOCK, Carole Rosemary, 81, Biscot Road, Luton. Killed by enemy action, at Luton, November 6th, 1944.

MOSS, Reginald Ernest, 86, Runley Road, Luton. L/Cpl., R.E.M.E. Killed in action, Burma, February 11th, 1944.

MOSS, Ronald Edward, 85, Langley Street, Luton. Pte. Killed in action, Italy, September 17th, 1944.

NELSON, Charles Richard, 42, Selbourne Road, Luton. Pte., Suffolk Regt. Died as prisoner of Japanese, Samoa, December 18th, 1942.

NEWTON, George Shepherd, 52, Hampton Road, Luton. Cpl., Seaforth Highlanders. Missing, believed killed, place and date unknown, 1940.

NIELAND, James Henry, 38, Bolton Road, Luton. Killed by enemy action, at Vauxhall Motors, Ltd., Luton, August 30th, 1940.

NORMAN, Roy, 74, Stratford Road, Luton. Gnr.-D.R., 419th Field Regt., R.A. Missing, presumed killed, Singapore, February 14th, 1942.

NORTHWOOD, Eric, 165, Dallow Road, Luton. Marine. Died on active service, June, 1942.

NORTHWOOD, R., 148, Milton Road, Luton. Sgt., R.A.F. Missing, presumed killed, July, 1941.

NUNN, Silas Henry, 42, Inkerman Street, Luton. Tpr., 1st Royal Tank Regt., R.A.C. Killed on active service, Ellon, France, July 12th, 1944.

O'BRIEN, Leonard David, Limbrick Hall, Harpenden, and B. Laporte, Ltd., Luton. Lt., Hertfordshire Regt. Died of wounds, N.W. Europe, September, 1944.

O'DELL, Edwin, 1, Burrs Passage, Langley Street, Luton. L/Sgt., Royal Corps of Signals. Killed in action, Sicily, July 17th, 1943.

O'FLAHERTY, Derrick Edward, 13, Luton Road, Cockernhoe, Luton Boys' Club, and G. F. Farr, Collingdon Street, Luton. Sgt./Pilot, R.A.F. Killed on active service, October 23rd, 1940.

O'NEILL, George Edward, 141, Chester Avenue, Luton. Sgt. W/Op., R.A.F. Missing, presumed killed, on operations, Dommartin, France, May 3rd-4th, 1944.

OAKLEY, Richard Hines, 473, Dunstable Road, Luton. Sgt./Pilot, No. 1 Squadron, R.A.F. Killed on active service, Purdis Croft, near Felixstowe, October 21st, 1941.

ODELL, Dennis Walter, 15, Jubilee Street, Luton. Sgt. A/G. W/Op., 37th Squadron, R.A.F. Killed in action, Orvieto, Italy, June 7th, 1944.

OGGLESBY, Frederick, 11, Stuart Street, Luton. L/Cpl., Wiltshire Regt. Died of wounds received in Germany, February 18th, 1945.

OLIVER, Dorothy Winifred, Hexton and Leagrave Post Office. First Class Airwoman, W.A.A.F. Accidentally killed, Wellington, Shropshire, August 23rd, 1942.

ORCHARD, DENNIS MALCOLM, 45, Trent Road, Luton. Killed by enemy action, at Vauxhall Motors, Ltd., Luton, August 30th, 1940.

ORDISH, CHARLES BRIAN, D.F.C., 39, Ludlow Avenue. F/Lieut., R.A.F. Killed on operations, December, 1943.

OSBORNE, FREDERICK WILLIAM, 26, Rothesay Road, Luton. Pte., East Yorks. Regt. Killed in action, Tunisia, April 6th, 1943.

OWEN, BRINLEY D., 173, Toddington Road, Luton. Gnr., 419th Field Battery, R.A. Lost at sea as prisoner of Japanese, September 12th, 1944.

OWEN, STANLEY JAMES, 418, Leagrave Road, Luton. Killed by enemy action in London, August 8th, 1944.

OWLES, AUBREY ERNEST, formerly of Luton, and late of 86, Poynters Road, Dunstable, and Vauxhall Motors, Ltd. Sgt./Pilot, R.A.F., 18th Squadron. Killed in air battle, August 31st, 1940.

PAGE, SYDNEY LEWIS, 5, Edward Street, Dunstable, and Vauxhall Motors, Ltd., Luton. Gnr., R.A. Died as prisoner of Japanese, Siam, April 13th, 1943.

PAIN, RONALD GEORGE, 38, Clevedon Road, Luton. Sgt., 35th Squadron Pathfinder Force, R.A.F. Missing, presumed killed, on operations over Kiel, Germany, August 26th-27th, 1944.

PAIN, STANLEY EDWARD, 38, Clevedon Road, Luton. Pte., 2/7th Queen's Royal Regt. Killed in action, Forli, Italy, September 27th, 1944.

PALMER, THOMAS SIDNEY, 51, Dudley Street, Luton. Air Mechanic, Fleet Air Arm. Lost with H.M.S. *Hermes*, Indian Ocean, April 9th, 1942.

PARKER, CHARLES O., 344, Beechwood Road, Luton. Gdsm., Grenadier Guards. Killed on active service, April 13th, 1945.

PARKER, EDWARD JOHN, 21, Boyle Street, Luton. Cpl., Corps of Military Police. Died as prisoner of Japanese, Siam, June 9th, 1943.

PARKER, KENNETH GEORGE, 484, Dunstable Road, Luton. Sgt./Pilot, R.A.F. Killed on active service, November, 1941.

PARR, HERBERT JOSEPH, 81, Saxon Road, Luton. Sgt., 279th Field Unit, R.E. Killed in action, Liessem, Holland, November 2nd, 1944.

PARROTT, ERIC HORACE, 58, The Avenue, Luton. S/Ldr., R.A.F. Missing from air operations, August, 1943.

PARSONS, FREDERICK WILLIAM, 150a, North Street, Luton. LAC., R.A.F. Died at sea while prisoner of Japanese, November 8th, 1944.

PATEMAN, VERA WINIFRED, 18, Midland Road, Luton. Killed by enemy action, at Luton, September 5th, 1942.

PAYNE, HAROLD VICTOR, 24, Beech Road, Luton. Spr., R.E. Killed at sea, Benghazi Harbour, December 28th, 1942.

PEACOCK, J., Beechwood Road, Luton. L/Cpl., R.A.C. Killed in action N. Africa, May, 1943.

PEARSON, W. L., 162, Marsh Road, Luton. Gnr., R.A. Died as prisoner of Japanese, Siam, 1944.

PEDDER, ROBERT EDWARD, 67, Ridgway Road, Luton. Flt./Sgt., R.A.F. Killed on operations, Germany, October 22nd, 1943.

PEPPER, HARVEY, London Road, Woburn, and Vauxhall Motors, Ltd., Luton. Pte., 2nd Battn. Bedfs. and Herts. Regt. Killed in action, Western Front, May 20th, 1940.

PERRY, EDWARD FRANCIS EDWIN, 17, Stockingstone Road, Luton. Sgt./Pilot, R.A.F. Killed on operations, November, 1940.

PERRY, SAMUEL, Breachwood Green and Percival Aircraft, Ltd., Luton. L.A.C., R.A.F. Killed on active service, Rangoon, November, 1945.

PHILLIPS, HERBERT LLEWELLYN, 13, Churchill Road, Luton. L.A.C., R.A.F. Killed on active service, Hadera, Palestine, January 17th, 1944.

PINNEY, DONALD FREDERICK, 139, Old Bedford Road, Luton. Air Mechanic, Fleet Air Arm. Killed on active service, January 14th, 1945.

PINNEY, GEORGE ROBERT, 34, St. Lawrence's Avenue, Luton. Pte., Suffolk Regt. Died as prisoner of Japanese, Chunkie, Siam, October 13th, 1943.

PITKIN, Archibald Henry, 159, Selbourne Road, Luton. Killed by enemy action, at Vauxhall Motors, Ltd., Luton, August 30th, 1940.

POLLARD, George Thomas, 112, Cowper Street, Luton. Gnr., 355/111th H.A.A. Regt., R.A. Killed on active service, Germany, November 29th, 1945.

POLLARD, Leslie Arthur, 29, St. Margaret's Avenue, Luton. Gnr., 148th Field Regt., R.A. Died as prisoner of Japanese, Siam, July 5th, 1943.

PORTER, Frederick Arthur, Swindon and Luton. Killed by enemy action, at Vauxhall Motors, Ltd., Luton, August 30th, 1940.

POTT, Ernest Charles, 22, Albion Road, Luton. Pte., R.A.O.C. Lost at sea while prisoner of Japanese, November 14th, 1942.

POULTON, Hubert William, 18, Kenilworth Road, Luton. Killed by enemy action, at Luton, September 25th, 1940.

POWELL, Edward Roy, 115, Marsh Road, Luton. Royal Marine, Landing Craft. Lost at sea, Walcheren Island, Holland, November 1st, 1944.

POWER, William Peter, 402, Dunstable Road, Luton. Gnr., R.A. Died as prisoner of Japanese, Batavia, September 1st, 1942.

PRATT, Arthur P., 18, Browning Road, Luton. Cpl., R.A.F. Died as prisoner of Japanese, Harrokoe Island, June 23rd, 1943.

PRATT, Walter William, 9, Windermere Crescent, Luton. Sgt.-Major, R.E.M.E. Killed on active service, Middle East, August, 1943.

PROCTOR, Richard George, 81, Blundell Road, Luton. Pte. Killed in action, Italy, April 7th, 1944.

PRUDAN, Noel, 7, Onslow Road, Leagrave, Luton. 1st Manchester Regt. Died on active service, August 10th, 1941.

PRUDAN, Raymond, 7, Onslow Road, Leagrave, Luton. Pte., 1st Manchester Regt. Died as prisoner of Japanese, August 13th, 1943.

PRYOR, Leslie Walter, 44, Devon Road, Luton. Sgt./Pilot, 17th Operational Training Unit, R.A.F. Died at Dalton, Lancashire, as result of war operations, May 21st, 1941.

PUGH, Cedric Ronald, 6, Limbury Road, Luton. L/Cpl., Corps of Military Police. Died on active service, August 14th, 1943.

RADDON, Edward C., "The Chalet," Derby Road, Luton. Third Officer, Merchant Navy. Missing at sea, Mediterranean, May, 1941.

RAINES, Elsie May, 58, Biscot Road, Luton. Killed by enemy action, at Luton, November 5th, 1944.

RAISBECK, Kenneth, 65, Blenheim Crescent, Luton. A.C.1, R.A.F. Killed on active service while training as pilot, Oswego, Kansas, U.S.A., June 26th, 1944.

RANCE, Derrick P., 92, Ashton Road, Luton. Sgt. W/Op. A.G., R.A.F. Coastal Command. Lost at sea, January 28th, 1944.

RANDALL, Frederick James, "Sugar Loaf," Leagrave, Luton. Major, 18th Reconnaissance Corps. Died of wounds, Alexandra Hospital, Singapore between February 5th and 15th, 1942.

RANDALL, Maurice Dean, 89, Alexandra Avenue, Luton. F/Lieut., R.A.F. Killed on active service, India, October, 1944.

RANDALL, Sidney, Trinity Road, Luton. Lost with H.M.S. *Exmouth*, January, 1940.

RAYMENT, Clifford George, 17, Tower Road, Luton. Pte., 2nd Battn. Devonshire Regt. Killed in action, N.W. Europe, August 12th, 1944.

RAYMENT, Harold Edward, 103, St. Margaret's Avenue, Luton. Pte., Bedfs. and Herts. Regt. Died as prisoner of Japanese, Siam, June 30th, 1943.

RAYNER, Sidney Francis, 66, Russell Street, Luton. Major, 2nd Battn. Bedfs. and Herts. Regt. Died of wounds, Italy, May 21st, 1944.

REES, Mrs. A., 83, Biscot Road, Luton. Killed by enemy action, at Luton, November 6th, 1944.

REID, David, 17, Hampton Road, Luton. Marine. Lost with H.M.S. *Royal Oak* September, 1939.

REYNOLDS, Frederick Horace, 6, Rosslyn Crescent, Luton. Pte., 6th Battn. D.L.I. Killed in action, San El Minerva, near El Alamein, July 27th, 1942.

RHODES, Thomas Geoffrey. Killed by enemy action, at Vauxhall Motors, Ltd., Luton, August 30th, 1940.

RICHARDS, Derrick Sidney J., 135, Dallow Road, Luton. Sgt./Pilot, R.A.F., Bomber Command. Missing, presumed killed, January 14th, 1944.

RICHARDS, John Thomas, 8, Medina Road, Luton. Flt./Sgt., R.A.F. Missing, presumed killed on operations, November, 1943.

RICHARDS, Wallace, 6, St. Augustine's Avenue, Luton. F./Lieut., R.C.A.F. Killed on active service, Canada.

RICHARDS, Walter Philip, 11A, Dunstable Road, Luton. P./Officer, R.A.F. Killed on operations, Torsken, Senja Island, Norway, May 21st, 1940.

RICHARDSON, Douglas Cameron, The Mount, New Bedford Road, Luton. Bdr., R.A. Drowned as prisoner of Italians when ship from Tripoli was sunk, November, 1942.

RICHARDSON, Joseph George, 74, Cromwell Road, Luton. Sgt., 101st Squadron, R.A.F. Killed in action, retruning from operations over Germany, August 19th, 1941.

RICHES, Leslie P., formerly Curate at All Saints' Church, Luton. Chaplain to the Forces. Missing, believed drowned, Dunkirk, June, 1940.

RICKARD, Sarah, 70, Biscot Road, Luton. Killed by enemy action, at Luton, November 6th, 1944.

RIGGS, George E., 33, Brook Street, Luton. L.A.C., R.A.F. Killed in action, August 30th, 1940.

RIXON, Cyril Jack, 74, Biscot Road, Luton. Died as result of enemy action, at Luton, November 6th, 1944.

ROBERTS, Alec Frederick, 258, Dallow Road, Luton. Dvr., H.Q., 4th Indian Corps, R.A.S.C. Died on active service, Bareilly, India, June 11th, 1943.

ROBINSON, John, 11, Court Road, Luton. Fusilier. Died of wounds, Italy, October 23rd, 1943.

ROE, Dennis Edward, 27, Cambridge Street, Luton. Driver, R.A.S.C. (Airborne). Missing, presumed killed in action, Western Europe, June 7th, 1944.

ROE, E. J., 323, Manor Road, Caddington, and 40A, Buxton Road, Luton. P./Officer, R.A.F. Missing, presumed killed, in air operations over enemy-occupied territory, June, 1944.

ROE, Harold William, 17, Dordans Road, Luton. Driver, R.A.S.C. Killed in action, Celle, Germany, April 13th, 1945.

ROOKWOOD, John William, 251, Dallow Road, Luton. Telegraphist, R.N., M.T.B. Killed in action, Mediterranean, July 17th, 1943.

ROSE, Carl, 19, Cardigan Street, Luton. Pte., Cambs. Regt. Died as prisoner of Japanese, Siam, June, 1943.

ROSS, James, 101, Selbourne Road, Luton. Killed by enemy action, at Luton, October 14th, 1940.

ROWE, Horace, 82, Argyll Avenue, Luton. 1st Class Stoker, R.N., H.M.S. *Acheron*. Lost at sea, December 17th, 1940.

ROWLAND, Albert H., 31, New Town Street, Luton. Pte. Died on active service in India, July 15th, 1944.

RUDD, Colin James, M.C. and Bar., 164, Dunstable Road, Luton. Captain, Northants. Regt. att. Staffords, and later att. Wiltshire Regt. Killed in action, Cleve, Germany, February 10th, 1945.

RUDD, Frank, 31, Biscot Road, Luton. Killed by enemy action, at Luton, November 6th, 1944.

SALE, Stewart George, 17, Avondale Road, Luton, and Lane End, High Wycombe. War Correspondent (Reuters). Killed in Italy, September 28th, 1943.

SALTER, Henry Ernest Richard, 107, Crawley Green Road, Luton. Gnr./Driver, R.A. (Field). Died as prisoner of Japanese, Burma, September 30th, 1943.

SAMWELLS, William Alfred, 42, Hazelbury Crescent, Luton. Army Pay Corps. Died on active service, May 15th, 1942.

SANDERS, Ernest Henry, 69, Maidenhall Road, Luton. Pte., 1st Battn. Dorset Regt. Killed in action, Caen, Normandy, 1944.

SAUNDERS, Albert James, 47, Sundon Road, Luton. Pte. Killed in action, Italy, October, 1943.

SAUNDERS, John H., Wingfield Close, Bedford, and Douglas Stratford & Co., Luton. Flt./Sgt., R.A.F. Killed on active service, October, 1944.

SAUNDERS, Kenneth Albert, 52, Trinity Road, Luton. L/Bdr., 75th Anti-Tank Regt., R.A. Died on active service, near Bremen, Germany, June 4th, 1945.

SAUNDERS, Leonard A., 43, Beech Road, Luton. Gunner, R.A. Missing at Singapore, 1942.

SAVAGE, Arthur, 25, Summerfield Road, Luton. Pte., 4th Battn. King's Shropshire L.I. Killed in action, Overloon, N.W. Europe, October 15th, 1944.

SAVAGE, George, 19, Grove Road, Luton. Pte., Army Catering Corps. Killed in action, Ainsy, Normandy, July 6th, 1944.

SAXBY, Albert J. W., 101, Third Avenue, Sundon, and formerly of Luton. Sgt., R.A.F. Killed on operations over Denmark, February, 1944.

SCALES, Barbara, 61, Wardown Crescent, Luton. Killed by enemy action, at Luton, October 14th, 1940.

SCALES, Henry Percy, 89, Hartley Road, Luton. Gnr., R.A. Died as prisoner of Japanese, Siam, August 6th, 1943.

SCOTT, Sidney R., 78, Dordans Road, Luton. Pte., 2nd Battn. Bedfs. and Herts. Regt. Killed in action, Florence, Italy, August 7th, 1944.

SCRIVENER, William George, 94, Pomfret Avenue, Luton. Accidentally killed while serving as a dispatch rider, Swindon, June, 1940.

SEAR, Joseph, 31, Lea Road, Luton. O/Seaman, R.N. Died on convoy duty, Mediterranean, April, 1942.

SHARP, George Ralph, 38, Rothesay Road, Luton. Sgt., 7th Squadron, R.A.F. Killed on operations over Berlin, January 29th, 1944.

SHAW, Arnold, 8, Stratford Road, Luton. Signm., R.N. Lost with H.M.A.S. Vampire, Colombo, April 9th, 1942.

SHAW, Gerald Charles Francis, 139, Beechwood Road, Luton. Able Seaman, R.N., H.M. Submarine P.165. Killed in action, April 18th, 1943.

SHAW, Ronald Bertie, 96, Lea Road, Luton. Sapper, R.E. Died on active service, January 14th, 1942.

SHEPHERD, Arthur, 28, Chobham Street, Luton. Gnr., R.A. Killed by mine explosion, December 24th, 1941.

SHEPHERD, Sidney, 28, Chobham Street, Luton. Gnr., R.A. Killed by mine explosion, Kent, January, 1945.

SHOTBOLT, Reginald Arthur John, 50, Winsdon Road, Luton. L.A.C., 6th Squadron, R.A.F. Killed on active service, Gunters Field, Alabama, U.S.A., April 7th, 1942.

SHUTTLEWORTH, Frank, Oldham, and Commer Cars, Ltd., Luton. Dvr., R.A.S.C. Died on active service, North Africa, October, 1943.

SILVER, Maurice, 64, Farley Avenue, Luton. Sgt./Navigator, R.A.F. Killed on active service, June 6th, 1944.

SIMKINS, Lizzie, 91, Althorp Road, Luton. Killed by enemy action, at Luton, November 6th, 1944.

SIMMONDS, Willis, 49, Trent Road, Luton. Bdr., 148th Field Regt., R.A. Lost at sea while prisoner of Japanese, September 12th, 1944.

SIMPSON, Charles William, Saxon Road, Luton. Gnr., R.A. Died on active service, June, 1940.

SINFIELD, John, 197, Biscot Road, Luton. Gnr., 148th Field Regt., R.A. Died as prisoner of Japanese, Siam, March 29th, 1945.

SING, Henry Lee, 13, Princess Street, Luton. AC/1, R.A.F. Killed on active service, Colombo, December 12th, 1945.

SKELTON, IVAN GEORGE, 45, Windmill Road, Luton. F/Officer, R.A.F. Missing, presumed killed, on operations over Germany, October 18th, 1944.

SKELTON, JOHN ANDREW GUTHRIE, 150, Wardown Crescent, Luton. Killed by enemy action, at Luton, August 30th, 1940.

SKINNER, FRED, 71, Trinity Road, Luton. Died on active service, July 15th, 1944.

SLATER, RAYMOND GORDON, 494, Dunstable Road, Luton. L/Sgt., 420th Field Battery, R.A. Died at sea as prisoner of Japanese, September 14th, 1944.

SMART, HAROLD ALFRED STEPHEN, 144, Richmond Hill, Luton. Bdr., 148th Field Regt., R.A. Died as prisoner of Japanese, Central Siam, December 31st, 1943.

SMITH, ALFRED ARTHUR, 47, Stanley Street, Luton. Pte., 2nd Battn. The Buffs. Killed in action, El Alamein, September 30th, 1942.

SMITH, AUBREY J., 16, Cardiff Grove, Luton. Pte., Suffolk Regt. Died as prisoner of Japanese, October, 1943.

SMITH, CHARLES, 11, New Town Street, Luton. Gnr., R.A. Died on active service in India, November, 1943.

SMITH, CHARLES EDWARD, 106, Willow Way, Luton. Sgt., R.A.F., Bomber Command. Killed returning from air operations, November 19th, 1943.

SMITH, DAVID, Barton, and Cundall Folding Machine Co., Luton. Gnr., R.A. Died as prisoner of Japanese, 1944.

SMITH, EDGAR GORDON T., 9, Conway Road, Luton. P/Officer, R.A.F. Killed on operations over Germany, December, 1941.

SMITH, FRANK, 19, Stockingstone Road, Luton. R.N. Lost with H.M.S. *Rawalpindi*, off Iceland, November, 1939.

SMITH, FREDERICK, 10, Hampton Road, Luton. Gnr., R.A. Killed in action, Italy, January 17th, 1943.

SMITH, GEOFFREY ARCHIBALD, 14, Broad Mead, Luton. Sgt. F/Engr., 15th Squadron, R.A.F. Missing on operations, presumed killed, September 10th, 1942.

SMITH, HAROLD WILLIAM, 9, Dudley Street, Luton. Gnr., R.A. Killed in action at sea, July 15th, 1941.

SMITH, JOHN HOLMES, 123, Runley Road, Luton. Killed by enemy action, at De Havillands, Hatfield, October 3rd, 1940.

SMITH, LESLIE, 9, Dudley Street, Luton. Gnr.-Dvr. i/c, R.A. Died of wounds, Italy, November 2nd, 1942.

SMITH, SHEILA ELIZABETH, 95 Harcourt Street, Luton. Killed by enemy action, at Luton, August 30th, 1940.

SMITH, STANLEY E. T., 30, Norton Road, Luton. Gdsm., Irish Guards. Died of wounds, Western Front, December, 1944.

SMITHAM, DANIEL, 35, Shaftesbury Road, Luton. Third Engineer, Merchant Navy. Lost at sea by enemy action, 1942.

SMYTH, WILLIAM J., 30, Dale Road, Luton. Gnr., R.A. Lost at sea as prisoner of Japanese.

SNOW, RICHARD JAMES, Warden Hill, Luton. Cpl., Cambs. Regt. Killed in action, Far East, January 28th, 1942.

SNOXELL, CHARLES HENRY, 45, Woodside Road, Luton, and employed at Luton Brewery. AC/1, R.A.F. Lost at sea, between Java and Japan, while prisoner of Japanese, November 23rd, 1942.

SNOXELL, GERALD JAMES THOMAS, 137, New Bedford Road, Luton. F/Officer, No. 1 O.T.U., R.A.F. Died on active service, January 13th, 1943.

SOTON, HENRY P., 21, Harefield Road, Luton. Killed by U.S. bomb lorry explosion, Offley, January 8th, 1945.

SPICER, JOHN ROBERT, 13, Letchworth Road, Luton. Pte. Died on active service in France, August 1944.

SQUIRE, LAWRENCE FRANCIS, 97, Wardown Crescent, Luton. P/Officer, R.A.F. Killed on active service, December, 1940.

SQUIRES, R. R., 20, Newbury Lane, Silsoe. Killed by enemy action, at Commer Cars, Luton, November 6th, 1944.

STADDON, ALFRED, 245, New Bedford Road, Luton. Signm., R.N. Lost with H.M.S. *Janus*, Mediterranean, February, 1944.

STANGHAN, ROBERT HORACE, 67, St, Catherine's Avenue, Luton. Sgt. A.G., R.A.F. Killed on operations, Northern Germany, June 23rd, 1942.

STOKES, FREDERICK CHARLES ALBERT, 29, Roman Road, Luton. Sgt. F/Engr., 427th Squadron, R.A.F. Killed on operations, Hamburg, Germany, July 29th, 1944.

STOUGHTON, LEONARD JOHN, 203, Cutenhoe Road, Luton. Killed by enemy action, at Vauxhall Motors, Ltd., Luton, August 30th, 1940.

STRATTON, BRUCE ALBERT, 104, Stanford Road, Luton. F/Sgt. W.Op., R.A.F. Killed on operations over Germany, February 20th, 1944.

STRONELL, NORMAN JOHN, 45A, Buxton Road, Luton. F/Officer, R.A.F. Killed on operations over Stettin, Germany, August 30th, 1944.

SUMNER, STANLEY ROBERT, 60, Runley Road, Luton. Sgt./Pilot, R.A.F. Killed on active service, October 16th, 1940.

SWAIN, DOUGLAS PHILIP, 23, Argyll Avenue, Luton. Sgt./Pilot, R.A.F. Killed on active service, at Tiddim, Burma, September 12th, 1945.

SWANNICK, NORMAN HARRY, 162, Baker Street, Luton. W/Bdr., R.A. Died of wounds, Italy, May 23rd, 1944.

TANSLEY, HIRAM JOSEPH, 46, Maidenhall Road, Luton. 1st Class Stoker, R.N. Killed on active service, N. Africa, August 23rd, 1943.

TAYLOR, DAVID ARTHUR, The Flat, Luton Town Hall. Sgt./A.G., R.A.F. Killed on active service, March 23rd, 1941.

TAYLOR, ROBERT C., 23, Moor Street, Luton. Sgt., Loyal Regt. Died of wounds, Italy, August, 1944.

TAYLOR, WALTER, 37, Duke Street, Luton. Pte., Cambs. Regt. Died as prisoner of Japanese, Siam, June 1st, 1943.

TEARLE, RAYMOND JOHN., 85, London Road, Luton. P/Officer, R.A.F. Accidentally killed on active service, near Sheerness, May 17th, 1941.

THOMAS, DOUGLAS A., 35, Ridgway Road, Luton S. Flt./Engr., R.A.F. Missing, presumed killed, on operations, August, 1943.

THOMAS, JOHN GLANFFRWD, 111, Chester Avenue, Luton. Killed by enemy action, at Vauxhall Motors, Ltd., Luton, August 30th, 1940.

THOMAS, PETER ANTHONY, 67, Elmwood Crescent, Luton. Sgt. W/Op. A.G., R.A.F. Missing, presumed killed, North Sea, February 25th, 1942.

THOMAS, PHILIP EDGAR, 67, Elmwood Crescent, Luton. Sgt. W/Op. A.G., R.A.F. Missing, presumed killed, Mediterranean Sea, July 25th, 1942.

THOMPSON, ANNIE ELIZABETH, 77, Biscot Road, Luton. Killed by enemy action, at Luton, November 6th, 1944.

THOMPSON, ARTHUR JOHN. Killed by enemy action, at Vauxhall Motors, Ltd., Luton, August 30th, 1940.

THOMPSON, BARBARA GLADYS, 79, Farley Avenue, Luton. Killed by enemy action, at Luton, August 30th, 1940.

THOMPSON, IAN WILLIAM, 79, Farley Avenue, Luton. Died, September 2nd, 1940, as result of enemy action at Luton.

THOMPSON, MATTHEW, 54, Ridgway Road, Luton. Pte., Pioneer Corps. Died on active service, September 17th, 1945.

THOMPSON, MAY, 79, Farley Avenue, Luton. Killed by enemy action, at Luton, August 30th, 1940.

THOMPSON, PETER DESMOND, 11, Morley Crescent, Edgware, and formerly of Luton. Sgt./Pilot, R.A.F. Killed on active service, October, 1941.

THORNTON, GEORGE FREDERICK, 86, Runley Road, Luton. L/Cpl., 17/21st Lancers, R.A.C. Killed in action, North Africa, April 8th, 1943.

TICKNER, WILLIAM THOMAS, 82, St. Michael's Crescent, Luton. Petty Officer, R.N. Killed on active service at sea, March 27th, 1943.

TOOLEY, Trevor James Francis, 219, New Bedford Road, Luton. Lieut., Suffolk Regt. Killed in action, Normandy, June 6th, 1944.

TOYER, George Frederick, 5, Stuart Place, Luton. Gnr., R.A. Lost at sea while prisoner of Japanese, September 12th, 1944.

TOYER, Reginald George, 22, Neville Road, Luton. Gnr., R.A. Died of wounds, Burma, March 6th, 1944.

TOYER, Ronald, 20, Maidenhall Road, Luton. A/Seaman, R.N. Lost in action at sea, September 19th, 1943.

TOYER, Ronald Derrick, 97, Boyle Street, Luton. Gnr., R.A. Died as prisoner of Japanese, Siam, August 19th, 1943.

TURNER, Harry Boyd, 87a, Albert Road, Luton. Sgt., 148th Field Regt., R.A. Lost at sea as prisoner of Japanese, September 12th, 1944.

TURNER, John, 106, Oak Road, Luton. Pte., Pioneer Corps. Died on active service, March, 1941.

TURNER, Rex, 159, Tennyson Road, Luton. Tpr., 10th Hussars, R.A.C. Killed in action, Libya, May 29th, 1942.

TYREMAN, Alan, B.E.M., 12, Durbar Road, Luton. Lieut., Royal Marines. Died on active service, May 23rd, 1945.

TYREMAN, Norman Allen, 33, Linden Road, Luton. Sgt., R.A.F. Killed on operations over Germany, September 3rd, 1943.

TYSOM, Ronald Francis, 12, Ivy Road, Luton. Gnr., 510 H.A.A. Regt., R.A. Died on active service, April 30th, 1943.

UNDERWOOD, C. F. W., 23, Durbar Road, Luton. P/Officer, R.A.F. Missing on air operations, September, 1942.

UPTON, Edward, " Sunnybank," Little Bramingham, Luton. Sgt. W/Op. A.G., R.A.F. Killed by enemy action, at sea, January 8th, 1942.

VARNAM, Frederick Leslie, 29, Dale Road, Luton. Pte., R.A.M.C. Killed on active service, Bayeux, France, September 13th, 1944.

VENTHAM, Reginald William, 52, Ivy Road, Luton. Pte., 2nd Battn. Royal Scots. Killed in action, Florence, Italy, September 3rd, 1944.

VEREY, Leslie Howard, formerly of 50, Newcombe Road, Luton. Spr., R.E. Killed during air raid while prisoner in Germany, December 2nd, 1944.

VERRAN, Reginald Stanley Edward, D.F.C., 78, Talbot Road, Luton. F/Officer, R.A.F. Killed on active service, Luneberg, Germany, October 17th, 1945.

VERRAN, Robert Claude, D.F.M., 18, Carlton Close, Luton. Sgt./Observer, R.A.F. Killed on operations, Catania, Sicily, January, 1941.

VICKERS, Frank, Luton Borough Treasurer's Department. Capt., R.A. Killed on active service, Germany, March, 1946.

WADDINGTON, William, 116, Runley Road, Luton. Killed by enemy action, at Luton, August 30th, 1940.

WAINWRIGHT, Alec George, 52, Old Bedford Road, Luton. P/Officer, 73rd Squadron, R.A.F. Missing, presumed killed in action, North Africa January 21st, 1941.

WALKER, William Charles, 17, Chester Close, Luton. Invalided from R.N died January, 1945.

WALLER, Eric Gordon, 10, Hillborough Road, Luton. Sgt., R.A.F., Bomber Command. Missing, presumed killed, Langensalza-Tour, March 23rd, 1944.

WALLINGTON, Raymond Arthur, 33, Harcourt Street, Luton. Gnr., 102nd (North Hussars) Field Regt., R.A. Killed in action, Tunisia, April 4th, 1943.

WALLIS, Alfred, 35, Essex Street, Luton. Killed by enemy action, at Luton, August 30th, 1940.

WANTLING, Arthur, 49, Bradley Road, Luton. Sgt. Killed in Normandy, July, 1944.

WARD, Eric Percy, 43, Selbourne Road, Luton. Killed by enemy action, at Vauxhall Motors, Ltd., Luton, August 30th, 1940.

WARDILL, John N., Stoneheaps, Kimpton, and formerly of Luton. Sub.-Lieut. (A), Fleet Air Arm. Missing, presumed killed, on operational duty, October, 1943.

WARDILL, Wilfred G., 16, Brantwood Road, Luton. Killed by enemy action, at Norwich, January, 1942.

WARNER, Cecil Charles, 42, Clarendon Road, Luton. Pte., Somerset L.I. Died of wounds, Western Front, October, 1944.

WARREN, Kenneth Henry, 106, Wardown Crescent, Luton. L/Bdr., R.A. Died of wounds, North Africa, April 30th, 1943.

WARREN, Ronald, 87, Russell Rise, Luton. Sgt./Pilot, R.A.F. Killed on active service, March, 1941.

WARREN, Wilfred Robert, formerly of Dunstable Road, Luton. Fleet Air Arm. Killed on active service, May, 1942.

WAYWELL, Gordon, 122, Dunstable Road, Luton. Cfmn., R.E.M.E. Died on active service, Done, N. Africa, May 17th, 1943.

WEATHERLEY, Alfred William, 75, Limbury Road, Luton. R.Q.M.S., 5th Training Battalion, R.E. Died on active service, March 4th, 1943.

WEBB, John Henry, 29, Kingsland Road, Luton. L/Cpl., R. West Kent Regt. Killed in action, Italy, January 8th, 1945.

WEDDELL, Irene Constance, 45, St. Martin's Avenue, Luton. Killed by enemy action, at Luton, October 14th, 1940.

WEEDEN, Henry John, 3, Chester Avenue, Luton. Died in hospital as the result of enemy action, at Luton, August 30th, 1940.

WEEDON, Douglas Henry, 30, Waller Avenue, Luton. Pte., Hampshire Regt. Killed in action, N.W. Europe, June 13th, 1944.

WEEDON, Jack William, 30, Waller Avenue, Luton. Gnr., 234th Battery, 77th H.A.A., R.A. Died on active service, September 4th, 1941.

WEEDON, Reginald Francis, 130, Waller Avenue, Luton. F/Officer, R.A.F. Killed on operations ; buried at St. Trond, Belgium, April 25th, 1944.

WELHAM, Robert William Charles, 9, Belmont Road, Luton. L/Bdr., R.A. Lost at sea as prisoner of Japanese, September 12th, 1944.

WELLS, Victor Charles, 142, Blundell Road, Luton. Naval Airman, Fleet Air Arm. Died on active service, June 30th, 1944.

WELLS, William (John), 8, Blyth Place, Luton. L/Bdr., 418th Field Regt., R.A. Died as prisoner of Japanese, Siam, December 12th, 1942.

WEST, Derrick, 6, Pirton Road, Luton. Killed by enemy action, at Vauxhall Motors, Ltd., Luton, August 30th, 1940.

WEST, Victor, 34, Marsh Road, Luton. R.A.F. Killed on active service, October 27th, 1940.

WEST, Walter Roy, 7, Welbeck Road, Luton. Killed in action, June 6th, 1942.

WHALLEY, George Thomas, 48, Gillam Street, Luton. Pte., 2nd Battn. Herts. Regt. Killed clearing minefield, Caen, Normandy, July 28th, 1944.

WHITE, E., 82, Lea Road, Luton. Pte. Killed in action, January 1st, 1945.

WHITE, George Robert, 461, Dunstable Road, Luton. Gdsm., 6th Battn. Grenadier Guards. Killed in action near Mareth Line, Tripoli, North Africa, March 17th, 1943.

WHITE, John Henry, 106, Hart Lane, Luton. Pte., 2nd Battn. Bedfs. and Herts. Regt. Killed in action, North Africa, April 13th, 1943.

WHITE, R. F., Rushden, and formerly of Luton. Lieut. (Leading Supply Asst.), R.N. Died on active service, June, 1942.

WHITELOCK, Robert Henry, 16, Essex Street, Luton. R.A.S.C. Died on active service, September 24th, 1942.

WHITTAKER, Arthur Thomas, 21, Oakley Road, Luton. Killed by enemy action, at Vauxhall Motors, Ltd., Luton, August 30th, 1940.

WHITTLES, Arthur Ernest, 114, Graham Gardens, Luton. Pte., R.A.M.C. Killed in action, N.W. Europe, June 10th, 1944.

WILCOCKSON, ROBERT, 29, Felstead Way, Luton. Sgt., R.A.F. Killed on operations, N.W. France, 1943.

WILLIAMS, DAVID GARFIELD, 35, Neville Road, Luton. Tpr., 15th Reconnaissance Regt. Died on active service, April 9th, 1943.

WILLIAMS, GLYN, Putteridge Park, Luton. F/Officer, R.A.F., 140 Wing 2nd T.A.F. Missing, presumed killed in action over Holland, December 3rd, 1944.

WILLIAMS, PHYLLIS MARJORIE, 120, Cowper Street, Luton. Killed by enemy action, at Luton, August 30th, 1940.

WILSON, ARTHUR GEORGE, 242, Crawley Green Road, Luton. Gnr., 419th Batty., 148th Field Regt., R.A. Died as prisoner of Japanese, Siam, September 16th, 1943.

WILSON, DENIS, 41, Lilley, and Geere & Co., Luton. Pte., Suffolk Regt. Died as prisoner of Japanese, Singapore, January 1st, 1944.

WILSON, FRANK, 24, Colin Road, Luton. Stoker, R.N., H.M.S. *Kingston Galena*, Dover Patrol. Lost at sea, July 24th, 1940.

WILSON, ROBERT, 42, Midland Road, Luton. Died September 6th, 1942, following injuries caused by enemy action, at Luton, September 5th, 1942.

WISE, DERRICK GEORGE, 125, High Town Road, Luton. Royal Marine Commando. Killed in action in Normandy, D-Day, June 6th, 1944.

WISE, PETER JOHN, 31, Biscot Road, Luton. Killed by enemy action, at Luton, November 6th, 1944.

WISEMAN, REGINALD WILLIAM, 65, Crawley Road, Luton. Dvr., Ayrshire Yeomanry R.A. Killed in action, Italy, August 7th, 1944.

WOOD, RONALD WILLIAM, 7, Chandos Road, Luton. Sgt., R.A.F., Bomber Command. Missing, presumed killed, February 25-26th, 1944.

WOODBRIDGE, FRANCIS ALLAN, " Woodville," Humberstone Road, Luton. Pte., 4th Battn. R. Norfolk Regt. Died as prisoner of Japanese, Taiwan, Formosa, January 1st, 1944.

WOODFIELD, RONALD GEORGE, 16, Belmont Road, Luton. Sgt., R.A.F. Killed in action, Denmark, April 4th, 1943.

WOODFINE, JOHN EDWARD, 56, St. Ethelbert's Avenue, Luton. Died as the result of enemy action, at Vauxhall Motors, Ltd., August 31st, 1940.

WOODS, RICHARD ANTHONY, 93, Selbourne Road, Luton. L/Cpl., R.A.S.C. Killed in action at sea, February 5th, 1942. Buried at Keppal Harbour, Singapore.,

WRIGHT, DENNIS WILLIAM, 102A, Midland Road, Luton. Flt./Sgt. Navigator R.A.F. Killed on operations, Stuttgart, July 25th, 1944.

WRIGHT, GEORGE J., 77, Pembroke Avenue, Luton. Dispatch Rider, Lothian Border Regt. Killed on active service, July 17th, 1940.

WRIGHT, JACK, 3, Clevedon Road, Luton. Pte., Highland Light Infantry. Killed in action, Germany, February 14th, 1945.

WRIGHT, KENNETH EDWIN, 67, Spencer Road, Luton. Pte., 2/5th Queen's Royal Regt. Died of wounds, Italy, December 6th, 1943.

WRIGHT, WILLIAM JOHN, 140, Kingsway, Luton. L/Bdr., R.A. Killed on grenade practice, Northumberland, January 20th, 1943.

YORK, HERBERT, 46, Cavendish Road, Luton. L/Bdr., R.A. Lost at sea as prisoner of Japanese.

YOUNG, J. H., 1, Albion Road, Luton. Tpr., Royal Tank Regt. Missing, presumed killed in action, Middle East, June 15th, 1941.

ZASTROW, W. R., 38, Fitzroy Avenue, Luton. Sgt. Flt./Eng., R.A.F. Missing on air operations, December, 1943.

Awards and Decorations

(The following is a list of Lutonians who have gained awards and decorations, either in the Services or in civilian life, during the war. In addition to the usual abbreviations, the initials M.D. are used to denote a " Mention in Despatches ").

ADAMS, H. S. B., 1, High Point, Farley Hill, Luton. Capt. **M.B.E.,** 1945, Italy.

ADAMS, NORMAN MARCUS, c/o Douglas Stratford & Co., Luton. Sergt./ Surveyor, 7th Survey Regt., R.A. **M.M.,** 1944, Holland and N.W. Europe.

ALDRED, R. A., Chas. Clay & Sons, Ltd., Luton. Lt.-Comm., R.N.V.R. **M.D.,** 1945 ; **D.S.C.,** 1946, Minesweepers.

ANDERSON, ERIC, 72, Adelaide Street, Luton. Tpr., R.A.C. **George Medal,** 1945, Italy.

ARNOLD, CECIL C., Wardown Crescent, Luton. F/Lt., R.A.F. **M.D.,** 1945.

AUSTIN, RUPERT FRANCIS, 216, Cutenhoe Road, Luton. Capt., R.E.M.E. **M.B.E.,** 1945, Italy.

BAKER, ALBERT HENRY, 13, Boyle Street, Luton. L/Cpl., 317th Coy. R.A.S.C., Att. R.A. **M.D.,** 1945, Italy.

BAKER, S. H., Luton. L/Cpl., R.A.S.C. **M.D.,** 1944, Italy.

BANKS, LESLIE J., Shell Mex & B.P. Oil Co., Luton. Lt.-Col., R.A.S.C. **M.D.,** 1943, North Africa.

BARRINGER, HAROLD WM., 25, Mixes Hill Road, Luton. L/Cpl., 77 (Br.) General Hospital (Field), R.A.M.C. **M.D.,** 1944, Normandy.

BARTLETT, CHARLES JOHN, Managing Director, Vauxhall Motors, Ltd., Luton. **Knighthood,** 1944.

BARTON, JAMES SYDNEY, 135, Beechwood Road, Luton. A/Ldg. Seaman, D.E.M.S., R.N. **M.D.,** 1943, N. Africa.

BATCHELOR, FRANK, 115, Alder Crescent, Luton. Able Seaman, R.N. **D.S.M.,** 1945.

BELL, ERNEST GEORGE, 55, Montrose Avenue, Luton. Signalman, R.N. **M.D.,** 1944, Normandy Invasion.

BENNETT, R., Luton. F/Lt., R.A.F. **Air Efficiency Award,** 1942.

BENSON, JOHN H., 111, Farley Hill, Luton. Sgt., R.A.F. **M.D.,** 1945.

BINGHAM, CYRIL, 71, Cambridge Street, Luton. Cpl., Suffolk Regt. **M.M.,** 1944, N.W. Europe.

BIRCHMORE, ROY BERTRAM, 25, Sunridge Avenue, Luton. F/Lt., 1940 (Meteor, Recon. and Special Duties) Flight, Pathfinder Force, R.A.F. **D.F.C.,** 1944 ; **Bar to D.F.C.,** 1945, Germany.

BLEANEY, ALBERT EDWARD, 17, Henry Street, Luton. Sergt., R.E. **M.D.,** 1946, N.W. Europe.

BLEANEY, BERNARD FREDK., 28, Woodland Avenue, Luton. Warrant Mech., H.M.S. *Valiant*, R.N. **M.B.E.,** 1945, S.E.A.C.

BLOW, KENNETH LESLIE OWEN, 390, Dunstable Road, Luton. Warrant Officer, R.A.F.V.R. Awarded **D.F.C.** Subsequently killed.

BOLTON, SAMUEL, 16, Bolton Road, Luton. Petty Officer, R.N. **D.S.M.,** 1942, Oran, North Africa.

BONNER, RALPH JACK, 73, Harcourt Street, Luton. Capt., 53rd Field Regt, R.A. **M.C.,** 1945, Italy.

BOOT, LESLIE, 69 Roundwood Lane, Harpenden and L.M.S. Goods Office, Luton. Staff-Sergt. R.E. **B.E.M.,** Egypt and Palestine.

BOSS, KENNETH, 117, Farley Avenue, Luton. Capt., R.A., Forward Observation Unit (Airborne). **M.C.,** June, 1945, N.W. Europe. Subsequently died of wounds.

BOULTON, FRANK PERCY, 44, Kimpton Road, Luton. Chief P.O. (E.R.A.), R.N., H.M.S. *Eskimo*. **D.S.M.,** 1944, N. Africa ; **B.E.M.,** 1944, Sicily.

BOYD-STEVENSON, Donald, 45, Chatsworth Road, Luton. S/Ldr., 104th Squadron, R.A.F. **D.F.C.**, 1943, Middle East.

BROWN, Gordon Percy, 63, Wychwood Avenue, Luton. Major, 1st Battn. Leics. Regt. **M.D.**, 1945, N.W. Europe ; **M.C.**, 1946, N.W. Europe.

BROWN, Willie Calvert, 90 St. Catherine's Avenue, Luton. Sergt., R.A.F. **M.D.**, 1943.

BRUMPTON, Charles Edward, 205, Runley Road, Luton. Cpl., Royal Marines (Combined Operations). **D.S.M.**, 1944, Normandy.

BURGOYNE, Ald. John, 228, Stockingstone Road, Luton. Chairman of Luton Emergency Committee. **O.B.E.**, 1946.

BUNNAGE, Ronald T., 63, Fountains Road, Luton. B.Q.M.S., R.A., No. 4 Military Dispersal Unit. **B.E.M.**, 1946.

BUNYAN, Reginald Arthur, 5, Trent Road, Luton. F/Sgt., No. 61 Squadron, R.A.F. **D.F.M.**, 1944.

BUXTON, S. L., Luton. Capt., 17/21st Lancers, R.A.C. **M.C.**, 1942, Middle East.

CARRUTHERS, Donald, 11, Brook Street, Luton. F/O., No. 35 Sq., R.A.F. **D.F.M.**, 1944, France and Germany.

CAWLEY, Alfred, 108, Graham Gardens, Luton. L/Sgt., No. 1 Air Support Signals Unit, Royal Signals (Army). **M.D.**, 1944, Italy.

CHANDLER, Geoffrey Graham, 222, Dunstable Road, Luton. Sgt/Artificer, R.A. **M.M.**, 1944, Italy.

CHANDLER, Graham H., Chiltern House, Markyate. Naval Armament Supply Officer, R.N. **M.B.E.**, 1942, Gibraltar.

CHESHIRE, Hettie, 30, Chandos Road, Luton. Chief Petty Officer, W.R.N.S. **M.B.E.**, 1945.

CLARK, William Henry, 10, Tower Road, Luton. Flt./Sgt., Security Police, R.A.F. **M.D.**, 1942. Subsequently killed.

COLEMAN, Arthur, 7, Dunstable Road, Caddington, and Percival Aircraft, Ltd., Luton. W/Officer, R.A.S.C. **M.D.**, 1945, Far East ; **B.E.M.**, 1946, S.E. Asia.

COLLIER, James Patrick, 98, Gardenia Avenue, Luton. Captain, 74 E. and M. Platoon, R.E., 21st Army Group, B.A.O.R. **M.D.**, 1945, N.W. Europe.

COLLINS, George Edwd., 29, Ivy Road, Luton. W/Sergt., 2902 Civil Labour Unit, Pioneer Corps. **M.D.**, 1945, Italy.

COOK, Leslie, 80, Kingston Road, Luton. Sub-Conductor (W.O.I.), R.A.O.C. **M.D.**, 1943, North Africa.

COOKE, John Douglas, 11, Douglas Road, Harpenden, and George Street West, Luton. Capt., Royal Corps of Signals. **M.D.**, 1940, Dunkirk.

COOPER, Philip Leslie George, formerly of 126, Oak Road, Luton, and now of 12, Beechcroft Gardens, Abington, Northants. Cpl., 5th R. Inniskilling Dragoon Guards. **M.M.**, 1945, Western Front.

COOPER, Philip Sidney, 160, Stockingstone Road, Luton. Cpl., Inniskilling Dragoons, R.A.C. **M.M.**, 1944, Normandy.

COOPER, Ronald, c/o Commer Cars, Ltd., Luton. C.P.O. (Ldg. Wireless Mechanic), R.N. **M.D.**, 1943, Far East.

CORNES, Geoffrey F., 319, New Bedford Road, Luton. Squadron Leader, R.A.F. **D.F.M.**, 1942, Battle of El Alamein ; **M.D.**, 1945, Western Europe.

COULSON, Leonard, 56, Chatsworth Road, Luton. Coder, R.N. **French Croix de Guerre**, 1944, Normandy.

COX Kenneth Victor, 45, Newark Road, Luton. F/Lieut., R.A.F. **D.F.M.**, 1941, Western Desert.

CRADDOCK, Joseph Percy, 31, Whitecroft Road, Luton. Sgt., R.A. **M.D.** 1944, Italy.

CRAIN, Frederick Chas., 6, Chandos Road, Luton. Cpl., No. 120 Sq., R.A.F., Coastal Command. **M.D.**, 1945, Battle of the Atlantic.

CROWNE, J. G., 16, Downs Road, Luton, and Eastex, Ltd., Guildford Street, Luton. Major, Nigerian Regt. **M.B.E.**, 1945, Chindits, Burma.

CRUTTENDEN, G. H., 83, Manton Drive, Luton. Major, R.A.O.C. **M.D.,** 1946, Central Mediterranean Forces.

CUNNINGHAM, John Crawford, D.S.O., 45, St. Margaret's Avenue, Luton. Major, 7th Bedfs. Battn. Home Guard, and Security Officer, Percival Aircraft, Ltd., Luton. **George Medal,** 1941, Parachute Mine incident.

CURRANT, Christopher, "Two Gables," West Common, Harpenden, and Currant & Creak, Ltd., Luton. W/Comm., R.A.F. **D.F.C.,** 1940, Battle of Britain ; **Bar to D.F.C.,** 1940, Defence of London ; **D.S.O.,** 1942, Northern France ; **Belgian Croix de Guerre,** 1942.

CURRANT, Eric James, Currant & Creak, Ltd., Luton. Lt.-Col. Indian Army Medical Corps, 14th Army. **M.D.,** 1944, Arakan.

DANDY, William Robert I., 51, Ludlow Avenue, Luton. Chief Special Constable of Luton. **M.B.E.,** 1945.

DANES, Bramwell Joseph, 51, Alton Road, Luton. L/Bdr., 23rd Field Regt., R.A. **M.D.,** 1945, Italy ; **American Bronze Star,** 1945, Italy.

DAY, Ronald Wm., 27, Douglas Road, Luton. T/Sergt., H.Q. 2nd Tactical Air Force, and H.Q., B.A.F.O., Germany. **M.D.,** 1945, Europe. **B.E.M.,** 1946, Europe.

DEAN, R., 9, Holland Road, Luton. Staff-Sergt., No. 8 General Transport Column, R.A.S.C. **M.D.,** 1945, Italy.

DEARMAN, Derek Roy, 93, Putteridge Road, Luton. P/O, R.A.F. **D.F.C.** 1944. (Previously killed in action).

DELLER, Sydney Stewart, 24, Ryecroft Way, Stopsley, Luton. Tpr., Northant. Yeomanry. **M.D.,** 1945, N.W. Europe.

DELME-MURRAY, G. B., 28, Conway Road, Luton. Major, 17th Dogra Regt. **D.S.O.,** 1945, Burma.

DENTON, Reginald, 25, Althorpe Road, Luton. Sergt., No. 156 Sq., R.A.F. **M.D.,** 1944.

DERBYSHIRE, Alfred Horley, Dunstable Road, Caddington and R. Colin Large, Ltd., Luton. F/O., R.A.F. **M.D.,** 1942.

DUDLEY, Eric Geo., 4, Greenhill Avenue, Luton. F/O., 44 Sq., R.A.F. **D.F.C.,** 1943.

DUNHAM, Peter B., formerly Stockingstone Road, Luton. Major, R.E. **M.D.,** 1945, Rhine and N. Holland.

EBERLIE, Elizabeth Mary Frances, 57, Crawley Green Road, Luton. Junior Comm., A.T.S. **U.S. Army Bronze Star,** 1945, S.H.A.E.F.

EGAN, Edwin Philip James, "The Sportsman," Stopsley, Luton. Seaman, R.N. **D.S.M.,** 1944.

ELLIS, Edward Sydney, 263, Marsh Road, Luton. F/Lt., R.A.F. **C.G.M.,** 1943, "Battle of Berlin" ; **D.F.C.,** 1944, Germany ; **M.D.,** 1945 Heavy Conversion Unit.

ELLWOOD, William Cyril, 6, St. Mary's Road, Luton. Sgt., Commandos. **D.C.M.,** 1943, Italy.

EMERY, Frederick William Douglas, 4, High Mead, Luton. F/Officer, 76 Squadron, R.A.F. **D.F.C.,** 1945.

EVANS, Evan A. C., Clerk to Luton Rural District Council. **M.B.E.,** 1946.

FALLER, Frederick, 170, Beechwood Road, Luton. Works Superintendent, Commer Cars, Ltd. **M.B.E.** (Civil Division), 1943.

FAUNCH, Sidney Chas., 74, Wychwood Avenue, Luton. L/Cpl., 240th Field Coy., R.E. **George Medal,** 1944, Normandy Invasion.

FARMER, Derrick, 100, Montrose Avenue, Luton. W.O.I., R.A.S.C. **M.D.,** 1946, North Africa and Italy.

FENSOME, Hubert Hedley, 79, Kent Road, Luton. L/Stoker, R.N. **M.D.** 1945, Northern France.

FIELD, Albert George, 11, Crescent Rise, Luton. Sgt., Lancers R.A.C **B.E.M.,** 1942, North African Convoy.

FLITTON, Stanley Charles, 25, Kingsland Road, Luton. A/Seaman, R.N. **M.D.,** 1944, Normandy Landing and Germany.

FRANKLIN, William Edward, 171, Dunstable Road, Caddington. Lieut., 7th Bedfs. Battn. Home Guard, Luton. **M.B.E.,** 1944.

FRANKS, Percy R., 72, Bury Park Road, Luton. Capt., Royal Signals. **M.D.,** Burma, 1945.

FREEMAN, Nelson Thos., 66, St. Ethelbert's Avenue, Luton. F/Sgt., R.A.F. **M.D.,** 1943.

FREER, Walter John Patrick, 148, Wellington Street, Luton. Sgt., 13/18th Royal Hussars (Queen Mary's Own), 10th Armoured Division. **M.D.,** 1944, N. Africa.

FRENCH, John W. L., Messrs. French & Co., Cardiff Road, Luton. F/Lt., R.A.F. **D.F.C.,** 1945.

FULLER, Desmond Chas., 136, Runley Road, Luton. S.Q.M. Sgt., 51st Royal Tank Regt. **M.D.,** 1945, Italy.

FYSON, P. A., Vauxhall Motors, Ltd., Luton. F/O., R.A.F. **D.F.C.,** 1944.

GAWLEY, Samuel, Woodside. Pte., 4th Bedfs. Battn. Home Guard, Luton. **B.E.M.,** 1944.

GINN, Robert James, 193, Cutenhoe Road, Luton. S/Ldr., R.A.F. **M.B.E.,** 1943.

GLANCY, J., Luton. Parachute Regt. **M.M.,** 1944, Northern France.

GLOVER, Thomas W., 21, Hastings Street, Luton. C.S.M., R.E. **M.D.,** 1945, Rhine Crossing.

GODDARD, Edmund, Lawn End, Harpenden, and Commer Cars, Ltd., Luton. Chief P/O., R.N. **C.G.M.,** 1944, Midget Submarine attack on the *Tirpitz.*

GODFREY, George Leslie, 37, Alton Road, Luton. L/Seaman, R.N. **D.S.M.,** 1940, Dunkirk Evacuation.

GOODMAN, F. Arthur, Commer-Karrier, Ltd., Luton. Lt.-Col., R.A.O.C. **M.C.,** 1940, s.s. *Lancastria.*

GRAVES-MORRIS, Philip H., Upper George Street, Luton. Lt.-Col., 2nd Worcs. Regt. **M.C.,** 1941, Middle East ; **D.S.O.,** 1945, Chindits, Burma.

GRIDLEY, John, Luton. Sgt., Wiltshire Regt. **M.M.,** 1944, Italy.

GRIFFITHS, Gerald, 37, Russell Rise, Luton. F/Sgt., R.A.F. **D.F.M.,** 1944, Berlin.

HAFNER, John Charles, 694, Dunstable Road, Luton. Lt., R.N.V.R. **Norwegian War Medal,** 1945, North Atlantic.

HANDFORD, Leslie, 57, Wardown Crescent, Luton. Capt., R.E.M.E. **M.D.,** 1946, N.W. Europe.

HARE, Louis William, 70, Blundell Road, Luton. Petty Officer, R.N. **M.D.,** 1943, Minelaying Operations.

HAWKINS, Austin Ralph, 58, Wardown Crescent, Luton. Major, Royal Marines. **M.D.,** 1943, M.E.F. ; **M.D.,** 1945, N.W. Europe.

HERBERT, Aston Arthur, 46, Butlin Road, Luton. Cpl., Royal Marines. **M.D.,** 1945, N.W. Europe.

HICKS, William Jas., 25, Mayne Avenue, Luton. Sergt., Bedfs. and Herts. Regt. **Belgian Croix de Guerre, (1940) with Palms** for service with 1st Battn. Belgian Fusiliers, 1946.

HILL, Arnold M., 17, Richmond Hill, Luton. F/Lt., R.A.F. **D.F.C.,** 1943.

HITCH, James E., 333, Dallow Road, Luton. Sgt., R.A.S.C. **M.D.,** 1946, Italy.

HOAR, Kenneth Sidney, 34, Carlton Crescent, Luton. W/Officer, R.A.F., Coastal Command. **M.D.,** 1944.

HOBBS, Peter Henry, 1, Brook Street, Luton. Major, R.A.V.C. **M.B.E.,** 1945, Burma.

HOBBS, Robert Brian, 20, Ashton Road, Luton. Petty Officer, H.M.S. *Belfast,* R.N. **B.E.M.,** 1942, Russian Convoys ; **American Purple Heart,** 1946, Normandy Invasion.

HUGHES, Clarence Lindsay, 30, Malvern Road, Luton. F/O., R.A.F. **D.F.C.,** 1944.

HUNTINGFORD, Frederick George, 44, Hawthorn Avenue, Stopsley, Luton. L/Seaman, R.N. **M.D.,** 1944, Light Coastal Forces ; **D.S.M.,** 1945.

HUTTON, D. J., B. Laporte, Ltd., Luton. S/Lt., R.N.V.R. **D.S.O.,** 1940, Dunkirk.

HYDE, W. J., Luton G.P.O. Major, R.E., i/c A.P.O. **M.D.,** 1945, N.W. Europe.

JENNINGS, Bernard James, Luton. Sgt., R.A.F. **D.F.M.,** 1941.

JENNINGS, Frank, 341, Beechwood Road, Luton. Lt.-Comm., R.N.R. **M.D.,** 1945, Normandy Invasion.

JOBLING, Joseph, 4, Wingate Road, Luton. Welding Shop Foreman, Electrolux, Ltd., Luton. **B.E.M.,** 1945.

JOHNSON, Michael Britton, 11, Bedford Gardens, Luton. Major, 34th Amphibian Assault Regt., Royal Marines. **M.B.E.,** 1945, Normandy Invasion.

JACKSON, Francis Chas., 23, Felstead Way, Luton. Sgt. (E.), R.A.F. **D.F.M.,** 1943. (Previously killed in action).

KEEN, Michael William, 97, St. Ethelbert's Avenue, Luton. Major, R.E.M.E. (Airborne). **M.D.,** 1945, N.W. Europe.

KELL, John, 38, Alexandra Avenue, Luton. Sgt., R.A.F. **B.E.M.,** 1946.

KING, Ronald Wilfred, 33, Argyll Avenue, Luton. F/O., R.A.F. **D.F.C.,** 1943, Anti U Boat Patrol.

KING, William James, Luton. Sgt., R.A.F. **D.F.M.,** 1941, North Africa.

KINGHAM, Jack, 464, Hitchin Road, Luton. F/Sgt., No. 115 Sq., R.A.F. **M.D.,** 1944, Germany.

KIRBY, Walter Jas. Fredk., 26, Brooms Road, Luton. Pte., 2nd Battn. Bedfs. and Herts. Regt. **M.M.,** 1944, Battle of Cassino.

KITCHENER, Ronald D., 51, West Hill Road, Luton. Lt. (E.), R.N.V.R. **M.D.,** 1944, Normandy Invasion.

LAMB, James Thomas, 29, St. Lawrence's Avenue, Luton. L/Sgt., 2nd Battn. R. Norfolk Regt. **M.D.,** 1944, Assam.

LARKMAN, Richard William, 72, Wychwood Avenue, Luton. Capt., R.A.O.C. **M.D.,** 1943, North Africa, followed by second mention.

LATHWELL, Reginald, 135, Farley Hill, Luton. Staff Sgt., R.A.S.C. **M.D.,** 1945, Normandy Invasion and Rhine Crossing.

LEGGATT, Henry John, 10, Tudor Road, Luton. L/Sgt., 6th Field Regt., R.A. **M.D.,** 1945, N.W. Europe.

LOOKER, E. M., Studham (formerly of Luton). Tpr., The Bays, Royal Tank Regt. **M.D.,** 1945, Italy.

LUCAS, Sydney Edward, 18, Grange Avenue, Luton. P/O., R.A.F. **D.F.C.,** 1944.

MacGEORGE, Jack Stephen, 123, North Street, Luton. Marine. **M.D.,** 1945.

MALSTER, Walter John, Divisional Commander, N.F.S., Luton, and Sub-Area Commander, Bedfordshire. **M.B.E.,** 1943, for general leadership during Eastern Region Blitz.

McPHEE, James, 80a, Castle Street, Luton. F/Lt., R.A.F. **A.F.C.,** 1944.

McPHEE, Thomas, 80a, Castle Street, Luton. S/Ldr., R.A.F. **D.F.M.,** 1941 ; **D.F.C.,** 1944.

MANDER, Arthur John, 9, Ashburnham Road, Luton. Colonel Commanding Beds. South Sector, Home Guard. **O.B.E.,** 1941.

MANDER, Stewart Tom, 21, Blundell Road, Luton. S/Ldr., P. and S.U., 84 Group, R.A.F. **M.D.,** 1945, France and Germany ; **M.B.E.,** 1946, France, and Germany.

MANN, Russell Frank, 22a, Norton Road, Luton. Sgt., Pioneer Corps. **B.E.M.,** 1943, Phillippeville.

MANSTOFF, A., Luton. F/Sgt., R.A.F. **D.F.M.,** 1944.

MARLOW, William Thos., 97, Boyle Street, Luton. R.S.M., Grenadier Guards, and Corps of Military Police. **B.E.M.,** 1945.

MARTIN, J., Luton. Sgt., 1st King's Dragoon Guards, R.A.C. **M.M.,** 1943, Middle East.

MASON, Frank, 110, Alexandra Avenue, Luton. F/Lt., R.A.F. **D.F.C.,** 1942, Middle East.

MATTHEWS, Dennis Edward, 61, Manor Road, Caddington, and Geo. Kent, Ltd., Hibbert Street, Luton. F/O., R.A.F. **D.F.C.,** 1945.

MAYES, Derek Leonard, 277, New Bedford Road, Luton. F/O., R.A.F. **D.F.C.,** 1943.

MAYLIN, John Horace Daniel, 3, Gloucester Road, Luton. C.S.M., 534th Tank Transportation Coy., R.A.S.C. **M.D.,** 1945, Africa.

MELLS, George Edward, Luton. L/Cpl., R.E. **B.E.M.,** 1944, Normandy.

MILLER, W. H., 97, Cowper Street, Luton. Sgt., R.A.C. **M.D.,** 1945, Italy.

MOCKERIDGE, Frederick Claude, 6, Montague Avenue, Toddington Road, Luton. C.S.M., Corps of Military Police. **M.M.,** 1940, Dunkirk.

MOODY, Leslie, 88, Elmwood Crescent, Luton. Major, Bedfs. & Herts. Regt., att. Monmouthshire Regt. **M.C.,** 1944, Albert Canal.

NUNN, Ronald A., 64, Crawley Road, Luton. Signalman. **Royal Victorian Medal,** 1945.

ORDE, Norman, 182, Beechwood Road, Luton. Sgt., 16/5 Queen's Lancers, R.A.C. **M.M.,** 1945, Italy.

ORDISH, Charles Brian, 39, Ludlow Avenue, Luton. F/Lt., R.A.F. **D.F.C.,** 1943. (Previously killed in action).

OWEN, Brian John, 78, Lea Road, Luton. F/O., R.A.F. **D.F.M.,** 1944, Germany.

PAILING, Rex, 199, New Bedford Road South, Luton. L/Bdr., 6th Searchlight Regt., R.A. **Belgian Croix de Guerre (1940) with Palm,** 1944, B.L.A.

PARFITT, D. W., 1, St. Margaret's Avenue, Luton. Capt., R.A.S.C. **M.D.,** 1945, N.W. Europe.

PARROTT, D. F., 134, North Street, Luton. L/Signalman, R.N. **M.D.,** 1940, Battle of the River Plate.

PARTRIDGE, J. E., Vauxhall Motors, Ltd., Luton. F/Lt., R.A.F. **D.F.C.,** 1942 ; **Bar to D.F.C.,** 1942 ; **D.S.O.,** 1943, Germany.

PEARSON, John, 1, Rothesay Road, Luton. M.S.M., R.A.S.C. **M.D.,** 1945, Italy.

PECK, David J., 99, Strathmore Avenue, Luton. Cpl., R.A.F. **M.D.,** 1944.

PHILPOTT, Reginald H., 35, Hartley Road, Luton. Driver, R.A.S.C. **M.M.,** 1946, N.W. Europe.

PICKFORD, James Thomas, 52, Browning Road, Luton. F/Sgt., R.A.F. **D.F.M.,** 1943.

PINKERTON, George Eustace, Limbury Manor, Luton. Capt., R.A.M.C. att. 1st Battn. K.O.Y.L.I. **M.C.,** 1944, Italy.

PLATER, Albert Jack, 57, Liverpool Road, Luton. Gnr., 99th Field Regt., R.A. **M.D.,** 1942, Western Desert.

PRATT, George Edward, 5, The Meads, Luton. Cpl., 111 Wing, R.A.F. **M.D.,** 1946, N.W. Europe.

PRIMETT, Ronald Murray, 137, Old Bedford Road, Luton. Lieut.-Col., R.A.O.C. **M.D.,** 1945, Italy.

PRYDE, Herbert Marshall, 31, Cardiff Road Luton. Master-at-Arms, R.N. **D.S.M.,** 1943, Malta Convoy.

PUNTER, Derek Hubert, 74, Manton Drive, Luton. Major, H.Q., 30 Corps District, R.A.O.C. **American Bronze Star,** 1944, B.A.O.R. ; **M.D.,** 1945, B.A.O.R.

RAMSAY, David B., 36, Castle Street, Luton. Capt., R.A.M.C. **M.D.,** 1944, Middle East.

REEVE, Leslie Frederick William, 7, Austin Road, Luton. L/Seaman, R.N. **M.D.,** 1945, Light Coastal Forces, Italy.

RICHARDSON, Keith R., 11, Humberstone Close, Luton. F/O., R.A.F. **D.F.C.,** 1945, Rhine Crossing.

RING, J. P., 76, Bradley Road, Luton. Cpl. **M.M.,** 1940, North Africa.

ROBERTSON, Ian Alex., 31, Felstead Way, Luton. S/Ldr., R.A.F. **D.F.C.,** 1941.

ROBINSON, Albert Edward, " Greenhills," Orchard Way, Luton. Capt., 15th Vehicle Park., R.A.O.C. **M.D.,** 1945, Italy.

ROBINSON, James, 40, Smart Street, Luton. Tank Shop Foreman, Vauxhall Motors, Ltd. **B.E.M.,** 1943.

RUDD, Colin Jas., 164, Dunstable Road, Luton. Capt., Northants. Regt. **M.C.**, 1944, N.W. Europe ; **Bar to M.C.**, 1944, Nijmegen-Arnhem Crossing, N.W. Europe. (Subsequently killed in action).

RUMBLE, Albert Edward, 10, East Avenue, Luton. S/Ldr., Special Duties List, att. M.A.P. **A.F.C.**, 1946, Test Pilot Duties.

SAUNDERS, William, St. Paul's Road, Luton. Sgt., R.A.S.C. **M.D.**, 1940, France.

SAVAGE, Arthur, 25, Summerfield Road, Luton. Pte., 4th Battn. King's Shropshire L.I. **M.M.**, 1944.

SAVAGE, John, 50, Chester Avenue, Luton. Sgt., Hampshire Regt. **D.C.M.**, 1944, Italy.

SEAR, Albert Joseph, Deputy Chief Constable of Luton. **George Medal**, 1941, Parachute Mine Incident at Percival Aircraft, Ltd., Luton.

SHANE, David Thos. Patrick, 1, Runfold Avenue, Luton. Able Seaman, Naval Diving Party " P " 2443, R.N. **M.D.**, 1946, Under-water Bomb Mine Disposal, Bremen, June, 1945.

SHARP, Leslie Alfred, 9, Surrey Street, Luton. Gunner, R.A. **M.M.**, 1942, Tobruk.

SIMKINS, Edward Wickens, 140, Cutenhoe Road, Luton. F/O., R.A.F. **D.F.C.**, 1944.

SINCLAIR, F. G., 95, Turners Road, Luton. Cpl., R.E.M.E. **M.D.**, 1946, Mediterranean.

SKELTON, Graham Clyde, 59, High Town Road, Luton. Flt./Lieut., 467 Squadron, R.A.F. **D.F.C.**, 1945.

SMITH, Walter R. S., 103, Chesford Road, Stopsley, Luton. Comm., R.N.V.R. **D.S.C.**, 1944, Normandy Invasion.

SMYTH, David P. W., 21, Walcot Avenue, Luton. Sgt., R.A. **M.M.**, 1943, North Africa.

SPIRES, John Henry, 11, Denbigh Road, Luton. F/Lt., R.A.F. **D.F.M.**, 1941, Malta and Middle East ; **D.F.C.**, 1944, France and Germany.

STANGHAN, Percy W., 74, St. Michael's Crescent, Luton. F/Sgt., R.A.F. **M.D.**, 1944.

STOKES, Cecil Sydney, " Bedfordia," Bramble Road, Luton. Sgt., R.A.F. **M.D.**, 1944.

STOTT, Gordon, 18, Alexandra Avenue, Luton. Sergt., No. 1 B.P.O., R.A.F. **M.D.**, 1944, M.E.F.

STRINGER, George, 98, Crawley Green Road, Luton. Senior Progress Man, Vauxhall Motors, Ltd. **B.E.M.**, 1945.

STYGALL, John Samuel, 29, Avenue Grimaldi, Luton. Assistant Production Engineer, Geo. Kent, Ltd., Luton. **B.E.M.**, 1946.

TAYLOR, Douglas, Town Hall, Luton. Sergt., 6th Armoured Divisional Signals. **M.D.**, 1943, Africa.

TEMPLEMAN-ROOKE, Basil Arthur, 49, Bishopscote Road, Luton. Wing Commander, R.A.F., formerly Leader of 576 and 150 Squadrons. **D.F.C.**, 1943, **Bar to D.F.C.**, 1945, and **D.S.O.**, 1945, all presented at one Investiture, 1945.

THOMSON, John, Inspector, Luton Borough Police, in charge of A.R.P. Department. **B.E.M.**, 1944.

THORNE, Frank Jas., 15, Priory Gardens, Luton. Captain, 31st Group, Pioneer Corps. **M.D.**, 1946, N.W. Europe.

TILDSLEY, William McKee Griffith, 45, Wimborne Road, Luton. W/Officer, 119th Coy. Pioneer Corps. **M.B.E.**, 1945, N.W. Europe.

TOFIELD, Claude Cecil L., 475, Dunstable Road, Luton. Col., R.E.M.E. **C.B.E.**, 1946.

TOWNSEND, Nigel H., 8, Priory Gardens, Luton. Capt., R.A.S.C. **M.D.**, 1945, Rhine Crossing ; **American Bronze Star**, 1945, Holland.

UNDERWOOD, Alan, 12, Durbar Road, Luton. Lieut., Royal Marines. **B.E.M.**, 1941, for bravery in air raid. Subsequently died on service.

VERGE, John, 16, Gardenia Avenue, Luton. Lt. and Q.M., 10th Hussars, R.A.C. **M.B.E.**, 1943, North Africa.

VERRAN, REGINALD STANLEY EDWARD, 78, Talbot Road, Luton. F/Officer, R.A.F.V.R. **D.F.C.,** June, 1945. Subsequently killed.

VERRAN, ROBERT CLAUDE, 18, Carlton Close, Luton. Sgt./Obs., R.A.F. **D.F.M.,** 1940 ; **M.D.** Subsequently killed in action.

VINCENT, H. C., Luton Borough Treasurer's Staff. Capt., R.A. **M.D.,** Burma.

WALLER, ROBERT BRUCE, " Fairholme," Hart Hill, Luton. S/Ldr., 418, A.S.P., R.A.F. **M.D.,** 1943, Western Desert ; **M.D.,** 1944, Sicily and Italy ; **O.B.E.,** 1945, Corsica and Southern France.

WALTHEW, HARRY F., 6, Manland Avenue, Harpenden, and Vauxhall Motors, Ltd., Luton. Lt.-Col., Herts. Regt. **O.B.E.,** 1946.

WEATHERLEY, ALFRED WM. GEO., 75, Limbury Road, Luton. Sergt., Special Forces (Airborne Signals). **M.M.,** 1944, Greece.

WELCH, ROY HECTOR, 12, Carlton Close, Luton. F/Lt., R.A.F. **A.F.C.,** 1944.

WELLS, HORACE GUY, 8, Blyth Place, Luton. Capt., 15th Parachute Regt. **M.D.,** 1942, N. Africa.

WERNHER, LADY ZIA, Luton Hoo. Leicestershire County President, St. John Ambulance Brigade. **O.B.E.,** 1946.

WHITE, CHARLES HENRY, 66, Frederick Street, Luton. Capt. and Q.M., Bedfs. and Herts. Regt. **M.B.E.,** 1942.

WHITEHEAD, JOHN FRANCIS, 60, Newcombe Road, Luton. Warrant Supply Officer, R. New Zealand Navy. **B.E.M.,** 1942, Indian Ocean.

WHITMORE, EDWARD RANDOLPH, 105, Montrose Avenue, Luton. Automatic Shop Foreman, Shefko Ball Bearing Co., Ltd., Luton. **B.E.M.,** 1945.

WICKHAM, CHARLES SYDNEY, 52, Sundon Park Road, Luton. LAC., 220 Squadron, R.A.F. **M.D.,** 1945, Azores.

WOODBRIDGE, PERCY HENRY, 121, Toddington Road, Luton. F/Sgt., R.A.F. **M.D.,** 1944.

WOODCRAFT, ERNEST, 183, Selbourne Road, Luton. Sgt. **M.D.,** 1944, Middle East.

WOODS, CHARLES MASON, 8, Weatherby Road, Luton. Stoker Petty Officer, R.N. **D.S.M.,** 1944, Battle of the Atlantic.

WOOLLFORD, ROY, 4, Beverley Road, Luton. W/Officer, R.A.F. **D.F.C.,** 1944, Germany.

WRIGHT, SIDNEY ARTHUR, 22, St. Monica's Avenue, Luton. Part-time A.F.S. Section Officer. **George Medal,** 1940, Thames Haven Oil Wharves.

Index

427

Glossary

A.D.C.C.	Air Defence Cadet Corps
A.R.P	Air Raid Precautions
Asdic	See page 180
A.T.C.	Air Training Corps
A.F.S.	Auxiliary Fire Service
A.T.S.	Auxiliary Territorial Service
B.B.C.	British Broadcasting Corporation
B.E.F.	British Expeditionary Force
C.N.R	Civil Nursing Service
C.W.S.	Co-operative Wholesale Society
D-Day	D for Day + Day
Ensa	Entertainments National Service Association
Fido	Fog Intensive Dispersal Operation
G.I.'s	Government Issue
Kangaroo	See page 174
L.D.V.	Local Defence Volunteers
N.F.S.	National Fire Service
Pluto	Pipe Line under the Ocean
R.A.F.	Royal Air Force
R.A.F.V.R.	Royal Air Force Volunteer Reserve
R.A.O.C.	Royal Army Ordnance Corps
R.A.S.C.	Royal Army Service Corps
R.E.	Royal Engineers
R.E.M.E.	Royal Electrical and Mechanical Engineers
R.F.A.	Royal Field Artillery
T.G.W.U.	Transport and General Workers' Union
U.S.A.F.	United States Air Force
V.E. Day	Victory in Europe Day
V.J. Day	Victory over Japan Day
W.A.A.C.	Women's Army Auxiliary Corps
W.A.A.F.S.	Women's Auxiliary Air Force Service
W.A.P.C.	Women's Auxiliary Police Corps
W.A.T.S.	Women's Auxiliary Territorial Service
W.M.S.A.	Wholesale Meat Supply Association
W.0.49	War Office 49, see page 179
Wrens	Women's Royal Naval Service
W.V.S.	Women's Voluntary Service

The earlier story of

LUTON AT WAR

is told in a first volume

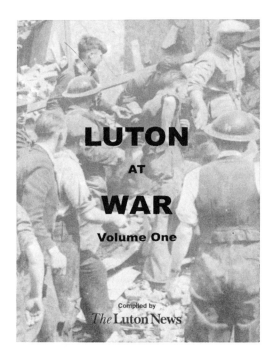

The contents are listed
on the next page.

Contents - VOLUME ONE

BEDFORDSHIRE'S YESTERYEARS
Volume 4
War Times & Civil Matters
by
Brenda Fraser-Newstead

Social history comes to life, first-hand and vivid, when seen through the eyes of those who experienced and shaped it. The ' Bedfordshire's Yesteryears' series contains many privileged glimpses of a way of life that has changed radically. Here is the generation of two World Wars; here are the witnesses to countless technological and sociological transformations. This volume highlights the angst of the Depression and the two World Wars, when the whole social fabric was disrupted but showed extraordinary resilience. It also traces another major feature of the twentieth century, namely the rapid development in all modes of transport - carriers and trams, airships and fire-engines, trains and automobiles. Route marches, the General Strike, the Home Guard, the munitions factory, the Land Army, barrage balloons, evacuees, G.I.brides, the Specials, steam fire-engines, double-decker trams, the concert party - just a few of the evocative words that roll away the decades.

The Book Castle

BUCKINGHAM AT WAR
by
Pip Brimson

Stories of courage, humour and occasional pathos as Buckingham people adapt to a state of war. How A.R.P., gas masks, blackout and mobilization were all coped with. How the Home Guard, Land Girls and the jobs women were directed to affected the town. The progress of war through those early years, including rationing and evacuation; the stories told by evacuees in the town. Read about the individual effort by those at home, and the town's fund raising events. When at last the end of the war approached, the blackout was lifted; the Home Guard, their job finished, stood down, and prisoners of war overseas began to return home to great rejoicing, which culminated on V.E. and V.J. Days. Servicemen too were slowly beginning to demobilize. Finally, everyone could sit back and take stock - attend to their losses and sadness, but feel proud of what had been achieved - and then, begin to prepare for the problems and happiness Peace would bring, after the long years of struggle and endeavour.

WINGS OVER WING
The Story of a World War II Bomber Training Unit
by
Michael Warth

For five years at the beginning of the 1940's the quiet countryside around the Buckinghamshire village of Wing was the scene of a period of activity not witnessed in those parts before or since. As with numerous other sites in the east of England an area of open field was selected for the construction of an airfield to be utilized by the RAF for the training of bomber aircrew. The peaceful country lanes were soon to be busy with the movement of men, women and vehicles whilst the skies above were filled with the many types of aircraft as they took off and landed at RAF Wing. The story of the airfield and Number 26 Operational Training Unit, which was based there, is one of great friendship and trust, courage and bravery, sadness and joy. The events of those few years shaped the lives of all who were there and their memories offer an insight into life in such an establishment in the extraordinary days of World War II.

The Book Castle

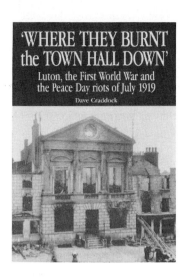

"WHERE THEY BURNT THE TOWN HALL DOWN"
Luton, The First World War and the Peace day Riots of July 1919
by
Dave Craddock

The weekend of 19/20th July 1919 was arguably the most momentous in the history of Luton. What began as an afternoon of peace celebrations marking the end of the Great War turned into riots that had by the Sunday morning left the Town hall a smouldering, gutted ruin, with the military in control of the town. Yet over the years, the story of the riots has been largely neglected. Drawing broadly on contemporary documents, witness statements and newspaper reports, the book gives a blow-by-blow account of the riots, their aftermath and subsequent trials. The hostility between the Town Council and ex-servicemen's organisations in the preceding months is also covered extensively, as is the impact of the First World War on Luton. Features of this book include informative appendices containing a wealth of information and over 50 illustrations.

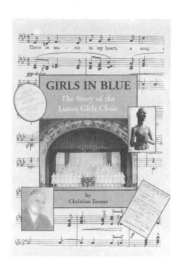

GIRLS IN BLUE
by
Christine Turner

The Luton Girls Choir started in 1936 and spanned 40 years of Luton's growth, making the name of Luton well known both in Britain and around the world. Even today the Luton Music Library receives requests for information and enquiries about its music. It was an amateur organisation, being a mixture of schoolgirls and young ladies under 24 who worked in local shops, offices and factories. However, there was nothing amateurish about their presentation and the girls sang with many famous people, appearing in a film and also singing at the Royal Command Performance. They toured Australasia and Denmark as well as singing in many towns in Britain. At its peak the Choir was often heard on the radio and seen on television, comedians joked about it and it featured in newspaper cartoons. Other choirs came and went, but the Luton Girls Choir survived for 40 years until the death of its founder Arthur Davies M.B.E. in 1977. For its members it was a unique experience and their story deserves a place in history.

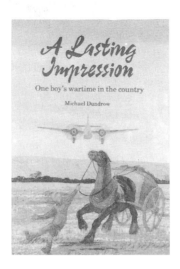

A LASTING IMPRESSION

by
Michael Dundrow

Michael Dundrow experienced an event in his formative years which strongly coloured or even completely changed the rest of his life.

This book describes one boy's overwhelming experience - wartime evacuation - which has left a truly lasting impression on his adult life. For this twelve year old from London's East End, to be dumped among a family of strangers on a large and busy farm below the Chilterns in Bedfordshire was a make or break experience of the first order.

Enriched by his years on the farm and in the village of Totternhoe, the adventures with new found friends, the sheer interest, fun and hard work of farm life and also the sowing of the seeds of appreciation of that lovely corner of South Bedfordshire, the details are all here, written with great affection. Although written fifty years after these unforgettable things happened, the story is undimmed by the passage of time.

In this evocative picture of wartime England are many glimpses of a way of village and farm life that has altered so dramatically in recent years as to be almost unrecognisable today.

COCKNEY KID AND COUNTRYMEN
The Second World War remembered by the children
of Woburn Sands and Aspley Guise
by
Ted Enever

On the evening of Saturday 7th September 1940, London's East End lay under a pall of smoke from heavy bombing by the German Luftwaffe. It was the beginning of what history was to record as the Blitz. Six year old Ted and his parents were victims of that first attack. With home and possessions lost, they left London to find safety, shelter and a new way of life in the villages of Woburn Sands and Aspley Guise. "Cockney Kid and Countrymen" is Ted Enever's story of that new way of life and a snapshot of the wartime years vividly remembered by the village children of the time.

Ted was educated at Bedford Modern School and entered journalism in 1951 with the Bletchley District Gazette. After two years national service he continued his career as a freelance journalist, with various large organisations. On retirement he was working for Milton Keynes Development Corporation. A founder member of the Bletchley Park Trust and now a Patron, Ted is author of "Britain's Best Kept Secret - Ultra's base at Bletchley Park."

Books Published by THE BOOK CASTLE

CHANGES IN OUR LANDSCAPE: Aspects of Bedfordshire, Buckinghamshire and the Chilterns 1947-1992: Eric Meadows. Over 350 photographs from the author's collection spanning nearly 50 years.

COUNTRYSIDE CYCLING IN BEDFORDSHIRE, BUCKINGHAMSHIRE AND HERTFORDSHIRE: Mick Payne. Twenty rides on and off-road for all the family.

PUB WALKS FROM COUNTRY STATIONS: Bedfordshire and Hertfordshire: Clive Higgs. Fourteen circular country rambles, each starting and finishing at a railway station and incorporating a pub stop at a mid way point.

PUB WALKS FROM COUNTRY STATIONS: Buckinghamshire and Oxfordshire: Clive Higgs. Circular rambles incorporating pub-stops.

LOCAL WALKS: South Bedfordshire and North Chilterns: Vaughan Basham. Twenty-seven thematic circular walks.

LOCAL WALKS: North and Mid Bedfordshire: Vaughan Basham. Twenty-five thematic circular walks.

FAMILY WALKS: Chilterns South: Nick Moon. Thirty 3 to 5 mile circular walks.

FAMILY WALKS: Chilterns North: Nick Moon. Thirty shorter circular walks.

CHILTERN WALKS: Hertfordshire, Bedfordshire and North Bucks: Nick Moon.

CHILTERN WALKS: Buckinghamshire: Nick Moon.

CHILTERN WALKS: Oxfordshire and West Buckinghamshire: Nick Moon. A trilogy of circular walks, in association with the Chiltern Society. Each volume contains 30 circular walks.

OXFORDSHIRE WALKS: Oxford, the Cotswolds and the Cherwell Valley: Nick Moon.

OXFORDSHIRE WALKS: Oxford, the Downs and the Thames Valley: Nick Moon. Two volumes that complement Chiltern Walks: Oxfordshire, and complete coverage of the county, in association with the Oxford Fieldpaths Society. Thirty circular walks in each.

THE D'ARCY DALTON WAY: Nick Moon. Long-distance footpath across the Oxfordshire Cotswolds and Thames Valley, with various circular walk suggestions.

THE CHILTERN WAY: Nick Moon. A guide to the new 133 mile circular Long-Distance Path through Bedfordshire, Buckinghamshire,Hertfordshire and Oxfordshire, as planned by the Chiltern Society.

JOURNEYS INTO BEDFORDSHIRE: Anthony Mackay. Foreword by The Marquess of Tavistock, Woburn Abbey. A lavish book of over 150 evocative ink drawings.

COCKNEY KID & COUNTRYMEN: Ted Enever. The Second World War remembered by the children of Woburn Sands and Aspley Guise. A six year old boy is evacuated from London's East End to start life in a Buckinghamshire village.

BUCKINGHAM AT WAR: Pip Brimson. Stories of courage, humour and pathos as Buckingham people adapt to war.

WINGS OVER WING: The Story of a World War II Bomber Training Unit: Mike Warth. The activities of RAF Wing in Buckinghamshire.

JOURNEYS INTO BUCKINGHAMSHIRE: Anthony Mackay. Superb line drawings plus background text: large format landscape gift book.

BUCKINGHAMSHIRE MURDERS: Len Woodley. Nearly two centuries of nasty crimes.

WINGRAVE: A Rothschild Village in the Vale: Margaret and Ken Morley. Thoroughly researched and copiously illustrated survey of the last 200 years in this lovely village between Aylesbury and Leighton Buzzard.

HISTORIC FIGURES IN THE BUCKINGHAMSHIRE LANDSCAPE: John Houghton. Major personalities and events that have shaped the county's past, including Bletchley Park.

TWICE UPON A TIME: John Houghton. North Bucks short stories loosely based on fact.

SANCTITY AND SCANDAL IN BEDS AND BUCKS: John Houghton. A miscellany of unholy people and events.

MANORS and MAYHEM, PAUPERS and PARSONS: Tales from Four Shires: Beds., Bucks., Herts. and Northants: John Houghton. Little known historical snippets and stories.

THE LAST PATROL: Policemen killed on duty while serving the Thames Valley: Len Woodley.

FOLK: Characters and Events in the History of Bedfordshire and Northamptonshire: Vivienne Evans. Anthology of people of yesteryear - arranged alphabetically by village or town.

JOHN BUNYAN: His Life and Times: Vivienne Evans. Highly praised and readable account.

THE RAILWAY AGE IN BEDFORDSHIRE: Fred Cockman. Classic, illustrated account of early railway history.

A LASTING IMPRESSION: Michael Dundrow. A boyhood evacuee recalls his years in the Chiltern village of Totternhoe near Dunstable.

GLEANINGS REVISITED: Nostalgic Thoughts of a Bedfordshire Farmer's Boy: E.W. O'Dell. His own sketches and early photographs adorn this lively account of rural Bedfordshire in days gone by.

BEDFORDSHIRE'S YESTERYEARS Vol 2: The Rural Scene: Brenda Fraser-Newstead. Vivid first-hand accounts of country life two or three generations ago.

BEDFORDSHIRE'S YESTERYEARS Vol 3: Craftsmen and Tradespeople: Brenda Fraser-Newstead. Fascinating recollections over several generations practising many vanishing crafts and trades.

BEDFORDSHIRE'S YESTERYEARS Vol 4: War Times and Civil Matters: Brenda Fraser-Newstead. Two World Wars, plus transport, law and order, etc.

DUNNO'S ORIGINALS: A facsimile of the rare pre-Victorian history of Dunstable and surrounding villages. New preface and glossary by John Buckledee, Editor of The Dunstable Gazette.

PROUD HERITAGE: A Brief History of Dunstable, 1000-2000AD: Vivienne Evans. Century by century account of the town's rich tradition and key events, many of national significance.

DUNSTABLE WITH THE PRIORY: 1100-1550: Vivienne Evans. Dramatic growth of Henry I's important new town around a major crossroads.

DUNSTABLE IN TRANSITION: 1550-1700: Vivienne Evans. Wealth of original material as the town evolves without the Priory.

OLD DUNSTABLE: Bill Twaddle. A new edition of this collection of early photographs.

BOURNE and BRED: A Dunstable Boyhood Between the Wars: Colin Bourne. An elegantly written, well illustrated book capturing the spirit of the town over fifty years ago.

OLD HOUGHTON: Pat Lovering. Pictorial record capturing the changing appearances of Houghton Regis over the past 100 years.

ROYAL HOUGHTON: Pat Lovering. Illustrated history of Houghton Regis from the earliest of times to the present.

GIRLS IN BLUE: Christine Turner. The activities of the famous Luton Girls Choir properly documented over its 41 year period from 1936 to 1977.

THE STOPSLEY BOOK: James Dyer. Definitive, detailed account of this historic area of Luton. 150 rare photographs.

THE STOPSLEY PICTURE BOOK: James Dyer. New material and photographs make an ideal companion to The Stopsley Book.

PUBS and PINTS: The Story of Luton's Public Houses and Breweries: Stuart Smith. The background to beer in the town, plus hundreds of photographs, old and new.

LUTON AT WAR - VOLUME ONE: As compiled by the Luton News in 1947, a well illustrated thematic account.

LUTON AT WAR - VOLUME TWO: Second part of the book compiled by The Luton News.

THE CHANGING FACE OF LUTON: An Illustrated History: Stephen Bunker, Robin Holgate and Marian Nichols. Luton's development from earliest times to the present busy industrial town. Illustrated in colour and mono.

WHERE THEY BURNT THE TOWN HALL DOWN: Luton, The First World War and the Peace Day Riots, July 1919: Dave Craddock. Detailed analysis of a notorious incident.

THE MEN WHO WORE STRAW HELMETS: Policing Luton, 1840-1974: Tom Madigan. Fine chronicled history, many rare photographs; author~served in Luton Police for fifty years.

BETWEEN THE HILLS: The Story of Lilley, a Chiltern Village: Roy Pinnock. A priceless piece of our heritage - the rural beauty remains but the customs and way of life described here have largely disappeared.

KENILWORTH SUNSET: A Luton Town Supporter's Journal: Tim Kingston. Frank and funny account of football's ups and downs.

A HATTER GOES MAD!: Kristina Howells. Luton Town footballers, officials and supporters talk to a female fan.

LEGACIES: Tales and Legends of Luton and the North Chilterns:
Vic Lea. Mysteries and stories based on fact, including Luton Town
Football Club. Many photographs.

THREADS OF TIME: Shela Porter. The life of a remarkable mother and
businesswoman, spanning the entire century and based in Hitchin and
(mainly) Bedford.

**STICKS AND STONES: The Life and Times of a Journeyman Printer in
Hertford, Dunstable, Cheltenham and Wolverton:** Harry Edwards.

LEAFING THROUGH LITERATURE: Writers' Lives in Herts and Beds:
David Carroll. Illustrated short biographies of many famous authors and
their connections with these counties.

A PILGRIMAGE IN HERTFORDSHIRE: H.M. Alderman. Classic,
between-the-wars tour round the county, embellished with line drawings.

THE VALE OF THE NIGHTINGALE: Molly Andrews. Several
generations of a family, lived against a Harpenden backdrop.

**SUGAR MICE AND STICKLEBACKS: Childhood Memories of a
Hertfordshire Lad:** Harry Edwards. Vivid evocation of gentle pre-war in
an archetypal village, Hertingfordbury.

SWANS IN MY KITCHEN: Lis Dorer. Story of a Swan Sanctuary near
Hemel Hempstead.

**THE HILL OF THE MARTYR: An Architectural History of St.Albans
Abbey:**
Eileen Roberts. Scholarly and readable chronological narrative history of
Hertfordshire and Bedfordshire's famous cathedral. Fully illustrated with
photographs and plans.

**THE TALL HITCHIN INSPECTOR'S CASEBOOK: A Victorian Crime
Novel Based on Fact:** Edgar Newman. Worthies of the time encounter
more archetypal villains.

SPECIALLY FOR CHILDREN

VILLA BELOW THE KNOLLS: A Story of Roman Britain: Michael
Dundrow. An exciting adventure for young John in Totternhoe and
Dunstable two thousand years ago.

THE RAVENS: One Boy Against the Might of Rome: James Dyer. On the
Barton Hills and in the south-east of England as the men of the great fort
of Ravensburgh (near Hexton)
confront the invaders.

THE BOOK CASTLE, 12 Church Street, Dunstable,
Bedfordshire LU5 4RU
Tel: (01582) 605670 Fax (01582) 662431
Email: bc@book-castle.co.uk